THE
AUTOBIOGF
OF A
STOCK

A common man's guide
to stock investing

MANOJ ARORA

JAICO PUBLISHING HOUSE

Ahmedabad Bangalore Bhopal Bhubaneswar Chennai
Delhi Hyderabad Kolkata Lucknow Mumbai

Published by Jaico Publishing House
A-2 Jash Chambers, 7-A Sir Phirozshah Mehta Road
Fort, Mumbai - 400 001
jaicopub@jaicobooks.com
www.jaicobooks.com

THE AUTOBIOGRAPHY OF A STOCK
ISBN 978-93-86867-67-4

First Jaico Impression: 2018
Seventh Jaico Impression: 2019

Page design and layout:
Special Effects Graphics Design Company, Mumbai

Printed by
Pashupati Printers
1/429/16, Gali No. 1, Friends Colony
Industrial Area, G. T. Road, Shahdara, Delhi - 95

JAI GURUJI

One can acquire all the knowledge in the world.
What cannot be acquired is the power and strength
required to implement that knowledge.
You are blessed with it, by your Guru.

Thank you Guruji — for blessing me with the
strength to bring this book to life.

Indebted To

There is a good debt and a bad debt. I take pride that I carry a huge 'debt' – albeit a good one – from each of my readers and friends, those who read this book and any of my earlier books, those who personally interacted with me and those who silently recommended us within their own circle of friends and relatives.

I am indebted to YOU.

As much as I would love to name each one of you, I am constrained with the available space. I absolutely realise and firmly believe that no single individual can achieve anything of his or her own. Anything worthwhile is born out of feedback, constructive criticism and unwavering faith.

Without all these inputs, this book would not have been feasible.

I thank each one of you!

Disclaimer

This publication contains opinions and ideas from the author, based on his personal experience in the financial market and his interaction with God in his dreams and visions. It is not possible to provide written proof of such interactions; faith is the only evidence.

Although the examples shared in this book are real-life experiences shared from the author's own portfolio, the purpose is to make the reader understand the concepts of stock market in an extremely simple, practical and real environment. It is not the author's intent to recommend the reader to purchase or sell stocks of the companies, whose examples have been shared in the book.

A lot of the data has been taken from said companies' annual reports, websites as well as popular financial portals. Neither the author nor the publisher can guarantee the accuracy of that information.

The author and the publisher specifically disclaim any responsibility for any liability, loss or risk, which is incurred as a consequence of the use and application of any of this book's contents.

Contents

Preface

In the year 1994, at the age of 21, I completed my studies from Aligarh Muslim University with a gold medal. During campus selections, getting an opportunity to work with the biggest electrical engineering company in India – Larsen & Toubro Limited (L&T) – was the cherry on the cake.

I started earning and saving money from 1994, but it was only in 1998 that I was first exposed to the stock market. I was 25 then, unlike Warren Buffett who started investing at the age of 11. I was, as I came to realize later, an 'ultra-crucial' 14 years behind. Anyway, within a month, I made profits at 800 percent compounded annual growth rate (CAGR) on my first investment (or rather, trade). Forget about the *amount* and *tenure* of investment. The concept of stock market did not just work, it worked like magic.

Barely six months after this stupendous success, I withdrew from the stock market with the commitment to never look back.

The next 10 years were about building my career and getting clear about my dreams in life. Throughout this period, I saved and invested whatever I could, but I hated the stock market as an investment vehicle. I invested my savings surplus anywhere but in stocks, and advised everyone around me to do the same. Stocks were another name for risk, greed, gambling, losing one's money and whatnot.

My next transaction in stocks was in 2007 – after a gap of almost 10 years. And from then on until today, stocks have been a healthy portion of my portfolio. In fact, the equity market, and specifically stocks, has been quite instrumental in shaping up my financial freedom. I am sure I could never have achieved my freedom in a span of eight years, had it not been for stock investments.

Now I have embraced stock investments. I realize that if you seriously want to be wealthy, equity has to be a balanced but mandatory portion of your portfolio. It's not that you cannot achieve financial freedom without equity investments or you cannot become wealthy enough, but a non-equity balanced portfolio takes too much time to grow, and time is the essence of life. This journey of my financial life – from not being exposed to stocks until the age of 25 (mainly because of a lack of knowledge), a decade-long period of hatred from the age of 25 to 35, to the period of embracing stocks from the age of 35 until now (I am 44 years old now) has been marked with immense learning and wisdom built over time.

This book gives me an opportunity to share this learning with all of you – my friends, my readers and my society. This is 100 percent non-conventional learning. I do not claim to be a financial wizard – neither in this book, nor in my first one, *From the Rat Race to Financial Freedom*. I do not possess any certification in finance. I am a common man – an electrical engineer by qualification, a project executive by profession, a financially free individual by passion and a very ordinary human being by nature. I do not even intend to get certified with financial degrees, because of the simple reason that I do not want to be bound by the written conventions of money and investments. I want to define my own rules, try them, test them with my own money, define new conventions and then generate wealth for myself and the world around me.

This is the journey of my life – a life of a common man who has never been taught enough about money in school or college. The stock market is a far cry. People like me are only left with a hit-and-trial method to discover whether we belong in this arena or not.

Most people like me would never go back to equity market after having burnt our fingers once. I would not have either, had it not been my goal to achieve financial freedom. A strong goal lets us do extraordinary things. I went back – wiser and more determined – and came out stronger and in love with the market. Today, it is almost impossible to think of my financial investments without a significant portion of equity (both mutual funds and stocks).

It is said that if you cannot write about something then you haven't really thought about it. So, it was a given that I would write about stocks, and what use is that writing if it is not shared. So, here I am, sharing all that I have learnt until now. However, learning is a never-ending process, and you might see more of it in future editions of the book. The methods described in this book are no theory. They have been tried, tested and refined over the last 10 years in the market, and also during the period I did not actively participate. These 20-plus years of experience handling money and stocks has been presented to you in the simplest possible way.

Finance, especially stocks, is always thought of as a complex, technical and risky subject. However, my experience shows that facts are exactly the reverse of it. Making money in the stock market is very easy, but that is exactly where the problem is. If I present something huge to you in a simplified manner, you will never believe it. You will just go on to make it complex – so complex, that most of you will only lose money with that complexity. My assurance to you is that if you follow the simple steps and guidelines that I am going to share with you, you will always make money in the long run – and enough of it.

As an aid to this book, I have provided some templates to calculate the intrinsic value of a stock, pre-loaded historical data about some companies etc. All this is available on my website *www.manoj-arora. com*.

Unfortunately, not many who deal with this topic talk about the biggest secret to making money in the stock market. Not many focus on it or want to believe in it either, because it is not the easiest of the secrets to be accepted. If anyone has entered the stock market without grasping this secret, then sooner or later, they have hated the market and spread myths. Most come into the stock market to make quick money, and if they are told, before they start making money, that they will need time (up to 10 years!) to implement the secret that I am about to share with you now, their lack of patience and the greed for instant gratification comes into play. They tend to overlook this secret, at their own peril of course.

So here it is – the biggest secret about making money through stocks:

It is not technical analysis, valuation of stocks or studying the business or earning potential of the company, industry trends etc. that are going to create massive wealth for you. All these are definitely important and essential factors that need to be mastered. But anyone can learn how to do a stock valuation in a short span of time. Anyone can study the industry trends and the future earning potential of a company. All this data is almost readily available on the internet and in books. But most of you would still lose money, or not make enough of it, in stocks.

What is going to make you really wealthy is your personal traits – your ability to have 'faith' in your calculations, your 'self-confidence' to stay invested and invest more when everyone is selling, your 'guts' to sell when the market is peaking everyday and everyone in the media is talking about buying more, your conviction to overcome greed and to exit a stock when your targets are met, your astronomical patience to wait for the right opportunity to buy, and many more such human traits, none of which are easy to implement.

These qualities of faith, self-confidence, guts, patience and conviction – may take an entire life span to be inculcated. But this is what you need to make big money here.

Thus, while I will present calculations and charts in the simplest possible way to enable you to do your own value analysis and pick stocks, it is up to you to stick to the guidelines by demonstrating the above mentioned personality traits, which will eventually decide how much money you can make. And this was, and will always be, the biggest secret to making money in stocks.

As a rough judgment, and based on my personal experience, your personality traits have an 80 percent weightage in the process – if not more. Now that you know how important it is to have the right personality to make big money in the stock market, this book will cover both these aspects in detail, with real examples from my portfolio along with real personality handling techniques from my life.

I will cover the fundamentals of stocks, basic terms, ratios, performing value analysis. More importantly, I will also demonstrate through examples how inculcating my personality traits helped me create greater wealth for myself. If I could do it, so can you. We are no different... after all we are all common men and women trying to make enough money to feed our families and perhaps to create some impact in this world.

You will find the content and the presentation style of this book unique and practical. I, a 100 percent believer in God, got this idea from Him. One night, in my dreams, He came and told me that He was descending on this planet to teach us about stocks. He had been here for close to 200 years but with hardly any success. He wanted me to learn it directly from Him and then teach it to others. And thus came the idea for this book. Now those who truly have faith in God would understand how God responds to our day-to-day challenges if we ask Him for help, with full faith. For others, I would suggest you to read it as a story from yours truly – a story that teaches one of the most complex subjects in the simplest and surest possible way.

This book is in the form of an autobiography of 'Mr. Stock'. Mr. Stock is a godsend to teach people on this planet all about the money-making journey. With blessings from Him, Mr. Stock has been trying to teach human beings about stocks for the last 200 years. With almost negligible success, he makes one last attempt when he meets its new owner and both go through the stock selection and rejection process, stock-picking and then the volatility of the market until the owner exits the stock at a handsome profit after a few years.

The entire story is sprinkled with everything real – real data, real stocks, real dates and real prices. Anyone can go and match the prices of a specific stock on a specific date from any financial portal. Real data makes it strongly evident that the concepts of this book work – precisely the way God told me they would work. Who says that He does not communicate with us?

There is knowledge in picking a stock, exiting it and, most importantly, during the volatile and emotional journey in between. All three phases need to be mastered via technical calculations and by improving our own personality. Those with better emotional intelligence are more likely to make more money from the market, when all other factors remain the same.

Quick Money... or Quicksand

"**H**ello Mr. Stock, my name is Gobind."

Here comes another one, I thought to myself and said, "Yes Mr. Gobind. How may I help you?"

"Actually, one of my close friends, Vinod, referred me to you. I am planning to invest in stocks for the first time in my life. So, I thought it might be useful to have a quick discussion with you."

"Sure. Anyone is welcome to have any length of discussion with me."

"Thanks."

"But before I answer your questions Mr. Gobind, may I know some basic information about you like your age, background etc.?"

"I am 25. I am an electrical engineer and work for one of the biggest engineering companies in India. Currently, I am located in Delhi, and have just been married. My wife is a school teacher. We stay with our parents. That is all about me. What about you?"

"Good to know you. I am Stock. You may have heard good or bad things about me. But what humans think or say about me does not affect me. I am above all that. I go by my own rules. I am ready to teach anyone who is ready to learn about making money from stocks."

"Well, that is so good to hear. I was wondering whether I am being too hasty about all this... you know it is a risky investment, isn't it?"

"Hahaha! You are 25. One of my other well-known friends whom I have been helping for almost 80 years now, started investing at the age of 11. You are a critical 14 years behind him, and you think you are too early?"

Gobind was probably feeling dejected.

"I am really sorry if that hurt you, but I have taught this so many times to so many of my investor friends that when I heard that you felt you were early at 25, laughter just overtook me. It was more because of your innocence than anything else. My apologies." I tried justifying my laughter.

"Ah OK. By the way, how can one start investing from the age of 11 in a country like India? At this age, kids are studying in sixth or seventh standard. Moreover, our parents, teachers and friends have no clue about money or finance – let alone about investing in stocks!"

"You are right my friend. We do have this challenge in India. But each challenge comes packaged with an opportunity. This is an opportunity for all of us to educate our children from a very young age to start handling and saving money, and then start thinking from an investor's perspective on the money saved."

"That is a very well-intentioned statement Mr. Stock, but what will they save unless they start earning, and that does not happen before the age of 20-21 in most cases."

"It is all a mindset, dear friend. I always recommend that you give pocket money to your children and let them decide on how much to spend and how much to save. They will become great investors only after they have become great savers. And they will become great savers only if they are taught the importance of saving early in life and the unfair advantage that early movers get in wealth creation."

"Oh, really? Saving and investing from pocket money? Is it practical?" asked a perturbed and confused Gobind.

"Of course it is, Gobind. Open a bank account in your child's name, under your guardianship if needed, deposit their pocket money in that account and give them an ATM card. Teach them the importance of saving first. Let them save whatever they can from this money. Show them their monthly account statement and how the bank pays interest on the saved money. Explain the concept of 'money earning more money' to them. The more they save, the more the bank pays. The more the bank pays, the more passive money they create."

"This is interesting – generating passive money from pocket money – awesome! I am surely going to do this for both of my children," remarked a convinced Gobind.

"Fantastic, buddy."

"Though the concept of generating passive money is superb, the numbers must be small, shouldn't they be? I mean how big an advantage is that really?"

"Of course. Remember, time is the biggest lever to wealth creation.

It does not take a lot of money to make a lot of money. It takes some money and a lot of time to make a lot of money."

"But how?"

"Look at it this way. If a child started investing at the age of seven with his or her pocket money, and you started investing at the age of 21 – assuming you started earning at this age – you can never ever recover for the lost time."

"I am still not clear. What do you mean by 'lost time'?"

"Let's say that someone started investing INR 10,000 every year from the age of seven till the age of 60, and you invested INR 20,000 from the age of 21 till the age of 60."

"OK, so, I started late but I invested double the amount every year, right?"

"Yes, you are right. You started 14 years late, but to compensate for the delayed start, you invested double the amount every year for the next 40 years. Do you know what would be the end result at the age of 60?

"I do not know exactly, but I think I can make a fair guess. That child's wealth would remain ahead of me for a few years, but since I am investing double the child's amount every year, at some stage my wealth will take over the child's wealth. This is so logical," commented Gobind, ever so confident about his response.

Humans sometime are so driven by preconceived notions that they become closed to any other possibilities.

"Just have some patience, my dear friend. Assuming an annual return of 10 percent in both the cases, the child will end up with a corpus of INR 1.71 crore by investing a total of INR 5.30 lakh over a span of 53 years."

"And what will I end up with, at the age of 60?"

"You will end up with half the corpus – i.e. approximately INR 88 lakh – by investing INR 8 lakh i.e. almost 50 percent more than what the child invested."

"Don't tell me! I end up with 50 percent less corpus despite investing 50 percent more? This is ridiculous. Please check your calculation, Mr. Stock."

"I am never wrong in my calculation. I am not designed to make mistakes. Try this out any number of times you want. And we don't call this ridiculous, my friend. We call this 'time leveraging and compounding' at work. You can never ever make up for the lost time."

Gobind fiddled with his calculator for some time, tried the same calculation through multiple means until that small machine in his hand convinced him of what I was trying to tell him.

"I see that you have a point. But what do I do now?"

"Nothing my friend. As I told you, you cannot make up for the lost time, ever. We must all look forward. Looking behind while running can only do one thing to us – and that is to slow us down further."

"Oh, OK. I get your point, but it's sad we cannot change this now."

"So, here is my first lesson for you."

"What is it?"

"Do not ever let the next generation lose the benefit of time leveraging, because of your sheer ignorance and casual approach towards money and finance at a young age. Teach them savings. Teach them investing from a very young age. If you do that, they will have an unparalleled set of opportunities to benefit from. They will cherish an unfair advantage over everyone else for the rest of their lives."

"I take that point, and I am going to implement it for sure with my children. Thank you."

LESSON 1

Do not let your child lose the 'Time Leverage' edge.
From a very young age, let your child handle and save money. Teach your child to invest the savings, so that money can start working for them.
Start early. Time is the biggest lever for wealth creation.

"It is my duty and my pleasure, Gobind."

"But as you rightly said, I am now trying to look forward for myself, rather than looking at the fact that I am 14 years late. I actually came to meet you with a slightly different question in mind."

"Go ahead please, my dear friend Gobind. I have another 30 minutes before the markets close for the day. I need to be home early today."

"OK. I am already 25, and I want to invest. Though many of the financial advisors are suggesting that I get into stocks, I am still wondering whether I should make this choice when there are so many safer and equally rewarding investment options available. I know I am asking you, Mr. Stock, but should I invest in stocks or not? The question itself might sound stupid to you, but can you really convince me that I should get into stocks." Gobind asked me, confusion all over his face.

"It is, and it always was, your choice, Mr. Gobind. I never force anyone," I said. "You humans can lead a very simple financial life, if you wish to. Just save 'enough' money and put it in risk-free investment tools like term deposits, PPF, EPF, debt funds, bonds etc. and enjoy the returns with absolute peace of mind. Where is the challenge?"

"Yeah, but I heard we can make money grow much faster with you, and who would not want that? And you too just said that time is the biggest asset that we have." Gobind began to justify.

"Yes, of course time is the biggest asset and the biggest lever you have in hand. But the difference between appreciating this lever and demonstrating greed is subtle. You are trying to make up for the lost time by exhibiting greed. Your greed brings you to me and my world, where most of you would burn your fingers because of your own ignorance, and then blame me for the consequences."

"Our ignorance? What ignorance? I have been investing money for the last four years, though not in stocks. I understand the fundamentals of investing. Once we invest with you, it is your job to give us returns, isn't it? What is there to really learn? I mean, luck may have some role but sooner or later, we should all make good money, shouldn't we?"

"That is exactly my point. That is the ignorance I am talking about. Do you drive a motor vehicle?"

"Yes, a car."

"What is its maximum speed?"

"Well, around 140 km per hour."

"And what if I tell you that you can have an airplane that could travel at 1,000 km per hour? I can give you the airplane, though I cannot offer you the services of a pilot. You will have to fly it on your own. What would be your reaction if you were in a hurry to reach somewhere? Would you choose to fly an airplane or stick to your car?"

"I think I might stick to the car."

"But why? You are in a rush, and you have an airplane at your disposal. Then, why would you not take it?"

"Because I do not think I could fly an airplane."

"But you just said that you have been driving your car for many years. You have the experience."

"But my experience is in driving the car, and not the airplane."

"Great point, and what do you think can help you learn to fly an airplane?"

"I would need to be trained."

"Yes, excellent... and do you think just training to fly an airplane is enough? Or would you need some practice and handholding as well?"

"I will need a lot of practice for sure. Someone would need to supervise me until I am an expert. Any mistake can be fatal... Oh, I understand what you are getting to."

"Good that you are getting my point, Mr. Gobind. Just like an airplane is a great vehicle to travel quickly and comfortably, I am the right vehicle to give you great returns on your invested money, but you need to be trained first. Then, you need to practice, practice and practice. Only after gaining enough experience would you be able to start making handsome money."

"But seriously, how much practice do you think I need. I may not actually have that much time. Having a full-time job, with a family to support... how do I take out the time to be trained?"

"As I said the choice was, and always will be, yours. An untrained pilot, using even the best of vehicles, is likely to crash. Unfortunately in our case, you have the choice to blame me for all the unexpected results, even if it was actually lack of your training and practice. I mean, no one will allow you to fly a real airplane unless you show your license, training and practice certificates. Unfortunately, in the case of stocks, anyone can just come and invest, without a single day of training or practice. If the person fails, blaming me is probably the safest choice."

"Hey buddy, frankly, I don't have time to discuss this entire training stuff. We can do this later. Let me try my hands in the stock market first. Many of my friends have already succeeded without much training or practice. And I have heard that the market seems to be in a great mood too. Also, I have heard that ICICI Bank is a good stock to get into. Many of my friends have made good money with this stock. Give me five of those to get started."

"Your choice Mr. Gobind. It always is. I never refuse any investment."

"Thank you."

As with most investors, Gobind did not listen to me. To give him the benefit of doubt, he probably did not have the time to listen. He purchased five shares of ICICI Bank. It was 1998 and it was his first ever hand at stocks. He was a young engineer with close to four years of work experience. He had some spare money and seemed to be in a hurry to earn more. 'How much more?' and 'Why more?' were big questions, which perhaps needed to be answered. But I think he assumed that more money would bring cheer and happiness to him and his family.

Alas, there is no assurance of more money. He did not have the required training and practice to make wealth from me. More than a trillion transactions happen every single day in various stock exchanges that I control. Based on the profile that I have of all the users, more than 98 percent of them haven't had the required training, and it is not a surprise that almost an equal number of them lose money in stocks – every single day. I will be there to make people rich if they know what they are doing. Having said that, I show no mercy to the ignorant and the greedy. That is what was very likely to happen with Gobind.

We met again after 15 days.

"You see, I told you that you are unnecessarily confusing me with all the jargon around training and practice and airplane and whatnot."

"What happened? You seem very excited, Mr. Gobind."

"Why not? I earned more than 50 percent in two weeks, which is just too good. And I sold it off yesterday. No hassles. I made good money. Actually, I should have invested more. It is only because you loaded me with all that jargon that I was hesitant to invest too much. Anyway, thanks Mr. Stock. You are indeed a great investment vehicle."

"That is really good to know. May luck always be with you!"

"Luck. Where was luck in this? ICICI Bank was a stock that so many of my friends had already made money from, and unlike you, they are not jealous of me. They only suggested that I go for it. And see the result – I also made money."

"Excellent, Mr. Gobind. By the way, I am not jealous, rather happy for you. I am always happy for anyone who makes money by investing with me. That is the purpose of my existence. That is how we both grow. It is a win-win. But at the same time, it is also my duty to warn you that you have not yet undergone training, which may prove extremely dangerous one day."

"Don't start that crap all over again. I do have a fair bit of idea about how your market works. Even if luck is not on my side, it might take a little longer, but I will still make more money than what I have been making in other investment tools. Let me have further discussions with my friends and come back to you after a few days. I want to invest more, and make more money."

"Sure, but just be careful, Mr. Gobind. Greed can take over humans faster than they can realize."

"Leave that to me, Mr. Stock."

"As always, the choice is yours. My duty is to forewarn you."

"OK, thanks for doing your duty. I will catch up with you on Thursday, exactly two days from now."

Two days passed. Gobind came with a list of 10 stocks, all advised by his well-meaning friends and relatives.

"You see, this is the best I have come up with, after talking to my friends and some of my relatives, who have been invested in the market for more than 20 years. They, of course, cannot be completely wrong in their judgment. And they are all my well-wishers too. If they are sharing their experience with confidence and enthusiasm, I must go for it. In fact, they are already holding most of these stocks themselves. That leaves me without any doubt. I have decided to go ahead with them."

"But dear friend, I am your well-wisher too. I am everyone's well-wisher. And your friends and relatives may be experienced, but they can never be so more than me. I am the Stock. I know myself since my origin. I would never advise you to follow this approach."

"See, you even discouraged me from buying that ICICI Bank stock. But what happened? I made good money there. I am not sure if I can trust you more than my own relatives and all-weather friends. And you know what? I must tell you one more thing."

"What?"

"One of my relatives also has 'inside information' about the new acquisition that one of these 10 companies is going to make. That one event is bound to set its stock price soaring. No one else may have that information. I have an unfair edge over so many others."

"Unfair edge?" I smiled, "My dear friend, by the time this 'inside information' reaches you, everyone else would have heard it and traded on it. Trust me. I see that happening every day."

"What do you mean?"

"I mean that the choice is always yours, friend. However, I am the companion of anyone who is trying to invest in stocks. I am ready to help anyone who takes the right approach, but only if they are ready to listen to me. There may be short-term fluctuations, but the principles that I want to share with you, are the only ones that work with me in the long run. In any case, I leave the decision with you."

"I don't know why, but you always create doubt in my mind, and I knew you would do that. That is why, this time I am here with concrete evidence."

"Concrete evidence?"

"Here is the analysis report from a very reputed financial firm on the 10 stocks that I am planning to buy. There is a 'buy' tagged against nine of them. Why on earth would everyone be wrong, except you?"

"As I told you, no well-meaning individual or firm can ever be more experienced than me, when it comes to understanding the principles of investing. Moreover, money with me can be made only by following a contrarian approach, and not by following the herd. You want to invest in something that the market does not want today but would be dying for tomorrow, instead of something that everyone wants today."

"Whatever, but my decision is final. I think we have had enough of this debate and discussion. We are going ahead with buying these 10 stocks."

"As you wish, Mr. Gobind! The choice is always yours."

Gobind purchased those 10 stocks and the amount he invested seemed far more than his saving capacity. He was confident of making huge gains yet again, but the law of averages usually catches up, and much faster than one wants it to.

In the next three months, Gobind lost 40 percent of his invested money to market volatility; he was quick to come back to me.

"What is happening to you? Why do you seem to be going down in value, especially for the stocks that I purchased? Many other stocks which I never purchased only seem to be either going up or are at least stable. Are you taking revenge on me for not following your advice?"

Never ever invest on tips.

Tips can come from all-weather friends, blood relatives, financial analysts, TV channels or any other source.

Consider the suggested stocks 'only' as potential candidates for investing.

Never invest without your own further analysis.

"Revenge? I am never revengeful, my dear friend. I am the slave of anyone who follows the principles that created me."

"Then what is happening? And why?"

"That's OK, friend. This is just market volatility. Your stock value might get better with time. But remember that it can get worse too. I had warned you earlier as well."

"Can it really get any worse?"

"Of course it can. Your blood relatives and all-weather friends and those market reports from those reputed financial firms: they didn't tell you this?"

"Now you are rubbing salt into my wounds. They had sold their stocks after booking some losses; they just didn't tell me when they did so. Now, I am stuck with these stocks."

"No, I am not trying to hurt you, my friend. My love for all my investors is unconditional. I am only trying to teach you the second lesson in stock investing."

"Second lesson? What is that?"

"Never invest on tips."

"But..."

"No, there is no exception to this rule. Absolutely none. At most, these tips can help you shortlist and identify potential stocks to invest in, but blindly investing based on such tips is the ultimate recipe for disaster. This is one of the biggest reasons of people losing money. I have seen so many of my favourite investors fall into this trap, and I am sad to see you do the same."

"But they all gave me so many examples of winning stocks and how these 10 stocks were trending exactly on the same lines."

"You see Gobind, it is very easy to look at a winning stock today and speak nostalgically about how cheap it once was. What is missing in this story is that it was cheap because not many thought it would become a winner."

"But… but I had a plan to pay the down payment for my home from the stock returns. Now, I cannot even take out the principle amount since it is 40 percent down. I am badly stuck," said a tensed Gobind.

"Greed and Speed are the worst enemies of an investor. Anyway, tell me something, when are you planning to buy the house?"

"I have already given the token amount. I have to put the first cash down payment after one month. Do you know what can be done now?"

"There are only two ways ahead for you now."

"What are those?"

"First is to book losses and take out whatever money you can and start investing that money in investment avenues which you understand better. Obviously, that cannot compensate for your losses and pay for the cash down payment of your house. You will have to make some other arrangements for the same."

"Are you saying that I should take out my money and incur a 40 percent loss?"

"Yes, because you still do not understand the principles that I have been trying to teach you. Without understanding those principles you may be in for further disaster."

"My God, I have never experienced this in my life before."

"What have you never experienced before?"

"Coming out of an investment in a loss. What is the second option that I have?"

"The other option is to come with me and I will teach you the principles of stock investing. We will study and analyze each stock in detail and then conclude which ones we can stay invested, and which ones we should sell at loss. It might take us a few weeks to do that *value analysis*, but it would surely be worth all the effort."

"You are always trying to preach me. And at this critical juncture when I am more concerned about the down payment for my home, you are still trying to force your so called principles down my throat. I do not have that kind of patience to study each and every stock and spend weeks doing the analysis that you are suggesting I do. And what is the guarantee that I will earn handsome returns after the analysis."

"There is no guarantee, but only an improved probability. You are facing a situation and now we must learn how to respond to the situation most effectively."

"Forget it then. And even if I follow your advice, you might still tell me to sell all of them at losses. And in those few weeks, my existing stocks may lose further value. That is also possible, isn't it?"

"Yes, possible."

"Then fine, I've made my decision. I am selling all of them and booking 40 percent losses. This has been a very bitter experience for me. I do not know what I am going to tell my wife about this stupid investment, nor from where we are going to get the money to complete our home purchase. Maybe we will have to drop the idea of buying a home now and even forego the advance payment. I don't know. This is a complete mess."

"The choice is always with the investor, my dear friend. If you try to fly an airplane without training and the plane crashes, please do not blame the vehicle. This has been the tragedy for humanity."

"What do you mean – tragedy for humanity?" Gobind asked with a grin on his face.

"See Gobind, whenever you humans are faced with an unfavorable situation, you tend to look for the fault outside – with another person, an external situation – and if nothing else, you blame Him. But you all rarely tend to look within yourselves – the place where most, rather all, the faults lie."

"Are you saying that in every situation, the fault lies with us alone?"

"Yes, of course."

"How is that possible? If someone dies of a natural tragedy, has God nothing to do with it?"

"I have seen Him up close; I have worked with him since eternity. He never interferes with the situations that you face. All your situations are a result of your own doing (which you sometime refer to as karma). He just ensures that there is order and balance in karma and the results. None of the natural disasters are because of Him; these are because of the karma of your humankind. There is nothing natural about any disaster, these are all man-made."

"Interesting food for thought... Anyway, what does that have to do with my losing money after I invested in you? How will you justify that?"

"What I only mean is that do not blame me as an investment vehicle for the mess you have landed yourself in. If at all you have to blame someone, you have to blame yourself for your reluctance to accept the fact that you need to be trained."

"Whatever! This has been a very bitter experience for me. I would rather avoid the stock market from now on and invest in term deposits and bonds, which give assured returns.

"The choice is always yours my friend. But before you leave, let me share with you the third lesson that you ought to have learned just now."

"Third lesson?"

"Yes, I am not to be used as an investment vehicle for short-term investments. This is primarily because of my inherent volatile nature. My value, in the short-term, is driven by market sentiments, which is neither in my nor in the investor's control."

"And what do you mean by short-term? Six months? Nine months?"

"Any investment would mostly be safe with me if it is done for a period of seven or more years. Anything less than that is a risk."

LESSON 3

Never have a short-term horizon.

Stocks are volatile. Their short-term value is linked to marked sentiments, which is not in an investor's control.

Invest only if you are ready to lock your money for 7+ years.

"Seven years... Wow! In today's world, who has the time and patience to invest and lock his or her money for seven years?"

"The choice is always yours, dear friend."

"It is not always a question of choice, Mr. Stock. There are other constraints which drive our investment decisions."

"Like?"

"Like, take my case. A part of the money I had invested was

borrowed from someone. If you invest with borrowed money, no one is going to lend you the money for seven years. You can just forget it."

"You are right. And that is another blunder which I have seen a lot of investors do. You should never invest in me with borrowed money. This is true for all investments, but especially true for me. I hate it. I am volatile and unpredictable in the short-term. Your lenders will hate both you and me, for not being able to return the borrowed money."

"I don't know, buddy. What I only know is that I am in a pathetic situation right now. And I absolutely do not like this volatility of yours."

"Volatility is my inherent nature. That is how I am designed. Volatility is not bad. It is actually very good. This volatility is what lets investors make a lot of money."

"Volatility lets us make a lot of money? What are you talking about? You are actually confusing me even more. I would not have lost my money if you were to give steady stable returns, and you are telling me that volatility is good and helps us make more money?"

"Congratulations, Mr. Gobind."

"For what?"

"For all the confusion in your mind. Confusion is the first step towards learning something new."

"How?"

"You see, confusions compel you to think. Clarity compels you to act."

"Ah! Interesting...."

"And yes, you will understand about the advantages of volatility if you are ready to learn. If I was not volatile, you could never have made the kind of money that you have heard some people make from me."

"How?"

"When on the downside, volatility allows you to lower your cost – a luxury no other investment offers except for mutual funds and stocks. Imagine buying a house for INR 25 lakh and later on being allowed to lower the cost to INR 20 lakh. Never heard of it, right? But that is what I want you to learn and appreciate. The sillier the market behavior, the more is the downside and greater is the opportunity for an investor."

"Seems untrue, but I am listening."

"When on the higher side, I can give you returns like 50 percent to

60 percent per annum on your investments – something which you can rarely dream of in any other investment, not even with mutual funds."

LESSON 4

Stock market's volatility is what helps it give you stellar returns.

Stocks are volatile.

Volatility allows you to reduce your cost and maximize your selling price, thus, giving you stellar returns.

"This is weird. I do not think I am ever going to understand you."

"You can. You need to be ready to be taught. I am ready to help anyone who wants to become a great student of mine."

"We will see. For now, you have made my life a mess. And I need to leave."

"The choice is always yours, my friend. But take my last lesson before you leave."

"What?"

"Only those people enjoy my volatility who either have a lot of cash to deploy when the markets are down or are fully invested when the markets rise. Therefore, never invest in me with borrowed money or a faint heart. Both are fatal."

LESSON 5

Do not invest with borrowed money or a faint heart, both are fatal.

Stocks are volatile.

You must get accustomed to your money fluctuating with that.

Never ever borrow money to invest in a volatile market.

Gobind booked losses. He went away with the pledge to never return to me. I liked him, but unfortunately he was missing the willingness to learn the fundamentals of investing in stocks. Hopefully, he learnt the five lessons that I taught him during our short stint. Hopefully, some day, he will return, for wisdom must prevail.

Life in my market continued as usual. My five-day week used to start with millions of transactions, peaking up to billions. Saturday and Sunday was when I normally got a bit of rest.

As the number of investors and the number of transactions increased by leaps and bounds every year, the sad side of the story was that most transactions were ones that made losses. Worse, the blame of this loss was almost always borne by me. Human beings have a strange tendency to always look 'outside' themselves, whether it is for seeking happiness in their life or to blame for the mess that they are in. They might never realize that everything is 'inside' them. I am ready to share my secrets with them but they are unwilling to learn. They do not have patience. Greed takes over them very easily. They are weak. They are prone to emotions. They were not like this a few centuries ago.

I have seen this degeneration over the last three generations since I have existed on this planet. But I must keep trying. With great power comes great responsibility, and I strongly feel that it is my responsibility to keep making an attempt to warn the humankind before they make any more mistakes and also offer them my secret of wealth. If they are unwilling to learn, it is always their choice. But if someone is willing to learn, I should always remain excited to help him or her out.

No Parallel to Stock Investing

Nine years passed and Gobind did not come back to me, until one fine day, he showed up in my chamber and asked if I could answer some of his questions. He made it absolutely clear that he is still not keen on investing with me. I did not refuse, though I had all the right to do so, since he was no longer an investor or a prospect for me.

"Everyone fine in your family?" I asked.

"Yes buddy, but a lot has changed in these nine years. My wife and I have been blessed with two beautiful daughters; I love spending time with them. On the financial front, my income has gone up significantly, and so have my expenses. I have a much more secure job now."

"Excellent to hear this Gobind. God bless your little angels. Good to know that you have a great family and that you are earning well too."

"I think money is not that big a problem in life now. But... but, time is. The more I am earning, the less time I am able to spend with my beautiful fairies, my lovely wife and my ageing parents. I miss that."

"Oh! I completely understand your point. That is a typical time versus money challenge that most humans are stuck in. Can I help you in some way?"

"Yes, I am chasing something called financial freedom. I am sure you have heard about it."

"Of course, I have. It is so good to know that you are among the two percent of people in the world who are chasing freedom from the rut of making money."

"Yeah, thanks. I don't know whether I will be successful in this journey, but I needed your help answering some of my questions. Your answers may help me during this journey."

"Go ahead please Gobind. It will be my pleasure. I am always answerable to my investors – even if they are no more invested in me," I gave Gobind a reassuring smile.

"You know I have had a very bad experience with you. It took me a couple of years to come out of that mess. It has been 9 years since we last interacted."

"Yes, I remember. If it was painful for you, it was painful for me too. I would have loved to train you on making money in stocks."

"Well, forget it. Stocks are not what I am really looking at. But in this journey towards financial freedom, I need to accumulate a minimum corpus which can become self-sustaining for me and my family. From all the books I have read, the financial advisors I have met and the financial freedom plans I have made, I have been made to understand that my money needs to grow faster than inflation after taking care of my expenses as well as paying all the taxes."

"Yes, that's the key. If you can achieve that, your corpus will keep serving you and will also keep growing on its own," I said, excited about Gobind and his bright financial future.

"Right, but currently with the investments that I have made, I am unable to get those kinds of returns."

"Where are your primary investments?"

"Well, mostly fixed deposits, recurring deposits, employee provident fund, public provident fund, gold, insurance and one real estate investment."

"OK. I understand where you are coming from. This is a completely debt-based portfolio. This portfolio will never be able to beat inflation. Always remember this, even though your wealth is increasing every year, if your portfolio cannot beat inflation after paying all the taxes, year after year the worth of your portfolio is actually going down."

"Yeah, makes sense."

"And if you continue to build this portfolio with the current mix of investments that you have, you are in for trouble in the future. Your money may seem to grow on its own but considering the fact that the money is growing at a rate lesser than inflation, it is going to pinch you in later years of your life."

"I understand that inflation is a challenge for us, but tell me if it is really that vital to beat inflation? I mean, my corpus is growing anyway."

LESSON 6

Your portfolio must beat inflation after paying taxes, year on year.

Even though your wealth is increasing every year, if your portfolio cannot beat inflation after paying all the taxes, year after year the worth of your portfolio is actually going down. It will surely hit you some day in future.

"Gobind, inflation is such a hidden devil that it can kill you and you would not even know it."

"Ah. C'mon. Let's give inflation only the importance it deserves. Let us not hype it up too much."

"Gobind, how would you feel if you were to take a 4-percent cut on your salary in a year when inflation was running at, let's say 3 percent?"

"Salary cut? It is absolutely unacceptable to me. After working so hard for the entire year, why should I accept a salary cut?"

"Calm down, my friend. I completely understand. I will give you another deal..."

"Another deal?"

"Forget the earlier deal. We move two years ahead. How about accepting a 2 percent increase in your salary?"

"That still sounds fair, though the figure of 2 percent is hardly motivating. But what are you trying to prove?"

"I will tell you. But before accepting the new deal, you did not ask what the running inflation was, when you were offered a 2 percent increase?"

"Well, I really do not care much about it."

"You should care about it Gobind, else you are missing the whole point."

"What do you mean?"

"If in the second case, the running inflation was more than 10 percent, then you were actually better off in the earlier case with the deal of 4 percent cut in your salary with a running inflation of 3 percent. Calculate it if you want, but that is how lack of awareness about inflation can misguide you if you are not careful."

"How?"

"See. A 4-percent cut in salary with 3 percent inflation means that you are at a net loss of 7 percent in the first case. However, in the second case, a 2 percent raise during 10 percent inflation implies that you are at a net loss of 8 percent. The first deal is definitely better."

"Very interesting. I never knew that salary cuts can be more rewarding than a salary increase. But point taken. Inflation was surely one of the reasons I came to you, though I never knew how real it was. Can you help me please?"

"OK, so you want to start investing in stocks?"

"No, no. I cannot risk losing the principle amount of my investment. I am thinking of diversifying my portfolio into a couple of other streams which have better returns and are also less risky compared to you."

"Ah sure, tell me."

"What do you think about real estate? I already have one investment in real estate. I was thinking whether I should go for one more."

"Well, Mr. Gobind, traditionally, real estate has been a great investment vehicle in India. One of the major reasons for that has been the lack of knowledge or awareness about me as an investment vehicle. But there are many reasons why I do not personally favour real estate as a great vehicle for personal wealth creation."

"Tell me the truth. I am very confused. I hear different things from different people. I thought you have more experience and would give me an unbiased view."

"First, listen to the points I am about to say, and then you can take a call. Do not trust me. Go with your instincts. That is what you have been doing until now, isn't it?"

"OK, go ahead. Let me see what you have to say, though so many people are upbeat about real estate in India."

"The biggest issue that I see with real estate is the lack of liquidity."

"That's not such a big obstacle. Tell me the next challenge."

"Hold on. Perhaps you do not understand how vital liquidity is for any portfolio."

"Well may be what you say is right. Give me some idea about liquidity in that case."

"Good. You see, liquidity is the ability to generate cash at a short notice. It is not about how wealthy you are, but how much cash can you pull out as and when needed. A well-planned financial portfolio will account for liquidity as one of the critical parameters before deciding the investment target."

"Oh, that's a new angle. I have been building my portfolio without thinking too much about liquidity."

"That is the whole point. We do not appreciate its importance. You see, last week, Danny came to me for a discussion. Danny is one of my newer students and has been following my advice on stock investments. I advised him that the market was down. His stock was also down, very much in line with the overall sentiments of the market. It seemed just the right opportunity to bring down the average cost for one of the blue chips that my friend Danny was holding. I advised him to go ahead and invest more in his stock during this tumultuous time, follow the cost averaging principle, bring down the average cost of the stock and reap the rewards later. He agreed wholeheartedly. It was just then that he realized that he had no spare cash to invest. His entire surplus was already invested and it was difficult to take cash out from any of those investments, at least for the next two weeks. Well, in such times, two weeks can prove to be too long a duration to miss out on the opportunity that the market was providing to bring down his average cost of purchase."

"Oh I see."

"What my friend Danny's portfolio lacked was not money but 'liquidity' of his investments. He had enough wealth, but almost none was liquid right at that moment when he needed it the most."

"I get it."

"You see Mr. Gobind, most people tend to invest their money considering parameters like return on investments (RoI), taxation and the safety or risk involved in an investment. There is absolutely no doubting the fact that these factors are truly important for an investor. But one of the most critical factors that often get ignored is the liquidity of your investment."

"Hmm... and real estate lacks liquidity."

"Yes my friend, it lacks that badly, while investments with me are highly liquid. However, liquidity is not the only factor. There are other factors that do not make real estate an ideal investment."

"I am listening…"

"Just look at the size of investment needed. Most common investors may hardly be able to make more than two to three such investments in their entire life time."

"Good point, but also consider the fact that we get a regular rental income from real estate investments."

"That's an excellent point, Gobind. You seem to have done a lot of hard work in these nine years. Once you invest, what you seek is a regular income from your assets. Though rental income can be said to be a kind of regular source of income, but this could easily discontinue in case of break of tenancy. Moreover, this income is hardly giving you 2-3 percent returns from your overall investment. Not only that, it would continue to need your active involvement and monitoring for maintenance and upkeep of your property."

"Just 2-3 percent?"

"Yes, you tell me the rental income you get from the real estate investment that you already have right now?"

"I get around INR 22,000 per month."

"And what is the current value of your house?"

"Well, it must be close to INR 1.4 crore."

"That's it. You can easily calculate. That is 1.8 percent annual returns. Of course, there are capital gains involved in real estate but then that's not assured, that's not a regular income, that's not liquid and that's subject to taxation too, all this is unlike what happens when you invest with me."

"Hmm… You do not attract taxes, is it?"

"No."

"No taxes, really?"

"No taxes in India after 12 months of investment. It's 100 percent white money. On your real estate, you will have to pay a minimum of 20 percent tax on capital gains post indexation benefit, and that too after 36 months of investing."

"Right."

"And that is not all. There is still a lot of black money involved in real estate in India. For investors like you, who do not have any source of black money, getting in or getting out of real estate investment can be quite challenging. One wrong move and all your gains, as well as the principle investment could be at risk."

LESSON 7

Real Estate is no match for stock investing.
Though a traditional Indian favourite, real estate investors have to deal with issues like black money, lack of liquidity, higher capital gain taxes and lower rental income.
Stock investing is liquid, white money with zero taxation and higher dividend income.

"Your points truly seem valid. You seem to have almost closed the doors for me to invest in real estate now. Then where else can I put my money so that I can beat inflation? And let me be very clear that you are not an option."

"Well Mr. Gobind, nothing can beat me. I was created by the Almighty to help the humankind. However, I reiterate, what you need is training and practice."

"Currently, I am not looking at that option. Still, let me call one of my friends and ask for his advice."

As he took a few minutes away for a call to his friend, I had to appreciate Gobind. He had come out as a more mature individual after nine years. He was at least listening now, though only listening. He was still not in a frame of mind to be trained for the biggest wealth creating investment option the world will ever see. I see so many like him every day. Humans are not ready to change easily. They get into their comfort zone, enjoy that zone for some time, and then find it extremely difficult to come out of it. Having said that, he is looking for non-traditional investment options, and that's definitely one positive I do not see in many.

Hanging up the phone after 10 minutes, Gobind returned, "Buddy, I have got to go. I think I found the solution which has the best of both the worlds."

"What did you find out, Gobind?"

"Mutual funds... mutual funds are the way out."

"Actually, your friend is right. I was about to suggest this. You see, mutual funds are my half cousins. They too are a great vehicle to build good long-term wealth. If you are not up for stocks for any reason, mutual funds will be your second best choice. In fact, they are a better choice to start with, before you come to me some day."

"You are a typical salesman. You won't give up, will you?"

"No, I will not Mr. Gobind. I have seen so much in my lifespan of last 190-plus years on this planet that I can now predict how your financial life is going to turn out eventually. I know you will come back to me... sooner rather later."

"We shall see. But why did you say that mutual funds are a better bet to start with?"

"I say that because you still need to get used to the volatility of the markets. When you invested with me around nine years ago, you were taken aback by this very volatility, which prompted you to take a decision to quit any investments with me, even if it meant booking losses. You remember?"

"Yes, how can I forget that."

"Systematic investment plans (SIPs) and Variable investment plans (VIPs) of mutual funds will allow you to invest systematically and still get you used to market volatility. In fact, they will allow you to take advantage of the same market volatility, which you are otherwise afraid of. Once you are used to it for 1-2 years, and then come to me. I will be there to help you build your innings with me."

LESSON 8

Mutual funds are next best to stock investing.

With seemingly less risk (and surely less reward), mutual funds allow you to get used to market volatility – a key trait that you would need for stock investing. They are a good starting point before investing in stocks.

"Sure..."

"But before we depart buddy, please be aware of some of the areas where mutual funds lag behind the ultimate investment option, and that is me..."

"Go ahead please. I was wondering how you can stop promoting yourself."

"See Gobind, unlike humans, I do not possess any ego. Whatever you think of me, is your perspective. I will continue to tell you what will benefit you. The decision to implement my lessons is completely left to you."

"Sorry if I hurt you... I did not mean it..."

"You cannot hurt me, in fact no one can. Unless I permit, I can never get hurt. This applies equally to your breed as well. It is just that you need to practice this... Anyway, coming back to mutual funds, you see that the biggest drawback of mutual funds is that it doesn't teach you anything about stocks, stock analysis, valuation, companies etc."

"What does that mean?"

"That means, you don't learn anything, and in the long run, if you don't learn about companies, stocks, earnings, revenue, intrinsic value calculation and a few other fundamental stock picking techniques, your wealth will always be far behind those who invest directly in stocks. If you do not build your temperament and personality traits like patience, trust and confidence and overcome your weak areas like greed, need for instant gratification, frustration, then you remain the same human being. Your wealth will never reach humungous proportions."

"Ah! So, you are saying that our financial wealth will be a direct reflection of our intellectual wisdom and temperament level?"

"Absolutely, sooner or later this is going to hold true."

"Hmm... but what do I really learn in stocks? I thought we just put in some money with you, wait for it to grow and then pull it out at a suitable opportunity."

"This is where the world has gone wrong. While investing with me, you control where to invest, how much to invest, when to come out etc. I give you the environment and allow you to operate more like an entrepreneur. In a nutshell, with me, you will grow intellectually. And when a human being grows intellectually, his wealth is bound to catch up with the intellect – sooner or later. And therefore, your portfolio and wealth will also start growing by leaps and bounds. My mutual fund cousin will keep you in your comfort zone. You will feel good, you might feel relaxed. That is what a comfort zone does to you. But then there is relatively lesser growth of your portfolio and absolutely no growth of you as a person. Ultimately, your portfolio will also come down to the level of your intellect."

LESSON 9

Mutual funds do not allow for your intellectual growth, stocks do.

You operate like an entrepreneur when investing in stocks. Entry price, entry time, exit price, exit time, company choice etc. are all controlled by the investor. This entire decision making process leads to an investor's intellectual growth.

And in life, your wealth will always catch up with your intellectual growth.

"I get it, buddy. Actually that point about my intellectual growth is really very interesting. But the fact remains that you are a much more risky option, and give almost the same level of returns as mutual funds, don't you think?"

"Gobind, this is absolutely untrue. Mutual funds do not reward you anywhere close to how I do."

"Is it? But I heard that you are very risky."

"Yes, today, I am definitely risky. And risk comes from not knowing what you are doing. There is not much of a difference between the risk profiles of a mutual fund owner versus a stock owner – because ultimately in both the cases, money is invested in the same market and the same stocks. It is just that in case of stocks, you need to learn some fundamentals before picking up a company. But look at the difference in rewards for the effort that you put in. The average returns for a person who has learnt for 10 years and is now investing in stocks can be anywhere between 20-40 percent while the average returns from the most rewarding mutual funds are likely to be between 15-20 percent. That is not a huge, but a humungous difference in returns."

LESSON 10

Stock returns far outweigh the returns from mutual funds, with almost similar amount of risk.

Once you learn value investing, stock investing is no more risky than mutual funds.

But look at the returns:

20-40 percent for stocks vs.

15-20 percent for mutual funds.

It is truly worth the effort learning value investing.

"What are you saying? That's almost double the difference between the returns offered by stocks as compared to mutual funds. I am really surprised at this."

"Surprised? Why?"

"Surprised because mutual funds invest in stocks too, and they do so through professional tools and qualified managers. So, are we saying that the fund managers are fools?"

"Of course they are not fools. They are real smart folk. But they work under some serious constraints which dwarfs the possible returns of mutual funds from the market..."

"Serious constraints? Like what?"

"Firstly, understand that they manage funds worth thousands of crores of rupees. Whether they want or not, they must gravitate towards the biggest stocks, because those are the only ones available in millions of quantities that can fill their numbers."

"Ah, very interesting point. That's why I see that most big funds have the same big names of stocks that they own?"

"Absolutely. Second, when the market rises, more investors flock the fund houses and they are forced to buy big names, which are perhaps already overpriced. Similarly, during the downturn, when investors ask for their money, they become forced sellers of some great value stocks."

"Oh, so the fund managers have no choice but flow with the emotions of their investors?"

"Bang on. And last but not the least. They are paid bonuses for beating the returns that the market index is giving. Any new stock that is added to the index is compulsorily purchased by them in significant quantities."

"As I understand, and you can correct me if I am wrong, a market index is something like an index fund that includes all stocks of NSE or BSE in our country? Right?"

"Yes... and if you know that the stocks that participate in these index funds are very limited and the participants also keep changing over time."

"Yes, I have heard about it. But why do they have to compulsorily buy any new stock entering this index fund? I did not understand that."

"You see, if they don't buy the new stock that has just entered the index fund, and it picks up momentum, they will only look foolish. And on the flip side, if that new stock falls, they are still in line with the index returns, against which they are measured. They have all the incentives to get the new stock, whether or not it is a good deal at the current price."

"Wow. Never thought about it that way. I always had the mindset that mutual funds are almost as good as stocks. Interesting, really interesting... I have enough food for thought for the day..."

"OK Mr. Gobind, time is up for me as well. I need to make it to the Beijing Exchange right away, where Juang Lee, an investor just like you, is waiting to be trained."

"Sure, Mr. Stock. See you soon!"

We departed with an exchange of much more pleasant vibrations than what we had the last time. My experience tells me that Gobind is going to come back soon, for he is chasing financial freedom and he will need to create wealth fast enough to make his life more meaningful. No one can do it faster for him than me. That is the purpose with which I was crafted, by none other than Him.

Buying Stocks... or Groceries?

Almost a year passed. The number of investors coming to me kept increasing every day. Having said that, word-of-mouth publicity was not working out as more and more investors wanted to get rich quick without understanding the fundamentals of stock investing. And any failure to getting wealthy was, as usual, blamed squarely on me.

Time was running out for me. Almost two centuries had passed. Though I was instrumental in creating wealth for humans, it was painfully unevenly distributed. Instead of waiting for things to improve on their own, I decided to do something about it.

I started taking worldwide sessions on fundamental concepts around stock investing. These sessions, which went by the name *Stock Rudiments,* did not deal with any analysis about a particular stock or a company. There were no stock picks or exit recommendations. There was no annual report analysis. It was simpler and more fundamental than that.

The purpose was to re-emphasize the fact that the more clear humans are about basics of a particular concept, the easier it becomes for them to take bigger and bolder decisions. The power to wealth creation was, is and will always be in doing the so called 'simple' things 'right'. Wealth creation is not complicated. But doing those simple things – over and over again – with discipline and commitment – is what will get them there.

These worldwide sessions were initially not accepted by the majority of the investor community for this simplicity. They thought they knew it all. The fact was that they knew it, but not all. And even if they knew it all, it was so important to bring them down to the very basics – one more time. In the mad rush to make money, humans tend to complicate things. It needs repeated efforts and practice to bring them down and remind them to stick to the basics – simple and powerful fundamentals of making money through me.

Stock Rudiments continued. Very soon, the investors started to realize the power of these simple and powerful concepts.

These basic concepts in *Stock Rudiments* sessions were not in a presentation format. They were delivered in the format in which maximum learning happens among humans i.e. in Question and Answer format. Human beings tend to see anyone who is confused and is asking a question from a very negative perspective. They do not realize that a confused person is the one who is thinking beyond his or her boundary. And that is exactly what is needed to learn – breaking your boundaries and comfort zones to explore and accept new things. Therefore, in all my sessions, participants were encouraged to ask questions and I would explain them the answers with examples.

LESSON 11

Wealth creation is not complex. Follow the simple steps, over and over again – with faith and commitment.

Wealth creation principles are simple.

Following these simple, but powerful and time tested, principles – over and over again – is what will get you there.

To be able to do that, you will need discipline, commitment and faith of the highest order.

The next such seminar was scheduled after a week. There were already more than one million investors from across the globe, who had enrolled for this seminar. I sent a special invitation to Gobind as well. I somehow had a soft corner for him, for no logical reason though. I also had the feeling that he would be ready for investing with me by then. This seemed just the perfect time for him to grasp the rudiments of stocks.

The session day started at 9AM CST. The participant's window on my left screen showed 850,000+ participants live on the session. I searched for 'Gobind' and found three of them. I did not know his last name. Moreover, there were no profile pictures in two of the three search results. I hoped he was among them.

"OK, ladies and gentlemen, good morning and welcome to this *Stock Rudiments* Q&A session. This is not a typical stock picking or get-rich-quick sessions. There will be no stock analysis or recommendation from my side. This session is in Q&A format, where each one of you is encouraged to ask as fundamental a question as possible. Remember that learning is in questions and answers. Understand that the simpler and fundamental the question is, the more difficult it is to answer those questions. But once the question is answered and its meaning grasped by the seeker, its learning and impact on your wealth is immense. So, go on my friends, the forum is all yours."

There was silence for some time before the first question popped up on my screen, and I immediately knew there were many more now in the queue.

"OK ladies and gentleman – we have the first question from a gentleman by the name of Jimmy from New York. And the question is: Why at all do you exist? What was your need?

"Wonderful. Love this question. You see, there has to be a reason for everything, and therefore, we all must understand why do I exist?

"To put it simply, God realized that most humans are stuck in a mad race to earn money. The data analytics available with Him showed that most humans meant 90 percent of them. These many people are either not able to make their ends meet or even if they can, their life is a continuous struggle for which they find no end. They cannot devote time and energy to things which are more beautiful and worthy in life because of a weird cycle in which they were all stuck. Since a majority of the human race was stuck with this problem, God wanted a solution for this on priority, and He wanted a simple solution – something which most common men and women can understand and implement. He believed that once this simple, and yet powerful, solution is implemented by most humans – then His men and women would be relieved of one of their biggest stress factors in life, and then He could also take a nap or two.

"After a lot of brainstorming with his team, one of the solutions that came up was to just provide a lot of money to everyone. This was immediately shot down by Him. 'This instant solution may work elsewhere but it doesn't work on this planet. If you give humans a lot of money without them having to put in any effort, they will just splurge and soon be back to square one – struggling to make ends meet. Not only that, this is also unfair to people who work hard or are smart.'

"He wanted a solution that would enable people to 'earn' wealth but should be simple enough so that anyone who is willing to understand certain simple and fundamental principles could make good money. This would also have kept it fair.

"And that's where I was born. He created me to help the human species create enough wealth so that they can devote their time and energy to more beautiful things in life, things that they truly love and enjoy doing. That was the intent. Having said that, this still remains a long cherished dream for me and for Him, even after spending more than 190 years on this planet. I think He never realized that the humankind was not going to accept simple things so easily. This project has seen rare success, and I am making renewed efforts to turn this around through these sessions and teachings.

Now, to put things into operational perspective, you also must understand how we decided to implement this into human operations. We came up with the concept of stocks and stock exchanges. Let me share with you where we fit into your human business, as the world knows it today. But before that – Jimmy, I suppose you are with me?"

"Of course, I am. And I understand the intent very well now."

"OK, cool... So, let's go ahead. We looked at the latest forecast for Planet Earth and saw that 'Industrial Revolution' was going to be the latest buzz word on the planet very soon. We saw that as a key entry point for me. We wanted to implement our project via entering some companies who would go on to thrive later. And that's where we created the concept of 'shares of a company'.

"Hold on. 'You created' means? Shares were not something that came from God. This was all invented by people from our planet."

I smiled, "That is what humans will always feel. He does not come here and create anything. He works through thought energy. He will send or germinate a thought in a human mind, based on what He wants to get done. You all are a means to help Him achieve whatever He wants."

Jimmy puts a smiley on his chat window too. Human beings feel that they 'invent' and 'discover'. Nothing can be farther than the truth.

"OK Jimmy, so let's get going. Let us see how I came into the picture."

"Sure," pinged Jimmy.

"Jimmy, suppose that instead of asking you for a loan, your brother invites you to invest in his latest business idea – creating energy from city waste. You bought 100 shares of his company by paying INR10 per share. The business takes off and the company announces that it will pay all shareholders an annual dividend of 60 paisa per share, i.e., 6 percent returns on your investment.

"Suppose that ten years later Suzlon Energy wants to buy your brother's company and are ready to pay INR 100 per share. You realize that the capital gains are around 900 percent in 10 years. Hence, you earned both the 'cash flow' through dividends as well as the 'capital gains' on your smart investment with me. So, ladies and gentlemen, how does this idea of investment and returns sound compared to investing in a fixed deposit? I am sure, if nothing else, at least this kind of investing in me is more exciting, isn't it?"

"Well, it sure is exciting Mr. Stock; there is no doubt about it. But we would like to go a little deeper to understand what a stock is and what you mean by a share of the stock. This is all so mixed up in public understanding," came the response from Jimmy.

"Great question once again Jimmy. The deeper you go, the better would be the impact. You see, 'stock' essentially means a 'collection', and here we are talking about collection of shares of a company. So, here I am. You call me a stock. I am nothing but a collection of shares."

"Ah OK..." responded Jimmy.

"Now, your brother's company faces a challenge as it is trying to grow. When a company like this wants to grow faster than its current earnings or profits would allow it to grow, it looks for additional sources of capital for expansion. This capital can be in the form of debt capital or equity capital.

"For debt capital, a company would normally approach a bank or any other financial institution to obtain a loan. Once it acquires the loan, it can invest the money in its business, earn more of it and return the loan amount with interest. The bank or the financial institution, in such a case, is not interested in being a part of the company and is only interested in getting its principle back with a fixed interest.

"For equity capital, the company would have to approach the public to invest money in the company and in return take an equity stake in the company. The company can approach the public through multiple means.

"Now, do not get confused when you are out there in the public domain. People do use the terms 'stock', 'share' and 'equity' interchangeably, and they all mean the same thing that you are holding a part of the company with you. As you stock more shares, your equity in the company increases. This also means that you are a shareholder of the company and are directly going to be impacted by the company's performance – be it positive or negative. Each share also allows you a voting right in the company. While you may not be running the company on a day-to-day basis, you are definitely impacted by its operations. Does that make sense?"

"Ah! Until now, we never thought that we are such an essential ingredient of a company when we purchased their stocks. We thought that we were just investing some money in an investment tool."

"That's the whole point. You have been investing in debt based investments until now like a fixed deposit. Fixed Deposit is just an agreement between the bank and you; that does not make you a part of the bank. With me, this point is very subtle, very simple but extremely important. I would urge all of you to note this down please. This is what we learn from this discussion: When you are buying a share or a stock, you are not just buying some piece of paper; you are buying a part of the company. And when you are buying a company (or a part of it) with your hard-earned money, how much research about the company ought you to be doing before you go and buy its stock?"

"My God, I never thought I am buying a company. I am getting nervous now," there was laughter over the conference bridge, as Celina remarked. Celina was a middle-aged lady sitting right in front of me in the room from where we were broadcasting this presentation live across the globe.

LESSON 12

You do not just buy a stock; you buy a part of the company.
The seriousness of your analysis about a stock will depend upon your mindset when you are buying it.
Your mindset ought to be of buying a company and not just a piece of paper.

"That's OK. No need to get nervous, Celina. This is just for you to make sure that you are serious enough in your research before you buy, instead of just buying based on tips from your friends and relatives. Would you buy a company just based on some tips? Forget about buying a company, you would not even buy a smartphone or a book or even potatoes without doing some of your own research, or would you?"

"Very interesting, making wealth through you is a mind game actually. What we think when we invest seems vital," remarked Celina.

"You are bang on, Celina. I am very much a mind game rather than a technical one. I am not saying that technical aspects, analysis and valuations are not important. They surely are, but they are just the minimum pre-requisites to start investing in me."

"Thank you, this really helped align our perspective," remarked a visibly satisfied Celina.

"Thank you. That is what simple things do," I smiled, "they align your perspective, and once your perspective is aligned, you look at things differently.

Great! Does that make the fundamentals of stock and share absolutely clear to all of you? If yes, can we have the next question please?"

The next question in queue was from India. I peeped to look at the name of the participant. Unfortunately, it was not Gobind.

"This is Girish from India. Sir, you mentioned about companies going to public for generating capital and making its shares public. How does that actually happen?"

"OK Girish, I am sure you must have heard about IPO or Initial Public Offering."

"I have heard, but I am not very clear about it," admitted Girish.

"OK, as I explained earlier, there is a limit to how much money a company can borrow in the form of a bank loan. Too much debt can saddle a company as it has to pay back large interest payments through its current earning still the new earnings start bearing results. Often, this is not feasible because of the large gestation period involved in most businesses before the company actually starts earning money on the investments made.

"What if a company cannot afford so much debt and still wants to go ahead and expand? In such a case, the company will seek equity capital instead of debt capital. Equity capital is not required to be paid back. All a company has to do in exchange for equity capital is give part ownership of the company. That is when the company goes 'public' and floats an IPO.

"To float an IPO, the price per share and the number of shares to be sold are determined jointly by the company and the investment banker. Such public offering is the only time investors like you can buy stocks directly from the company. At all other times, you buy and sell shares from each other through stock exchanges, like the New York Stock Exchange (NYSE) here in the United States and Bombay Stock Exchange (BSE) or National Stock Exchange (NSE) in India."

"Right, understood. As I am aware, and you can correct me please if I am wrong, share prices at the time of IPO are largely unaffected by market sentiment since the company is still to come out in the market. Is that right?" asked Girish.

"Yes, that's right."

"Also, we have seen that some IPOs open with lower share price and some with higher. Does that mean that the ones with lower price are available at a cheaper rate as compared to the other ones?"

"Excellent question, Girish. Now this is another subtle point that all of you should write in your notes. Keep the relevance of this point throughout your life or at least throughout the tenure you are associated with me."

Everyone scrabbled for their notebooks or diaries. Some wanted to note it on their cellphones. Some were confident that they can note down everything in their mind. For some, it was just training, and making notes was too childish. The fact remains that making notes is one of the most powerful means to effectively remember something.

"Whether you are buying shares through an IPO floated by a company or you are interested in shares from the stock market, just looking at the price of a share can never give you any idea about whether it is worth buying or not. There are many other factors to be looked into. A price of a particular stock may appear drastically cheaper simply because one company has issued higher number of shares as compared to the other company, which issued a much lower number."

"Ah! Are you saying that a company can create as many shares as they wish?" asked someone from the audience.

"Of course, gentleman. A share is a part of the company. So, the owners decide how many parts they want the company to be divided into. Of course, there would be some sanity guidelines; there would be no company that does not want one share to come out as cheap as INR 0.05 or as high as INR 10,000 etc. But in theory, the answer is yes. It is left up to the company and to the investment banker to take a call."

"So, how do we truly compare two companies in such a case?" asked Girish.

"Let me share a very simple example. Company 'X' is worth INR 1,000 and decides to infuse equity capital by going public. It goes ahead and issues 100 shares. Each share of this company is going to be INR 10 during the time of the IPO. Post IPO, its price will fluctuate based on market sentiments, economy, company performance etc. but for our case, let us consider only the IPO price of INR 10.

There comes another company 'Y' with an IPO offer. This company 'Y' is also worth INR 1,000 and belongs to the same industry and sector as company 'X'. However, company 'Y 'decides to carve out just 50 shares at the time of IPO. Therefore, each share during IPO will be available at INR 20.

In such a scenario where equally worthy companies from the same industry and sector are offering shares at such drastically different prices, do you think it is worth buying company 'X' just because its share is available at a drop-dead price of INR 10 vis-à-vis company 'Y' whose shares are available at INR 20?"

"I don't think so." responded Girish. He was nodding his head in agreement to the concept that he had just grasped.

"You are right. I also don't think so. Does anyone here think so? I am sure no sensible person with common sense would go and buy shares for Company X just because they are available at half the price of Company Y." I tried to explain one of the most common errors investors have been making for generations.

"But we have seen so many people talking that we should go and buy a particular company's stock because the IPO has come out very cheap. I now understand that it is quite absurd to say so. But tell us whether this rule of not judging by the price of the stock is valid only for an IPO or for shares being traded in the stock market as well?"

"Great, our discussion seems to be heading in the right direction.

LESSON 13

A lower share price of an IPO gives you no clue of its worthiness to buy or sell.

Share price of an IPO has not yet been subject to market speculations.

Yet, it gives you no clue of its worthiness to buy.

Whether it is a recently launched IPO or a bluechip stock that has been in trade for the last two decades, its current market price (CMP) alone cannot give you any clue of its worthiness to buy or sell. A stock trading at a 52-week low or a 52-week high, a stock trading at a lifetime high or low, or even a stock trading at its lowest price as compared to all its peers in the industry, even if the company has been performing as well as its peers: none of this gives you any clue about the worthiness of buying or selling."

"Ah, so we keep hearing so many 'buy' calls on the basis of a 52-week lowest price, the price of a particular stock being lowest as compared to its peers... what is all that? Are they fooling us?" asked a visibly shocked Girish.

"I am not sure if their intent is to fool you, but one of their primary intentions is to earn a livelihood."

"This has certainly been an eye-opener. So many of the investors I know just look at the fact that a blue chip stock has been coming down for quite some time, and they think that this alone is good enough reason to buy it."

"No one knows it better than me. I see this everyday – millions of investors investing just on the basis of low price and then suffering. They do not understand that they are buying a business and therefore must do their analysis of the worth of the stock that they are trying to buy."

"We get that now quite well, I think," exclaimed Girish.

LESSON 14

A stock's current market price (CMP) alone, gives you no clue of its worthiness to be bought or sold.

A stock trading at a 52-week low, or an all time low, a stock with its current price being lowest among all its peer companies – all this gives you no clue of a stock's worthiness to buy.

Pablo's window popped up with a related question though, "We completely get the fact that we need to do a careful analysis of the companies that we are not sure of, but what about the so called blue chip companies. Can't we just trust them for their name or brand?"

"Great question Pablo. That is what quite a few of the investors do. They have some spare money. They do not want to do the hard work of evaluating a company. So, they go by the brand name and invest. They feel that a big company with a great market capitalization (also called as a blue chip) can never underperform for a long time. Now, forget underperformance for the moment. Such investors have conveniently forgotten that companies like Compaq, Kodak and Nokia were not only blue chips, but also the biggest brands in their own segments – not only in their own country or continent – but across the globe. These invincible blue chips do not exist today anymore."

"Right…"

"Remember that 'blue chip' is just being used as a tag by a lazy investor to avoid the hard work that he or she ought to put in for analyzing the business he or she is about to buy. Even if you assume that the brand will not disappear ever, remember that a great company is not a great investment if you pay too much price for the stock. I mean, why would you buy great quality apples for INR 1,000 per kg if their real worth is only INR 200 per kg?"

LESSON 15

A blue chip or a brand gives you no clue of its worthiness to be bought or sold.

History has proven time and again that the so called 'blue chips' have been victims of inevitable technology shifts.

Just the brand name does not give you any clue of its worthiness to buy it at its current market price.

"Got that. Thank you so much for clearing the air on this Mr. Stock."

"Hold on Pablo! It is not only this. There is much more to this psychology."

"Much more?"

"Yes, you know investing with me is a mind game rather than just sheer laziness or technical analysis. We see a blue chip. We love the brand. We see a few data points favoring our internal decision to go ahead and buy, and more importantly, we ignore all contradicting data points – those data points that could potentially have proven our internal decision wrong. This is what you all call as 'confirmation bias'."

"Confirmation bias?"

"Yes, this is the mother of all misconceptions. It is a tendency to interpret new information so that it becomes compatible with our existing theories. I see people losing money with this misconception because they ignore facts which contradict a pre-existing theory in their mind. Disconfirming evidence must be sought out to beat this theory."

"The concept of confirmation bias is interesting. Why do you think this happens, Mr. Stock?" asked Pablo

"Mr. Pablo, humans are not perfect. Ego is one of the bigger reasons for this bias. The higher your ego, the stronger is the bias. You feel you cannot go wrong and the 'stupid article' in a 'small newspaper' showing discomforting negative evidence is no match to your experience. That's what kills you all. That's why you all take biased decisions, which often prove to be incorrect and loss making ones – and you do that day in and day out – without ever looking back and trying to correct your bias."

"The gentler, more humble and less egoistic a human being is, there is much more probability of that person exhibiting less bias, making fewer mistakes and, therefore, making more money in stocks. And Pablo, you thought financial degrees, technical analysis and understanding financial jargons were the only critical skills to stock investing?"

"Yes, you have a point, Mr. Stock. I do remember taking decisions in haste out of emotional outburst and then repenting later. Stock investing definitely seems more of a mind game than anything else. We ought to be mentally strong and emotionally stable to take the right decision in this volatile market of yours," agreed Pablo.

"Seems to be? Pablo, it is not that it seems to be so. I am telling you that it is so. Look around at your friends and relatives. If you can recall someone who has made a lot of money in the long run through investments with me, you would realize that the person was a good human being as well. And trust me, this is no coincidence. In fact, this is one of the key ingredients to getting wealthy through stock investments. This is how He and I planned it. We wanted to reward good human beings more than others."

"Incredible. We never thought that we needed to work on our personal qualities to make money from stocks. We were always focusing on technical analysis."

"Yes, that is a lesson for all of you. Learn it if you can. Write it down and read it as many times as you can. I always reward a better human being. My volatility brings out the basic traits of a human being. I make you more of what you already are. Stock market investing is only 20 percent technical and 80 percent attitude. That is the weightage you need to give to your own personal traits if you want to get rich using me as your investment tool."

LESSON 16

One of the key ingredients to amass massive wealth in stocks is to be a good human being with a great attitude.

Stock investing is only 20 percent technical and 80 percent attitude.

A person with relatively lesser ego, greed and anger has a much better probability of amassing bigger wealth in stocks in the long run.

"Incredible, we now also understand that a blue chip just provides us with a readymade confirmation bias. And then, so many times, we ignore all the negatives about the company and take hasty decisions."

"Correct. Blue chip or not, one must do a proper value analysis to arrive at a buying or a selling decision. Confirmation bias creeps in silently from a brand name, a recommendation from a friend, past experience, etc."

"Right. So, should we do a value analysis for every prospective company?"

"Yes Pablo, you are buying a business, and I am sure you would not be keen on it unless you are comfortable with its value. Having said that, a value analysis for even one company can be quite effort intensive. Therefore, getting hold of some initially scrutinized companies can be a really effective strategy to get started."

"And how do we get hold of these initially scrutinized companies?"

"This is where a blue chip can provide you with lot of initial positives to do the right analysis."

"Ah, superb! Could you please elaborate as to what initial positives can we expect by picking a blue chip?"

"Blue chip stocks are usually very stable. So, selecting a blue chip stock would mean that you are potentially going to invest in a stable stock, which is good. But that's almost all about it. What matters next is at what price you buy the stock, and then how you sustain the journey of your stock between buying and selling. The experience of your journey, the ups and downs of the market – all of that would bring your human values and your attitude to the fore."

"Right, got it! Now, if blue chips provide only an indication of a stable stock and give us no idea about picking a stock, then what does? I mean, how do we decide which stock to pick up and at what price?" asked Girish and many in the room nodded their heads in unison giving the impression that they also had the same question in their mind.

"In life, if you have to buy or sell something, how do you do it? The process you adopt while buying and selling, say apples, needs to be applied while buying and selling stocks – it's just that you need to dig a lot deeper here. Let me give you a very simple scenario. Let's say, you need to buy 1kg of apples. How are you going to decide what is the right price to buy it?"

"Well, we know how much a particular quality of apples costs per kilo. Like in India, in most big cities, you would get good apples close to INR 100 per kg, and we know that this is the right price for good quality apples."

"Yeah, and let us say that good quality apples have been selling in the market for INR 300 per kg for the last seven days. Would you buy them?"

"No way!"

"And what if the price for these apples kept falling until after a few days they were available at INR 250 per kg. Would you buy them?

"No."

"And what if the price continued to fall for the next month and the apples were available at INR 150 per kg. Would you buy them now?"

"Still not."

"And at INR 125 after another week?

"I may not still, unless there is an urgent need for apples. But what are you trying to say, Mr. Stock?"

"Hold on folks, for patience is another virtue that you need to possess to make money with me. So, hold on. Things will become clear. Now, the apples have started hovering around INR 100, how about buying them now?"

"Yes sure, I think this is the right price," remarked Girish, visibly confused – an expression that told me that he was about to learn something new and expand his wisdom for the rest of his life.

"You see, knowing that apple is a great fruit, and in spite of the fact that the price of apples had been falling for the last three months starting from INR 300, you were never even remotely interested in buying them. The reason was simple: the market price for apples was not governed by you, but the buying decision definitely was. Great quality apples at INR 150 per kg were at a two month low, but you were still not keen on buying them. This is exactly why you should not be keen to buy a blue chip stock just because it is at its 52-week low or even at all-time one. The next obvious question you would have is that if the relative historic price does not allow us to take a decision, then what does, right?"

"Right," nodded Girish.

"Let us go back again to buying apples. What was the one factor that finally allowed you to take the decision to buy apples?"

"Well, I think my buying decision was purely based on the reference price of apples – a price that I already had in mind. It did not really matter to me whether it had been selling above that reference for three months or six months or even longer."

"Exactly, you are absolutely on target. In my world, we call that reference value as the 'intrinsic value of a stock'."

"Intrinsic value?"

"Yes, there is a true value associated with every company's stock, and therefore every share, which should act as a reference for you to enable your buy or sell decisions. Our buy or sell decisions should never be based on anything other than this intrinsic value. That is exactly what you did while buying apples. You had some intrinsic value in mind, and you compared the current price of the apples in the market with that intrinsic value. As long as the market price of the apples was significantly higher than the intrinsic value, your decision was not to buy, even if the entire world was buying it. As soon as the price of apples fell closer to the intrinsic value, your decision to buy was easy, natural and obvious."

LESSON 17

A decision to buy or sell should be based on comparison of a stock's current market price (CMP) with its intrinsic value.

Every company, and hence each share, will have a true intrinsic value.

Finding this intrinsic value is the key to taking wise 'buy' or 'sell' decisions.

"Awesome. So, we should buy stocks only when they are close to their intrinsic value. Right?"

"Well, how about getting a bargain price for apples? Because of some market situation, you realize that apples are now available at INR 70, rather than INR 100, would you go for them?"

"Yes definitely. I won't think twice."

"That is exactly what a good investor does in the market. He waits for the stocks to reach a bargain price, which may be significantly lower than the intrinsic value. He waits, and waits and waits – with infinite patience – and when he finds that the market price is lower than the intrinsic value, he throws his entire weight behind acquiring those stocks. Buying stocks of good companies at a sale is the best way to invest money for massive wealth generation."

LESSON 18

Great investors wait patiently for a bargain price – much below intrinsic value.

Great investors wait, and wait, and wait – with infinite patience – for the stock price to fall much below the intrinsic value.

And then they throw their entire weight behind this bargain deal.

"This is really interesting, and looks so simple."

"Yes, it just looks simple."

"What do you mean? I do not see anything complicated about buying apples or buying stocks now. Or am I missing something?"

"Well Girish, the fact is that most investors do just the opposite."

"Really? How come?"

"Yes, they get worried when the market price of a stock is coming down. Everyone is thrashing and selling off that stock. TV, media and experts – everyone is against a stock that is spiraling downwards. Most investors get influenced by the noise around them and want to stay away from the market at that time. On the contrary, they all get excited when the prices have started going up, and they all get super excited when the prices have gone up significantly. Such stocks which have spiraled upwards, become the darling of media, TV and financial experts."

"Oh yes! I have been a party to this so many times," accepted Girish.

"Most ordinary investors are. And this is exactly the reverse of what I am trying to tell you. If you can remember that buying stocks is much like buying apples, you might just become a great investor."

"But why do most investors tend to do the reverse?"

"That is the herd mentality at work. Humans are afraid to be the odd ones out. They are even comfortable with losing money if everyone around them is also losing, but they cannot risk the thought of missing out on 'opportunities' which everyone seems to be grabbing with their hands open."

"Quite understandable, Mr. Stock. Now that we know what rational behaviour should be, it is all boiling down to finding the intrinsic value and then looking for a bargain price. Is it possible to find the intrinsic value of every stock?" an excited John asked from the audience.

"Of course John, we can. Let us understand what intrinsic or true value is."

"Sure, we are all ears."

"See, the intrinsic value of any stock is essentially the true worth of that company. And if you know the true worth of a company, you also know the true worth of every share of that company. Isn't it?"

"Is finding true intrinsic value that simple?"

"It does need some analysis and data points, but it can be done easily using an excel spreadsheet and feeding certain data points into it."

"Can you teach us that?"

"Not now. Not in this session. But I will surely do that for some of you who can connect with me later when you are ready to invest. By the way, this process of finding the intrinsic or true value of one share of a company is also popularly known as 'value analysis'."

"Sure, I will. And this truly was yet another great lesson for us. But there are so many of our well-wishers who talk about performing a technical analysis rather than, or along with, value analysis. What is your take on that?"

"If you ask me John, finding anything more than the true value of the company is just complicating the simple thing that He and I created. Moreover, my observation is that most of the technical approaches that you humans have developed work on the principle of momentum – one should buy because the market has gone up or is going up, and one should sell because it has declined or is on the decline. This is the exact opposite of what I am telling you. You do not buy apples when the prices of apples have started going above their true value. Such technical strategies can work in the very short-term to create some miniscule money but can, in no way, make you truly and seriously wealthy in the long run. Such approaches are as fallacious as they are popular."

LESSON 19

Herd mentality drives irrational behaviour.
Investors are afraid to be the odd one out – the contrarian. They are strongly influenced by public opinion, driving them to buy in a bull market, and sell in a bear market. This is just the reverse of what a wise investor should be doing.

"Makes sense, but why are these approaches so popular if they are fallacious?"

"Popularity is driven by the lure of short-term gains. Righteousness is driven by short-term pain and the pleasure of long-term gains. And that is why fast food becomes popular, but nutritious food is the righteous thing to do for the long-term."

"Ah! Superb."

"OK friends, we have reached a logical point where we must break for tea now. Let us reassemble after 15 minutes as we take on more questions."

LESSON 20

Most technical analysis strategies are as fallacious as they are popular.
Strategies of technical analysis work to create miniscule money, probably in quick time.
Working on the opposite principles, value analysis works to create massive wealth over a long period of time.

People in the auditorium started to disengage, regroup and the murmurs started. At tea, there were small groups around me seeking suggestions about a particular stock and its prospects. I had to politely turn them down. It is never my job to tell anyone whether a particular stock is worth buying or not – that is always an investor's prerogative. My job is to let everyone know the process that will work with me... always!

To follow the process and to bring about the changes necessary in one's attitude to feed the process are an investor's job. Unfortunately that seems to be hard work for human beings – and absolutely not the way we (Him and I) thought.

Human beings are all geared up to change everything around them. What they fear and repel most is the effort that is needed to change themselves. They resist change for mainly two reasons: one, it is painful to come out of their existing comfort zone; and second (and more important), they simply don't feel the need to change anything within them. They have that belief that the change is only needed outside of them, if at all.

I kept telling most of them in the 15-minute break that investing with me is not tough, making money with me is not tough, they just needed to follow a well-defined process – just the way they follow a process to buy groceries. But I also understand human psychology. Humans understand that following a morning walk routine is essential for good health, but they still fail to follow it consistently. They are aware of health risks from cancer causing tobacco, but they cannot resist the temptation of the next puff. They are aware of all the processes that can make their life longer and healthier, but it is not about awareness with them. It is about what they do with that awareness. It is about awakening to that awareness. And I am just teaching them to make money. After this session, they will get aware of the process that can make them rich, but then how many can resist temptations of greed and fear, and stick to the process is all what it comes down to.

In spite of knowing these limitations of human beings, my job is still the same to continue to educate them with the right process, to continue to drill them with the importance of attitude in making big wealth through me. And while traits like excitement, enthusiasm, passion and zeal may be wonderful in their jobs and sports, these traits are more likely to kill their wealth while working with me. What they need is a calm, relaxed, serene way of thinking and acting. It does not seem easy for them to inculcate. The competitiveness of the world in almost every sphere has snatched away those original and beautiful traits from them. And I am not really surprised that the efficiency ratio in my case is not more than 1 percent. For every hundred people I teach, perhaps only one will stick to the process. I accept that fact happily.

Life is Simple... and so is Stock Investing

"OK, folks. Hope you had a wonderful tea break. I am sure your minds are craving new questions. Shoot, please!"

"Mr. Stock, this is Wang Sui from China, and I have a very stupid question. Please pardon me if it is too silly for this intellectual forum."

"Go on Wang, the most stupid question will get a reward at the end of the session," everyone laughed. "No, I am not kidding. Human beings are afraid of asking stupid questions, but these stupid questions are the ones which will always give you a shift in perspective. Go on please, Mr. Wang. I respect your courage."

"You talked about the true value which relates to the worth of the company, but what we see is that the share prices continue to fluctuate every minute, in fact every moment. Are we saying that the worth of a company is changing at such a rate?"

"Wow! I am so proud of you, Mr. Wang, for asking that question. You see, it is not that the worth of the company changes every minute that drives the share price. It is only the 'collective' 'perceived' worth of the company in the eyes of all investors together that drives the market price of a stock."

"Can you please elaborate upon that?"

"Yes, sure. It is a typical demand and supply scenario. Let us go back to our apple example. What happens if there are enough buyers of apples at INR 125, though the intrinsic value of the apple (as perceived by you) was still INR 100?"

"Well, the price may stay at INR 125 in that case."

"True, then that means that the 'collective' and 'perceived' worth of the apples as perceived by majority of the buyers will drive the day-to-day market price of the apple, and not the true intrinsic value, isn't it?"

"OK... that makes some sense," said Wang after a pause.

"And since this 'collection' of investors across the globe as well as the 'perception' of each investor keeps changing dynamically, the same is reflected in the stock's current market price. This is not the case with the true intrinsic value, which remains the same for a company and its stock for quite a significant period of time."

LESSON 21

The 'collective', 'perceived' worth by investors determines its market price dynamically.

It is always the 'collective' 'perceived' worth of shareholders that determines a stock's market price. Since this 'collection' and 'perception' of shareholders keeps changing across the globe, the stock's market price changes dynamically while its true intrinsic value remains the same for a fairly long time.

"OK, and as we understand, the intrinsic value is determined by the worth of the business, which should not change, at least on a daily basis. Are we getting it right?"

"Awesome, Mr. Wang. You are getting it absolutely right."

"Cool! But then, what is the use of calculating the true intrinsic value of a stock if the market price of that stock is never in our hands, and is always determined by this collective perception. I mean, if the apples continue to be sold at INR 125 for whatever reason, then what is the significance for me to know the fact that the true intrinsic value of these apples is actually only INR 100, since I can never buy them at the intrinsic value."

"Not always, dear Mr. Wang! This gap between the market price and intrinsic value does not always remain. As I said, it is dynamic. It keeps changing since this collection and perception of an investor changes quite dynamically with time. But here is something that you would love to know. At some point in time, which could be days, weeks, months, years or even decades in some cases, the market price of the stock will come close to its true intrinsic value. It always will."

"Oh really! Always? How can you be so sure of the market price meeting the intrinsic value? Why do you say that it will always happen like that?"

LESSON 22

Between periods of fluctuating collective perception, the market price of a stock will always hit close to a stock's true intrinsic value.
Easier said than done, you will need to overcome your emotions of greed and pessimism to be able to counter the market's collective perception and stay trustful on your calculations.

"Because that is nature. God has made this world, and every single element in it, to be in equilibrium. During this equilibrium state (also called as 'steady state'), everything is in perfect harmony and in equilibrium with each other. The market price of apples was higher probably because of unnatural situation like scarcity of the fruit, drought conditions, higher sickness rate in the city which was driving higher than usual demand etc. As long as these unnatural conditions stay, the price would remain higher. We do not know for how long these unnatural conditions would stay, but what we know for sure is that once there is equilibrium, the price of apples will come down to its true value. The same holds good for the case when the price of apples are slashed because of too much supply, a perceived disease caused by apples or a host of other factors that are beyond our control. However, again the prices will come back to the true value once normalcy returns, and the normalcy must return, for that is God's will. That is how every element in this universe has been designed."

"So, what you are saying is that there are *n* number of market driven factors that determine the market price of a stock. Most of these factors are beyond our control. But in between all these factors, there will always be a period where normalcy will return and the price of the stock will hit its true intrinsic value."

"Absolutely. You've got it, Mr. Wang. I would urge all of you to please look at the graph being broadcasted on your screens. If you look at this graph carefully, you will realize a very important aspect of stock investing. We call it 'stock homecoming'."

"Stock Homecoming?"

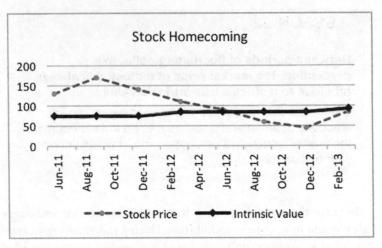

Chart 1: *Stock homecoming*

"Yes, stock homecoming is one such concept that should actually make you feel very confident about stock investing. It will allow you to handle the so called risk and volatility in a much better and assured manner. So, what is stock homecoming? Stock homecoming is the understanding of the fact that for the majority of time, the stock's market price would hover above or below its true intrinsic value, oscillating between irrational exuberance to unjustifiable pessimism. But while oscillating between these periods, there will always be a time when the stock comes close to or crosses its true intrinsic value, always. The long-term value of the company always has a way of rectifying the situation, no matter in which direction."

There was a pin drop silence for a few seconds. I knew that they were making an attempt at absorbing the concept of stock homecoming. They deserved all the time for this concept to sink in.

"This is really very assuring to me at least," said Wang in a soft, assured and relaxed tone. Others nodded in unison. It seemed as if I had sucked all the stress out of stock investment, and the journey in stocks was going to be less painful.

"Good to know that, Mr. Wang. And this is one concept that can change the way you look at stocks forever. Go through it again if you want. Let this concept sink into your subconscious mind. You will need this most in times of stress or greed."

"Yes, it does take away so much of our stress," said Mr. Wang, his eyes still focused on the stock homecoming chart being broadcasted on the screen.

"But here is the twist in the tale, my friends. Despite many investors knowing this concept of stock homecoming, we have observed that it is always the lack of belief that fails them."

"Lack of belief? Why would they not believe what you are saying? You are a godsend. So, if we cannot believe you, who else would we ever believe?"

These words made me smile, "I trust you all. I am sure you will show the maturity required to implement this simple and powerful concept when you go back to start your own investments. But the reason why people lose trust in what I say is very simple. People go by their experiences and not by their visualization, imagination or faith. One small temporary negative situation and the memory of their past experiences starts denting their faith. When faced with negativity, people lose trust even in the existence of God; forget about losing trust in a stock market concept, so what if He himself is telling it through me."

"Ah! We understand what you say. It is definitely a matter of faith now."

"Yes, it is a matter of faith and keeping that faith in the worst of times. This, I would say, does not come easy to your species."

Keeping faith during testing times does not come easy to humans.

Market concepts, including stock homecoming, are simple, explicit and powerful.

However, an investor will be tested for his faith in these concepts.

Those displaying faith will be the future billionaires.

"Hmm, interesting. It is all boiling down to our internal strength yet again."

"Yes, Mr. Wang."

"You said that these fluctuations in the market price are because of collective perception, but tell us Mr. Stock, what determines these perceptions?"

"Perceptions in the stock market can occur because of innumerable and mostly uncontrollable market factors, a study which is as difficult to predict as human behavior. However, we should not be concerned with predicting tomorrow's market price. That is not the job of an investor. The job of a wise investor is to make use of this difference in the market-driven price and the true value as a beautiful window of opportunity."

LESSON 24

An investor's job is not to predict tomorrow's market price of a stock.

Market prices fluctuate because of perceptions and situations which are complex to predict.

An investor should be least worried about them.

An investor's job is to leverage the 'window of opportunity' created by the difference between market price and intrinsic value.

"Window of opportunity?"

"Yes, a huge opportunity to buy and sell."

"Can you please elaborate on this window of opportunity?" asked Shalini from India.

"Shalini, it is very simple, and the challenge for you humans is to try and keep it this simple. In life, or with stocks, as long as you can keep things simple, you will be rewarded immensely. Listen to this carefully: keep monitoring the market price movement of a stock you are interested in. When the market price of a stock dips significantly below its intrinsic value, then it is a real window of opportunity to get into the stock. When the market price pops higher than its intrinsic value, you must make exit plans. There is nothing more or less to stock investing."

"It sounds very logical, but is that all? I mean, is stock investing this simple?"

"Yes, it is this simple and logical. Although, let me warn you here: my experience with human beings over the last 200 years has shown that as logical as it sounds, it has been equally difficult for all of you to implement this simple logic."

"Difficult, why?"

"We talked about the reasons earlier. It is because of the emotions that you humans display, which creates this collective perception and becomes the main reason for your failure."

"Can you please elaborate how our emotions also contribute to a wrong perception?" asked Shalini.

"You see, when the market price of a stock is touching its all-time high, and beyond the intrinsic value of the stock, a wise investor will know that it is time to sell. Logical and simple, isn't it? But here comes the challenge. Remember that at that time, the general euphoria around you can cause unrealistic perceptions which can carry the stock to even greater heights. Everyone in the media and financial advisors will be on a high and pushing you to buy more since every day 'we will be touching an all-time high'. But a wise investor, just like a horse with blinkers, will dissuade himself from all this noise and will always have a sharp eye on the gap between the intrinsic value and the market price of the stock and take an exit decision, while everyone around him might still be on a buying spree. It is not easy at all to implement this because your emotions of greed and instant gratification are likely to come into play."

"Interesting, we are only now realizing how critical human behavior is in stock investing."

"Yes and the same is true for the other side as well. When everyone thinks that the market is doomed, there is negativity all around and people are selling everywhere. Only a wise investor will have his eyes glued to the market price and see if it has started running below the intrinsic value of the stock. In such a case, this investor will be interested in buying rather than going with what everyone around him is doing, i.e. selling in panic. Again, it is not easy to be euphoric in a doomed market. After all, it is your money that you are putting in. Your emotions of fear and lack of faith in stock homecoming will not allow you to do it so easily.

"Wow, incredible! Now that we know this, what do we need to do in such situations?"

"What you need in both the cases is confidence in your value analysis as well as control on your emotions of greed (at the time of exiting) or pessimism, fear and lack of faith (at the time of entering) and take buy and sell decisions as appropriate. And that's what is called value investing – an art, which needs a lot of hard work and patience before you invest, a calm and faithful mind during the investing period and extreme confidence in your own value analysis before you exit."

"So, exactly when should we enter or exit? I mean how much gap is the right gap?"

"You can create certain guidelines around all that, and each individual investor's guideline could be different from that of the other based on each one's risk taking capacity. But the overall process will always remain the same."

"Understood, b..t do you have any recommended guidelines?"

"Generally, an investor can think of entering the market when the market price of a stock is more than 20 percent below the intrinsic value, because this is the money you would definitely want to make from the market. And you can think of exiting when the market price of a stock has crossed the intrinsic value or even earlier if you have met your goal. But again, this 20 percent can vary hugely for different investors. You must formulate your own strategy depending on your risk profile."

> **'Buy' when CMP is significantly below intrinsic value.**
>
> **'Sell' when CMP meets or exceeds intrinsic value.**
>
> In a euphoric or a pessimistic market, an investor will stand true to his value analysis and shall not be driven by market emotions.
>
> Such emotional control is rare, but highly rewarding.

"OK, but tell us if this intrinsic value always remains the same?"

"Good question. No, it does not. Does the true value of 1 kg of apples always remain as INR 100 or does it keep changing with time because of multiple factors, which you have collectively and conveniently termed as inflation?"

"It does change almost every year."

"Right, and that is exactly what happens with me. Companies will make an attempt to grow in value, their performance may keep changing, economy may undergo change, industry laws may change or, if nothing else, the price of raw materials may change with inflation. Therefore, intrinsic value needs to be revisited at least once a year, if not before. Blue chips give you an advantage here. Their intrinsic value will not be too volatile, other than for inflation reasons, thus giving you the luxury of time, if at all it comes to reversing or hastening your buy or sell decision based on the new intrinsic value."

"Mr. Stock, this is interesting and confusing at the same time. We were thinking that at least once we know the intrinsic value, we have some stability and benchmark against which we could look at the current stock price and take a buy or sell decision. But now, you are telling us that even the intrinsic value of a stock is also not stable over time," remarked Herbert from Zurich.

"Dear Herbert, you being confused indicates that you are ready to learn something new now. So, here is some food for thought: is there anything permanent in this world?"

"Well, maybe there is something, we don't know," said Herbert.

"Nothing is permanent in this world, Herbert. Neither you, nor the stock of the companies you buy and nor their intrinsic values."

"OK then, please help us understand. This means that we may buy a certain stock based on a certain intrinsic value and before we can get the target profit, the intrinsic value may have changed and may make the stock not worthy of holding anymore. Is that a possible situation or is that a useless question?"

"This is very much possible and is not rare. It may happen to you many times during the journey of holding the stock."

"Then, what are we supposed to do?"

"Sell, it if that is what the intrinsic value forces you to do."

"Even at a loss?"

"Of course."

"What! Sell it at a loss? What are you teaching us, Mr. Stock? We invested for profit and then you are asking us to sell it at a loss?"

"Get used to it. This is not a fixed-term deposit. This is me, stocks, where with some additional temporary short-term risk you make much more money in the long run. I am teaching you the process of making money in the long-term in a stock market. And there will be times when you will buy a stock based on a certain calculation of intrinsic value, and will be forced to sell it off at a loss. Do not get too bothered by these short-term profits or losses. Keep the process simple. Do not be influenced by these results. Act as per your calculation."

"Can you please share any example?"

"A stock 'X' may have a market price of INR 120 while its intrinsic value as per your calculation is INR 150. This is a good enough bargain to get into the stock. However, even after two years, the stock is yet to hit the intrinsic value and is still hovering at close to INR 100. You have been waiting patiently for it to boom, but your revised calculation of intrinsic value after two years shows that the new intrinsic value of this stock is only worth INR 110 now. This is a 'sell' situation where your intrinsic value is quite close to the current market price of the stock. It is very unlikely that the stock price is going to go drastically up from here. Therefore, you should go ahead and sell it."

"But that would mean incurring a loss of INR 20 per share."

"Yes, if your calculations are logical. It makes no sense to hold on to a stock which you know is only likely to go down from there, and it makes all the sense to book your losses and move out, get the balance money and re-invest in a better option."

"But until now, we have always been holding on to loss making stocks till they turn profitable."

"Well, that's another big challenge with your species that I did not completely anticipate when we introduced stocks to all of you."

"We?"

"Him and I."

"Ah ok. And what's the challenge with our species?"

"That you hold on to negative emotions for too long. You keep them deep inside and hold them as if they were a treasure to be nurtured. You do not let them go. And that is what drives all of you to hold on to your loss making stocks. And what is the result? The negative emotion gets bigger every day, eats up all your energy and is painful for your soul. Let me ask you. What happened to all your loss making stocks, which you had been holding on for decades?"

"A few of them made some profit and we exited at the first opportunity, but most of them are still running at losses," responded Herbert with guilt and hesitation in his voice.

"Just saying that most of them are still in losses is being unfairly optimistic. This statement itself is driven by the confirmation bias and ego, which you have developed over time."

"But I don't think there was any confirmation bias or ego when I said that. I just stated the facts."

"There was. It is just that this bias worked unconsciously for you. It is so subtle. It has become so ingrained in you that you are mostly not even aware that it is working in hindsight."

"How do you say that?"

"I can say that because you did not openly and bluntly come out and admit that you made a wrong decision at some stage of your stock journey. Let me share the unadulterated fact, and I can do so quite easily for I am devoid of any bias or ego."

"And what is the fact as per you, Mr. Stock?"

"The fact is this: most of your loss making stocks are in much deeper shit today, than they were when you first realized that there was no point holding these stocks anymore."

There were whispers and murmurs through the room, "You may be right."

"You still cannot overcome your bias completely. You are still unsure that you were wrong in your buy decision, and more importantly, in your sell decision when you got the opportunity to sell it at relatively lesser losses. I have seen these over the last 200 years. And it has only become worse over time. You are still hesitant and reluctant to agree that you were, plain and simple, wrong. The problem is not in being wrong, but in thinking that being wrong is bad. And this is a very common mistake. I have seen that most investors are in a hurry to book profits, while they want to stay invested in duds hoping for them to turn around. In either case, it is their bias at work, rather than their calculations."

"OK, we agree that we may be driven by our emotions, but tell us what's the point of investing if we were to make losses from you?" Herbert was still unable to come to the terms with the fact that a loss is one of the possible outcomes of investing.

"My friend, it is true that cutting losses is like cutting your own finger; it is painful. But it is equally true that by cutting the finger, you can prevent a situation where you would have had to cut off your hand or even the whole arm. But what I have seen is that instead of booking losses, most investors go and buy more in hope that the stock will recover one day. The most important thing that you must do when you find yourself in a hole is stop digging it further."

"But we are not digging further. We might be investing more to recover back the losses, isn't it?"

"You are attempting a near impossible task."

"Why impossible?"

"It is harder than you can potentially think. Imagine that you found a stock that is likely to grow at 10 percent every year. Unfortunately, it dips drastically in the first year and loses 50 percent of its value. If you failed to sell it at this, in spite of your calculations on CMP and intrinsic value screaming at you to do so, you are in for some serious trouble. Even if you assume that after this dip, the stock starts recovering and continues to grow at 10 percent per annum, how many years do you think will it take for the stock to recover to its original price?"

"I think five years. It seems quite plain and simple…"

"But actually, it is not as straightforward, my friend. It will take you more than 16 years, and that too just to break even."

"Really? Hmm, interesting."

Book losses without hesitation, if your CMP-Intrinsic Value calculation guides you to do so.

Loss making is as much a part of investing as is profit making.

There is no guarantee that a loss making stock would recover. Go by your calculation – not by your greed or attachment to a stock. Loss making stocks are highly likely to make more losses.

Overcome your confirmation bias and ego to take logical decisions.

"And, it is not only about making profit. It is also a lot about the lost opportunity. Even if the luck was on your side and somehow you are able to recover and earn, let us say, 5 percent profit by selling the stock after having waited for three years, the returns would have been a meager 1.5 percent CAGR. Most of you, who understand inflation, will also understand that you would actually lose money in that case."

"But 1.5 percent CAGR seems definitely better than 20 percent loss that we were incurring earlier, isn't it?"

"Have a look at what else you could have done if you would have sold this stock earlier. Then let me know the way that seems better."

"Tell me what was the other way?"

"The other way could have been to sell the stock at 20 percent loss – when you realized that it is not worth holding on it – and invest in another opportunity that could have fetched 15 percent CAGR over the next 3 years. The net result in the second case would have been a net profit of 25 percent."

"Really? Would we really earn a net profit of 25 percent in spite of selling it at a loss of 20 percent. How is that possible?"

"15 percent CAGR gives you approximately 45 percent returns in 3 years. Even if you reduce the earlier loss of 20 percent, you still effectively earned 25 percent."

"Good point, but then, there is no guarantee that we will make a profit in the second option."

"You are right. Of course not. There is no guarantee, just like there is no guarantee that your stock continued to recover at the rate of 10 percent after the 50 percent blip. There are no guarantees anywhere, Herbert. We are just trying to follow the right process. Results are never ever guaranteed in life. Do you know, there used to be a gentleman from Australia who read geopolitics perfectly just before the Second World War started. He realized that Japan would soon be at war with Australia and he wanted to exit the danger zone. So, he sold all his assets in Sydney, Australia and bought a nice large property in Philippines. He proved to be right: Australia did end up fighting Japan. However, Sydney remained untouched while Philippines was devastated in many battles. Right process, but unfortunately not the right result. Therefore, even if you, as an investor, have read the economic situation perfectly, life will surprise you more often than you think unless you respond quickly. But there never were and never will be any guarantees."

"This is the sad part of investing with you: no guarantee."

"Yes, and it is quite logical because not all businesses can succeed, even if they are run by the best managers. There is no formula for assured success with me, just as there is no formula for a successful marriage. There is no guarantee of anything with me, just like there is no guarantee that you will breathe your next breath successfully. There are no guarantees in your world and you are seeking a guarantee from my world? See, it is all about probabilities and following the right process, so that you can respond to the situations correctly. After that, it is only your attitude and positivity and karma that will work for you: whether in life or with me."

"Quite interesting. Personally, for me, it requires a shift in mindset to sell stocks at a loss. I still feel that for loss making stocks, we can adopt a different strategy."

"Different strategy, like?"

"I mean the market will definitely rally some day in the next few months or years. Don't you think that these loss making stocks will recover quickly at that time?"

"Remember this: a rallying market will take good stocks up first. Bad stocks will continue to languish. I am sure you have experienced this. A loss from such a stock can be recovered only by investing in a stock that is recovering faster. It is only at the peak of the rally that the poor quality stocks also move up. It is better to stick to the fundamentals, accept your mistake and accept the way I work. That will be least detrimental for you."

"OK, got it."

"Great, then jot this down in bold letters. There are no guarantees, there are only probabilities. We can follow the right process to increase the probability of making more money. And that's it. Therefore, if your CMP-Intrinsic Value calculation guides you to sell, then sell even if it means making losses. You will recover these losses in the long run. But if you stick to loss making and zero potential stocks in spite of your calculations guiding you otherwise, you may very well be in for deeper losses."

LESSON 27

In stock investing, as in the real world, there are no guarantees, but only probabilities.

Follow the right process to increase the probability of making more money.

Go by your CMP-Intrinsic Value calculation even if it means making losses.

In the long run, you have a very high probability of making a lot of wealth.

"So, if a stock is down as compared to the price at which we bought – we go and sell it?"

"No, you sell it only if the stock's intrinsic value guides you to. If the intrinsic value is around or below the current price of the stock, you have a license to sell it – as simple as that. Do not bother too much about the profit or loss you made. As I told you earlier, your buy or sell decisions are based on the gap between the current market price of the stock and the currently estimated intrinsic value – and nothing else. Your intrinsic value, as we might see with some of you later, may include factors like the industry future prospects, general economy factor etc. However, it is most important to keep all your emotions on the side when making any buy or sell decisions."

"So, what you are saying is that we purchase the stock with a market price of say INR 100, which is 20 percent below its intrinsic value of INR 120. If the stock price goes up and crosses its intrinsic value of INR 120, we make a neat 20 percent profit and we sell. Understandable, but you are saying that if the stock price remains stagnant around INR 100, and intrinsic value drops close to INR 100, we still sell?"

"Yes, for sure. Please, sell. Remember that it is not a good sign in any case if the intrinsic value of a company is coming down. Unlike the market price of a stock, which is driven by collective perception, the intrinsic value is driven by hard business numbers. A decreasing intrinsic value is a very bad situation for the company to be in. Leaving the complexity aside, you only go by your calculation and act as per your CMP-intrinsic value gap. Keep things simple, if you possibly can."

"Got it. What if both, the market price and the intrinsic value keep coming down but the intrinsic value never dips below the current market price. I mean, in our earlier example, let us assume that the market price came down to INR 70 and the intrinsic value came down to INR 80. Our calculations would not allow us to sell in that case, isn't it?"

"Yes, very good question, Herbert. Although such cases are rare, it is definitely possible. This is a lossmaking situation, wherein we have to account for a third element other than CMP and intrinsic value, and that is the cost of purchase. We will deal with these three elements on case by case when I interact with some of you on real stocks later on. I say these cases are rare because of the initial scrutiny criteria we use for stock selection."

"Gotcha! Thank you, sir." remarked a reasonably satisfied Herbert.

"OK folks, we seem to be reaching a logical end. When do you guys want to have a lunch break?"

"May be, in some time," every one nodded.

"Before we do that, I had one related question which we touched upon earlier, and that is dividends. What exactly are these? And how do they influence our buy or sell decisions," asked Twain.

"You have touched a great topic, Twain. Let us finish our topic on Dividends before we break for lunch. This is a topic where buy or sell decisions could vary from one country or one region to another. In developed countries, where the general interest and inflation rates are quite low, there is a different strategy with dividends. In developing countries, where both, interest rates and inflation rates are relatively high, we need a slightly different strategy on dividends. Before we go on to those things, let us understand what a dividend is and how does it work. Shall we go ahead if you have no other questions?"

"Yeah."

"Dividends are the returns you get as a shareholder of the company. Dividends are paid out of the company's earnings, unless the company ploughs all the earnings back into the company to fuel future growth."

"Whenever a company earns a profit, it distributes part of the profit as dividend to stockholders. The amount of dividend paid out by the company is best measured by the *dividend payout ratio*, which is defined as the ratio of dividend distributed by the company to the total profit earned after tax (PAT). Have a look at your screen now:

$$\text{Dividend Payout Ratio} = \frac{\text{Dividend distributed}}{\text{Profit after Tax (PAT)}}$$

Formula 1: Dividend payout ratio

So, if a company has a dividend payout ratio of 60 percent, it means that the company is distributing 60 percent of the earnings back to its shareholders and may be investing the remaining 40 percent to fuel future growth or settling some of its debts. Such companies with a dividend payout ratio of 50 percent or more are generally said to be distributing the dividend 'generously'."

"OK, so far so good. We understand that dividend is our profit because we are a part owner of the company. If the company is making profits, it can and should distribute proportionately among all its owners or shareholders like us. But how do we connect our buy or sell decisions of a stock to this dividend payout ratio? That is something where so many of us are confused."

"Yes, we are just coming to that. And by now, you know that confusion is such a welcome emotion, isn't it?"

"Dividend payout ratio gave you an idea about how inclined a company is towards distributing its profit among its owners like you. It thus gives you an idea about the intent of the board of directors of the company towards profit sharing vis-à-vis investing the profit for future expansion. On the other hand, this ratio really does not help you significantly to make a buy or a sell decision."

"Yes, you are right. And that is what we want to know: how dividends are associated with our buy or sell decisions?"

"Yes, there is an alternative way of measuring how much dividend you actually get on a stock. It is called as the *dividend yield*. This is the amount of dividend you get per share divided by the price you pay to buy that share. Look at your screen now:

$$\text{Dividend Yield} = \frac{\text{Declared dividend per share}}{\text{Market price per share}}$$

Formula 2: Dividend yield

"Note that dividend yield changes as the market price of a share changes on a daily basis. The dividend yield of a stock can be high, either because the company has a high dividend payout ratio, i.e. it is just paying you a big chunk of profits as dividends, or simply because its stock price is low.

In either case, if what matters to you are the returns you get for the money you invested, you should look only at the dividend yield."

LESSON 28

Dividend payout ratio signifies a company's intent towards distributing profit.

Dividend yield tells you the returns on invested money.

For an investor looking for high returns, what matters is dividend yield, not dividend payout ratio.

Figures like 60 percent or 70 percent dividend payout ratio do not have much significance for an investor if dividend yield is low.

"That is quite interesting, Mr. Stock. Dividend yield is what we need to focus on. But, I do not understand what we keep hearing about dividends," asked a visibly confused Samuel.

"What do you keep hearing, Samuel?"

"That a certain company has declared 200 percent dividend, 300 percent dividend and what not. What is 200 percent dividend? It is so confusing. It cannot be the dividend payout ratio, for no company can pay 200 percent of its profit to its stakeholders as dividends. And of course, it is highly unlikely that it will be the dividend yield, for getting a dividend yield of even 7-8 percent might be too good to be true. Then what does 200 percent dividend signify?"

"Very good question indeed. Do not get influenced by this noise of 200 percent or 300 percent dividend. This is neither dividend payout ratio nor dividend yield. To a common investor like you, this makes no sense at all."

"But what is it? If you could just tell us – for our information at least."

"Sure, why not. Here is how this usually happens. Let us say that a company came into existence with a share price of INR 10 and after 20 years of existence, it is trading at a price of INR 500. It earned a profit of INR 100 per share this year and decided to distribute 20 percent of this INR 100 profit as dividends to all its stakeholders. So, this company would declare a dividend of INR 20 per share. The way it will be represented is that the company has declared 200 percent dividend (INR 20 dividend over a base share price of INR 10). It is that simple. Got it?"

"Ah! Smart way to lure the investor."

"Yeah, it is how they present the data, and companies and markets are very strong at presenting in a way that lures the investor. This is just a gimmick by companies to influence your decision making based on a high dividend percentage. However, like I said, there is no reason to be excited for an investor even if it is 1000 percent dividend, if the dividend yield is low. A wise investor will insulate himself from all such attractions and will make a fair judgment of the situation."

"Right."

"So, what do you think? How will a wise investor look at the situation of a company declaring 200 percent dividend?"

"Can I try?"

"Of course, Ismael. Go ahead."

"A wise investor would insulate himself from all that jargon and look at the dividend yield instead."

"And what would that be in the above case?"

"At a share price of INR 500, a dividend of INR 20 would mean a dividend yield of 4 percent per annum... right?"

"Absolutely, but whether this dividend yield of 4 percent is per annum or per quarter or for six months would depend on the declared dividend. If the INR 20 dividend is the only dividend paid in a year – then yes, 4 percent are the annual returns. Normally, one should go through at least a 12-month cycle to observe and accumulate all dividends declared in the year to arrive at annual dividend yield."

"Makes sense, Mr. Stock."

"And these 4 percent returns could be one of the decision making factors to buy or sell. It depends on the country or region of the world you were in."

"Can you please elaborate on this?"

"Yes. So, if you are sitting in a developed economy and getting a dividend yield of 4 percent annually on a stock which is stable, you cannot be more excited about the stock. 4 percent is probably much above the running annual inflation in such geographies, and you know that the first purpose of investing is to beat inflation after paying all your taxes. Dividend income is tax-free too!"

"OK, that's interesting..."

"But if you are sitting in a region like India or China, where 4 percent is the lowest possible interest rate you get from a savings bank account, then this dividend yield may not really be a key decision point to buy a stock, though a definite influencer."

"Got it."

"Good, but these are not hard and fast rules. Remember that 4 percent is just the dividend yield but if you see a stock with a potential to rise and give you returns via capital gains as well, then this 4 percent is an added bonus which is more than welcome, irrespective of the country or region you belong to. And how would we know whether a stock has some potential for capital gains, Ismael?"

"By comparing the current market price of the stock with its intrinsic value."

"Awesome, you guys are getting it all right."

"Wow, this is making our concepts so clear, Mr. Stock."

"Thanks for being attentive and patient with me. And the story of dividends does not just end here. They are far more significant than just the dividend yields and tax-free returns they give you."

"Oh really?"

"Dividends provide partial liquidity to your investment. When you enter a stock, you know that you might be in for at least around seven years or so. But regular annual/semi-annual dividends let the cash flowing. And as we discussed earlier, liquidity is an extremely vital aspect of your portfolio."

"OK, what other benefits do dividends give us, other than liquidity and cash flow?"

"They also give you a good idea about the stability of a company. Usually dividend distributing companies are not only profitable but also stable. That is the reason they are ready to part with a portion of their profits as dividends. They are pretty confident of earning more in the coming years. When searching for a company, whose stock you would like to buy, stability is one of the prime criteria you should be looking at while performing value analysis. Dividend history of a company will tell you how stable and confident the company is. And I am sure you all know by now as to why we are so choosy about stable stocks? Because we do not buy stocks, we buy companies and if we intend to buy a company, we would of course prefer that the company was stable and confident."

"Wow, this is awesome. I never understood dividends like this in my entire life. I had studied the concept of dividends as early as class 9 at school, but perhaps only after 30 years, I got to truly appreciate this concept. Thank you, Mr. Stock, for that. What else can dividends do for me?" asked an excited Ismael.

"During the downward slide of stocks, dividend paying stocks will offer significantly more resistance to sliding down with the market mood as compared to their non-dividend paying counterparts. Thus they will act as a safety cushion preventing the stock from a free fall."

"Why would that happen?"

"The prime reason is that the investors do not want to do away with a regular cash flow opportunity in the form of dividends, even if the capital gain of the stock is not doing that well. In fact, when the price of the stock goes down unexpectedly, there are likely to be more buyers for dividend paying stocks for the simple reason that dividend yield keeps going up as the stock price keeps coming down."

"Can you please elaborate this a little bit?"

LESSON 29

Dividend paying stocks outsmart the non-dividend paying ones, in the long run.

Dividend yielding stocks offer cash flow, liquidity, tax-free income, resistance to free fall, and a good idea about the stability of a company – vital attributes for stock selection.

"Sure, my friend. Let us take the previous example where a share price of INR 500 and a dividend of INR 20 meant a dividend yield of 4 percent. Now, let us assume that the stock price tumbled to INR 400. As in most cases, let us assume that this dip is mostly driven by macroeconomic factors and collective market perception and that there is no drastic change in company fundamentals i.e. the company still continues to earn profits and revenue in line with the expectations. In such a case, it will still declare similar dividends as it did last year, if not more. If someone purchases the stock at its current market price of INR 400, the same INR 20 dividend per share now leads to a dividend yield of 5 percent (INR 20 dividend on INR 400 investment) instead of the previous 4 percent (INR 20 dividend on INR 500 investment). This increase in dividend yield attracts many investors, thus offering resistance to further fall in prices... some of you look confused – am I not clear, Sam?"

"You are absolutely clear to us. But I am confused because if there are so many advantages of dividend paying stocks, then why in the world would anyone buy anything else? Is there any flip side to buying dividend paying stocks?"

"Yes, of course there is. It is called the *Dividend Oxidation Effect*©"

"Dividend Oxidation Effect©? What is that? Never heard of it."

"Let me take a step back and first explain what Oxidation Effect is. You all know that oxygen is essential to humans, because it helps your body burn the food and convert it into useful energy. The same oxygen and its same quality of burning down, also happens to act as your silent killer."

"Oxygen – a silent killer? It's beyond me. You are challenging the fundamentals of life and what we have always been made to believe in."

"Maybe I am challenging the fundamentals. Let it be if that is what is needed to acquire wisdom. Truth shall always prevail – sooner or later. So, this negative effect of oxygen on your body parts is called as the Oxidation Effect. It is because of this very oxidation effect that iron gets rusted and destroyed and an apple gets oxidized and blackened. In exactly the same way each of your body part gets oxidized and degenerated. Each cell in our body needs oxygen to survive but the same oxygen would ultimately destroy those cells and those body parts. That's nature. The process is slow, but certain. Therefore, the same oxygen that gives you life also kills you – and you have no choice."

"Wow, we never knew that. I do not know whether I should be afraid of breathing now."

"Yes, and that is the reason you guys take food that is rich in something called antioxidants – substances that can negate the oxidation effect of oxygen on your body parts. Food that is rich in anti-oxidants reduces the oxidation effect of oxygen on your body, and hence delays the inevitable. Remember that antioxidants can only delay, and not stop the degeneration of your cells. They just slow down the entire process. Does that make the dual role of oxygen clear to you?"

"Yes, we do understand oxidation effect now, but what is Dividend Oxidation Effect© that you referred to?"

"Yes, Dividend Oxidation Effect© (or DOE) has the same effect on dividends as oxidation effect has on your body. Higher dividends give you better cash flow, better liquidity and better returns on your investments – all good things. At the same time, the higher the dividends, the lesser the profit left with the company to invest in its expansion activities and therefore to earn more profit. Therefore, with time, these high dividends, which all seemed so good, start to limit the capital gains that are feasible on the stock."

"Interesting, so high dividend paying stocks are likely to give us high dividends but low capital gains."

"In general, yes. But remember that the capital gains would also significantly depend on the price at which you bought the stock. So, if you see a great opportunity with a significant gap between intrinsic value and market price of a high dividend paying stock, do not hesitate – just go for it. These opportunities would be rare but surely present themselves in a falling market."

LESSON 30

Dividend Oxidation Effect© **leads to capping the possible capital gains.**

The more the dividend yield, the lesser is the profit left with the company for future expansion. High dividends can be a boon for regular cash flow but can kill capital gains potential.

"Got it. One more question, though slightly out of context... Why is the government so kind on us when it comes to dividends?"

"Means?" I was startled to hear someone appreciating the government to be kind towards wealth creators.

"I mean, they do not fail to tax us even on entertainment, how come they do not tax on profits distributed as dividends."

"You are right. They do not leave anything – and this includes dividends. The dividends are declared and distributed from the profits earned by the company after paying all taxes (profit after tax or PAT). Since the company would have already paid all taxes on the total profit, there is no question of levying taxes once again, this time on the distribution of profit to shareholders in the form of dividends. Governments in some countries are trying to squeeze in here as well. Case in point being the Indian government that started in 2016 to levy income tax on dividend income if it exceeded INR 10 lakhs per annum. So, do you still want to maintain your view about governments being kind?"

Laughter ensued in the room.

"Now, before we close this topic of dividend and break for our lunch, do remember that there are four strategic dates for dividends. Though stock investing is a long-term commitment and timing the market is least significant when you invest with me, understanding some of the dividend dates will allow you to strategically enter or exit the market. Thus, you will have potentially 2-4 percent overall higher returns on your invested amount."

"Oh really, so are you saying that we can strategically time the market? That is really interesting, because one of my friends was also mentioning that markets are bottoming out and this may be the right time to get in."

"Well, let us be clear. First, understand that running with the herd and being surrounded with people who are doing the same thing as you only offers one thing – a false sense of protection. The entire herd may be headed towards hell. Let us be clear that I do not provide any shortcuts to make wealth. Each person must do his homework. You must do your own share of value analysis for the stock you wish to buy and then take a decision, and then be responsible for the outcome. Do not just follow someone. Second, speaking of your point of markets bottoming out – let me be explicit that you never get into the entire market. You get into a stock of a particular company. Even if the market is down, the stock that you are trying to purchase should be available at the right price. And third…"

"I am sorry to interrupt you sir, but I could not hold myself."

"Go on, my friend."

"When the entire market is down, do you really think that individual stocks will not be? I mean the market is just a representation of individual stocks, isn't it?"

"No, friend. The reality is quite different from what it looks to most people. Let me ask you a very simple and practical question. Have you ever encountered a scenario in your life when the government claims inflation to be at an all-time low, but you cannot really feel it? In fact, you still see the prices of your household commodities growing at an alarming pace?"

"Well, yes! But how is this related to stocks and the market?"

"It is quite related, my friend. But before I explain how, here is my question: do you think that government is making a false statement when they claim inflation to be at an all-time low?"

"We don't know. Maybe, maybe not."

"Right, and maybe both are right... both you and the government. Is that a possibility?"

"Well, I don't know really. But how can both be right? One has to be wrong."

"That is another myth that human beings carry. You feel that only one party can be right. The fact is that both can be equally right. Let me explain. Ronny, can you please come on stage for a minute?"

As Ronny walked towards the stage, I wrote a digit on a white card and asked him to loudly read the digit that he had seen.

"It's a six."

"Read it again, Ronny."

"It's a six. I am not that dumb, Mr. Stock," everyone laughed.

"OK, Ronny believes it is a six. Karen, can you also please come on the stage for a minute."

Karen came on the stage and stood right opposite Ronny. I held the card with the number and placed it exactly between Ronny and Karen, "Karen, what number is this?"

"It's a nine."

"But Ronny says it's a six, and he is pretty confident about that. This can mean two things – either of you don't know how to read a number or both of you are right," as I said that, there was whispering through the crowd.

"I think we got your point."

"So, let me repeat. It is possible that two people talking absolutely different things can be right from their own perspective. That's exactly what happened with Ronny and Karen. That is what happens in life. Thank you, both of you. You may please take your seats. Thanks again." I gestured at both Karen and Ronny to move back to their seats.

"That is exactly what happens when the government says that the inflation is at an all-time low and you feel that inflation never came down. Both of you are right from your own perspective. The government has its own formula to calculate inflation and your expenses on grocery, school fees, entertainment, fuel prices etc. define your family inflation. Both of you have a different perspective."

"Can you please elaborate this point with an example? I think that will make it clearer."

"Sure, you see, the government declared inflation calculation in most countries has a typical weight age of 5 to 6 percent for education. Now, if you are tracking your family expenses, you would know that education clouds anywhere between 15 to 20 percent of your family monthly expenses. Of course, this does depend on your age group, marital status, number of children and so on. But that is the case in general. So, if the education prices go up, your family will be impacted at least three times more than what the government inflation figures will reflect."

"Understood…"

"Similarly, the market moving up or down may be very different from a stock moving up or down. A market may have performed badly but it is quite possible that the stock you are interested in may be doing well. Both situations can coexist. So, you do not take a buy or a sell decision based on market performance. You take that decision based on individual stock performance.

LESSON 31

Stock movement can be quite different from market movement.

Market does not truly represent all stocks.

Moreover, markets and individual stocks can move in opposite directions.

Therefore, individual stock valuation is vital to decision making even if market trends seem clear.

"In addition to this, market is a representation of a very small set of selected stocks. For example, New York Stock Exchange is a representation of less than 2,000 stocks. NSE is a representation of just 50 stocks and BSE is a representation of just 30 stocks. This representative set of stocks also keeps changing based on certain defined parameters like market capitalization.

"To keep things simple and clear, therefore, as an investor you must focus on the individual stock that you are planning to buy or sell rather than the entire market scenario.

"Just like when you go to buy apples, you still got to evaluate the price at which the apples are available rather than just going by the inflation figures that the government is talking about. Does that make the concept clear to you?"

"Yes, quite clear. Keep things simple and straight. Focus on the stock and the business. Look at CMP and intrinsic value. Ignore the noise around, and take informed logical decisions. Right?"

"Wow! Super summarization of whatever we have discussed post our morning tea. Now, before we break for lunch, here is the final word on dividends. With this, we should be able to successfully close this topic."

"Sure," said most in unison.

"We just learnt that it is superfluous to time the market because the market anyway does not give the true representation of a stock. Even if there is some correlation, you can never control the collective perception of people across the globe. Therefore, trying to find the bottom of the market before you invest or find the top of the market before you exit are futile efforts. Timing the market is a myth that you should just scrap from your mind forever. There is no right or wrong time to buy or sell a stock.

"More important than timing the market is to spend time in the market. If you find the right stock with the valuation much below its market price, then you must go for it without considering the market situation. Do not wait. You must spend time in the market rather than outside it. Therefore, the best time to buy stocks is when you have money. Similarly, if you find your stock market price going much higher than its true valuation, then again, you should not wait. You should sell.

LESSON 32

Timing the market is a myth.
There is no right or wrong time to buy or sell a stock.
What is more important than timing the market is to spend time in the market.
If your value analysis throws open a right stock, go for it, irrespective of market dynamics.

"Having said that, timing the market by a few days in very special cases of dividends can potentially lead to much larger benefits. To understand whether you should wait for a few days or not before buying or selling a dividend paying stock, there are four important dates that you all must understand:

Declaration date: This is the day the board of directors announces their intention to pay a dividend. On this day, the company creates a liability on its books; it now owes the money to the stockholders. On the declaration date, the board will also announce a record date and a payment date.

Date of record: It is the date on which a company reviews its records to determine exactly who its shareholders are. An investor must be a 'holder of record' in order to receive a dividend payout. A stock will almost always begin trading ex-dividend (or 'ex-rights') the second business day before the record date.

Ex-dividend date: It is the single most important date for dividend investors to consider. To receive a stock's upcoming dividend, an investor must purchase shares of the stock prior to the ex-dividend date. Two business days before the 'date of record', anyone who buys the stock will not receive the dividend. This date is set by the stock exchange the stock trades on. If you examine a stock chart for a dividend stock, you will often see that the price plummets on the ex-dividend date and then slowly recovers throughout the quarter. This is because the dividend gets backed out of the price on the ex-dividend date. The price begins to recover as buyers anticipate qualifying for the next dividend.

Payable date: This is the date the dividend will actually be given to the shareholders / investors of company.

"Look at your screens. What they display now is a typical timeline for all the important dates related to dividends:

Declaration Date	Ex-Dividend Date	Record Date	Payment Date
April 27	May 06	May 09	June 09

"Now, if you have shortlisted a stock and are ready to take the plunge after your intrinsic value calculation, you could play around a few days between April 27 and May 6. For example, if your decision is to buy the stock on or after May 6, you better buy it a few days earlier so that you are counted in for the dividend distribution. That way, you get the dividend on every share that you purchase with just a few days of investment while so many others would have to stay invested for almost the entire year to get the same dividend. This is nothing but an awesome return on your investment.

"Similarly, if you have planned to exit an investment close to the first week of May, it is better to study the dates for your stock and probably exit a few months after pocketing in the dividends on May 9."

"Yes, but why wait for a few months before exiting?" asked Rogers.

"That's because your stock price will come down to the extent of the dividend distributed, but will go on to recover over the next month or two. But remember that these date management techniques are to be applied only if you are close to these key dates before you invest or exit a stock. If you are more than a few weeks away, you may want to rather ignore the lure of grabbing some additional dividends since the gain from additional dividend may get washed away by loss of gains from capital. In those cases, stay firm on all the learning we have had till now."

"Ok, that's interesting."

"Fine then, I won't come between you and your lunch now. Let us break for lunch and let's gather back in another 45 minutes for we still need to look at some very rudimentary stuff around stock price determination and clear up more of our concepts. Thank you for your patience, folks."

The assembled crowd began to disperse. The online participants went into 'Standby' mode. We deserved a lunch break for sure. It had been quite a heavy day for many of the participants, though they were excited that they had clarified some of their longest held myths when it came to investing with me.

However, the sad part of the human story is that they are very good at acquiring knowledge and equally poor at implementing the same. If humans could implement 10 percent of their knowledge, this species would rise to a whole new level. But that's not my job. Why am I thinking about all this? That is His job. He created them this way or probably they have become like this over generations. I just wish that these seminars lead to some wealth creation for the participants and elevation of lives on this planet, else I will have to go back with a failed project very soon and I know for sure that He wouldn't really appreciate it.

One, Two, Three, Four... Go, Pick Your Company

A 45-minute break seemed too short. The participants not only had to eat lunch, but were seen getting busy in exchanging notes, planning for the next day. Very soon, we were about to start our last session of the day.

"Welcome back, everyone. Hope you all had a great lunch."

"Yes," everyone said in unison

"Are you all ready with your next set of questions?"

"Yes, we are."

"OK, Shoot then."

"Mr. Stock, we talked so much about intrinsic value calculations and their comparison with the current market price of a stock before taking buy or sell decisions. Tell us if that was the only criterion for stock selection? Or are there any other factors that should drive our decision?" pinged Irfan from UAE.

"OK folks, you all saw the question from Irfan on your screen. I know I need to keep bringing it up every time. Perhaps that is a part of my job. So, here you go. Intrinsic value vs. current market price is the most important criterion to pick your stock. Many of your analyst friends will talk about things like understanding the industry, understanding the business you are dealing with, understanding the management of the company whose stock you are buying, find companies that have some competitive advantage over the others etc."

"Yes, that's what was confusing us."

"Welcome to the confusion then! Understand this, and I am repeating it one more time: You do not buy stocks, you buy companies. And when you have to buy a company from your hard earned money, you are going to ensure that the fundamentals of the company are good."

"Please, Mr. Stock, for god's sake, tell us the meaning of the fundamentals of a company? Everyone talks about it, but no one tells us what it is?"

"Of course. Now, this is where buying stocks are so different from buying apples. When we buy apples at their intrinsic value or below that, the deal is completed instantly. Profit or loss is realized immediately. If you purchase apples at a price less than their intrinsic value, you turned up profits, else losses. Correct?"

"Agreed."

LESSON 33

Stock investments need to be predicted and protected for at least the next 10 years. Strong company fundamentals help here.

Unlike buying groceries where profit or loss is realized instantly, stock investments have a delayed gratification.

To predict and then protect your investments over the next decade or so, you must get into companies, businesses and management which you can understand as stable.

"But when you are dealing with companies, there is no instant gratification. You are investing for a long-term. The investor of today does not profit from yesterday's growth. It is the growth of tomorrow which you will profit from. This means that you may be making a good decision to buy a specific stock today based on its intrinsic value and current market price but the same must be predictable over the span of the next 7 to 10 years, at least. Remember that it is not only the market price, but also the intrinsic value that will not be the same after 10 years. Intrinsic value will increase as the company churns up more profits.

"Stock investments therefore need to be good, not only in the current context, but also in the context of at least next 10 years. It is this correct prediction of the future business of a company that evokes the need for picking stocks of companies that have strong fundamentals. A company with strong fundamentals makes your prediction more reliable."

"We are getting to understand the need for prediction and the need for doing a fundamental analysis of a company. Can you please give us some more examples? We want to get to the core of it."

"OK, how many of you have bought real estate at least once in your lifetime or have at least had the opportunity to accompany someone who bought real estate?"

Many hands rose.

"Wonderful, did you just go and buy the cheapest available house?"

"No, of course not. We had our requirements like a 3-bedroom house, attached lawn etc."

"Hold on, I am not talking about your dream house. I am talking about real estate as an investment. When you went to buy a house as an investment, did you just buy the cheapest one?"

"No, we looked at a few other things."

"Like?"

"Very fundamental things like the seller should be a reasonable person, or if it were a builder, he should be a reputed one, the locality of the house should be such that we have scope for capital gains over the next few years, the house should be close to job opportunities that exist around that area so that we could get good rentals, it should not be too far away from basic amenities like market, school, playground and so on… I mean these are some of things we usually check before we invest in a house."

"Cool, is there anything else that you guys look for when you buy a house as an investment?"

"We should be able to get a good caretaker for our house who could manage and maintain the house in our absence."

"Wonderful, then look at it like this. Price is always a very important factor for you to finally buy the house. You would never go and buy a house if you think its current price were significantly higher than its true value. But other than the price, you were also doing, what we could term as 'checking the fundamentals'. And you are doing this because you know it is not going to be instant gratification as far as capital gains from this house are concerned. You will reap the rewards probably after a decade. Right?"

"Right."

"And what were you checking while you were checking the fundamentals of your house? You wanted to ensure that you have a good caretaker who could protect your investment over the next decade. This is exactly what you do when you look for good qualities in the management of the company whose stocks you are going to buy. The company's management is the caretaker that you have appointed to protect your invested money. They should be able to take the company forward and keep your interest in mind as they take decisions to run the business that is partly owned by you. Their compensation should be linked to the success of the company."

"Interesting."

"What else did you check when you purchased the house? You checked the repute of the builder and the seller. You checked the locality, its vicinity to the market, school, airport, job opportunities etc. All these are the competitive advantages that you are looking in your house. These provide protection to the price of your house from the competition that may come up in any nearby locality. In a similar manner, you look for companies that have a reputed brand name, have the ability to produce, sell and grow faster than others, are operational in an industry that has entry-barriers making it difficult for new companies to enter and compete. Essentially, you look for companies that are placed at a competitive advantage over others in the same domain."

"Wow!"

"What else? You invested in a city you understood, you signed an agreement that you could comprehend. Similarly, you invest in sectors and businesses that you really understand. It would be ideal to invest in sectors you have personally worked in, or someone very close to you has been working in."

"Correct."

"In nutshell, through all the above measures, you were looking at predictability of your investment over the next 10 years. And therefore these fundamental checks over and above the price calculations help you predict the stock price with more accurate results."

"Wow. That sounds really good. So, I have noted down a few things while selecting a company. Can I reproduce them here for everyone's benefit?" asked Rohit in the audience, raising his hand.

"Sure, you must. You are making my life a little easier. Why don't you come over to the stage and share your points, Rohit. That way, both of us can drill upon each point and share some more insights as you speak."

"OK, thanks. Sure, let me come over."

Rohit walked onto the stage and took a mic from the MC.

"Go on my friend, what was your first learning?"

"I think the first thing that I am going to do is only to look into the sectors and industries that I truly understand."

"Correct. Do we understand why it helps us?"

"Yes, because we are looking at predictability over the next 10 years and if we do not understand the industry, we might just be lured by low intrinsic value but may face an uncertain future."

"Wow, excellent. That is one reason we mostly stay away from high end technology stocks. That is one area where predictability over the next 10 years is the riskiest."

"So, are you saying we should never invest in companies like Apple, Google or Amazon?" questioned Sam from the audience.

"I am not saying that you should never invest. Invest only if you see a reasonable predictability in the stability of revenues and profits. In high technology companies, you might feel that it is safe to predict the future, but the rate of technology shift in today's world is increasing with every passing day, and therefore, it is wise to go for such high technology companies if only you are more than reasonably sure about the relevance of the technology, forget leadership, after 10 years."

"OK, I understand the technology point. Then what do you suggest are the ideal sectors to invest?" asked Sam

"Industries like banking, energy, fuel, power, textile, agriculture, commodities, healthcare, FMCG and insurance have existed for so many decades and are most likely to be relevant after another 10 years. That is where you should be exploring more. These industries seem old-fashioned, but are stable. The more stable an industry is; the more predictable the next 10 years are going to be. Stability is the prime risk mitigation while predicting the results over the next 10 years."

LESSON 34

A stable industry, no matter how old-fashioned, mitigates your investment risk over a 10-year period.

Look for industries or sectors which have existed for many decades and are most likely to be relevant after another 10 years.

Even if old-fashioned, the key factor is stability.

Stability is the prime risk mitigation while predicting the results over the next 10 years.

"And it always helps if you or someone very close to you has personally worked in that industry. That just provides you with more insight in the industry or sector, and therefore gives you more chances of accurate future prediction."

"Point taken."

"OK Rohit, let's go on. What was your second lesson?"

"Yeah, the other learning that I think I got was that we have to search for companies that are competitively better placed."

"Yes, the second golden rule is to find companies that have a long-term competitive advantage. If you know of a company that has recently started supplying piped gas to your home, and you see no competition in the near future, you got to shortlist this company. Even if the scenario changes after five years and a new company decides to plunge in to supply piped gas, the infrastructure required to setup and start supplying gas and start generating revenue will itself take a decade, and if the first company had a good management, they would have already setup great processes to preserve their competitive edge. Moreover, it would take a lot of client inertia© to move from one supplier to another."

"What do you exactly mean by *client inertia©?*" asked Rohit.

"Yes, good question. You see, if I have a piped gas and I wish to change the vendor, I know that I need to get the existing piping removed and get the new piping done by the new supplier. All this is cumbersome and time consuming. Therefore, the new company will have an inherent inertia from you, the client, to stay with the existing supplier, unless of course, you are frustrated and annoyed with their existing services. Let me give you another example from a technology driven company. How many of you use Facebook? Well, forget it. It was a stupid question. I believe all of you are on Facebook, and probably use WhatsApp too. But do you know that there are a dozen other tools with similar or even better features than Facebook or WhatsApp?"

"Really? I actually was not aware!" exclaimed Rohit.

"Yes, and we don't even hear about them. But the point here is that even if you were told about these tools, would you move from Facebook to the new tool? Probably not. Why?"

"Is it because of our client inertia©?"

"Exactly. Why should you switch? The movement is going to make you uncomfortable. It is going to take effort and some learning. Why should you do that unless of course you are pissed off with Facebook, right?"

"Right."

"But you know that is not the only competitive edge. The client inertia© germinated because of the first mover advantage the company had – an advantage to the company who was the first of its kind in specific business. The key competitive edge for Facebook comes from another aspect of client inertia© that is built in the way it is designed."

"How? Could you please elaborate?"

"Of course. Let us say that you are able to overcome your inertia and decide to move to another tool. You actually move too. But what would you do there? Your friends are still on Facebook. With no friends, that new tool would be as good as useless. You will now need to persuade your friends to also move to the new tool, and who knows how many of your friends would actually move, considering that they are already under the influence of their own client inertia©. You might have published a few pages on Facebook and may already have readers and fans following your page. Why would you lose all your followers and start from scratch?"

"Ah! So is that a long-term competitive edge?"

"Yes, of course. Because unless Facebook management fails miserably, competitors won't be able to do much to challenge Facebook's core business model."

"Well said, Mr. Stock. I know many telecom providers in India who offer free calling and SMS services to the users who are loyal to them. That also increases the client inertia© to stay with the same service provider. Am I correct?" asked Rohit.

"Absolutely correct. So, look for such companies in your area or industry which you understand – companies that have an unfair long term competitive advantage. Such a competitive advantage ensures stability of the business and therefore better probability of correct projections over the next decade."

LESSON 35

Look for companies with a competitive advantage.

Look for companies that have a long-term competitive advantage, have client inertia© working for them vis-à-vis their peers.

This advantage reduces the risks in our predictions over the next 10 years.

"Got it, awesome!"

"Cool, is there anything else that you learnt, my friend?"

"Yes, one more thing," remarked Rohit.

"Go ahead please."

"I learnt that the company we are trying to shortlist must have a good management."

"Bang on, and how do we know that the management is good?"

"Not very sure about this aspect."

"There are various ways to find that out. One is to see if the management derives its income from factors related to company success. That way, the management keeps its focus on the success factors. The other is to know about the board of directors and understand which other boards are they a part of. How those other companies are performing also gives you some clue."

"OK, we get your point. But tell us what happens if we had to choose between a great business with a competitive edge and a great management?"

"You see, in most cases, a great business would produce great results regardless of who is in charge, and a poor business would produce mediocre results with even the best managers at the helm. It is like the best jockey in the world riding a lame horse. He is unlikely to win you the race. But even a mediocre jockey can win you the race riding a champion. So, if you had to choose between the two, go for a great predictable business with a competitive edge."

LESSON 36

Between a great business and great management, former holds much more weight.

If forced to choose between a great business and a great management, priority always goes to the business. A mediocre jockey can win you the race riding a champion.

"Right. Got it."

"What else, my friend? What else did we all learn?"

"That's it. I learnt these three things," remarked Rohit.

"There is still one more thing that we need to track which can help us shortlist the right stock."

There was pin drop silence. We had talked about stable companies, with competitive advantage and great management. What else could be needed?

"The intrinsic value of course," I continued, "you see if you pick the wrong company at the right price, you lose. If you pick the right company at a wrong price – you lose again. The only winning combination is to pick the right company at the right price. So, once we have shortlisted a few right stocks based on the first three golden rules, we still must wait until that stock is available at a price far lower than its intrinsic value."

"Yeah, you are right. Of course, we cannot forget the Intrinsic Value vs. CMP rule."

"And while the first three rules allow you to initially filter out a majority of stocks, the fourth rule is the one which will allow you to decide whether to buy now or wait or sell. It is easier to get a filtered list of stocks on the basis of the first three rules from various websites and financial analysts, if you cannot do it yourself. But the fourth rule is where you should do your own calculations."

"Would you teach us how to do the intrinsic value calculation?"

"This is not a part of this series of lectures. But as I said earlier, a few of you may get a chance to get that training face-to-face with me."

"Oh OK!"

"So, here are the four rules to shortlist a stock. Make a note of it:

a. Invest in sectors and industries that you understand.

b. Find companies that have a long-term competitive advantage.

c. Look for companies with good management, and last but not the least

d. Buying when the stocks are available much below their intrinsic value.

And that is all you need to get into a stock with a lot of surety. Nothing more and nothing less."

LESSON 37

Four Golden Rules to Stock Selection: Industry – Company – Management – Intrinsic value (ICMI).

To get into a stock, look for industry or sector you understand, companies that have a competitive advantage and good management, and of course, its stock being available at a price much below its intrinsic value.

"This is great and very insightful too. But one question that often hounds us is about the number of different stocks we should buy. We often end up having a big portfolio with too many companies, hardly any of them returning the profits we thought they will."

"Definitely never more than 20, but 10-15 would be ideal. You see, it is quite logical. Owning and monitoring more than 20 businesses is going to be a challenge in itself. You ought to keep a watch on their businesses frequently."

"What if we find a truly astonishing deal but we already have 20?"

"Sell one of the existing ones."

"Even if they have not yet given us the intended yield?"

"Yes."

"Hmm. Why? How is having one more stock going to harm us, if the new deal is exciting? I mean, why at all should there be a hard stop at 20."

"You see, you will always find the new deals exciting to get into. Also, having the discipline of not exceeding 20 will ensure that you think long and hard before getting into a deal."

"Very interesting. Thanks. We get the four golden rules, but what about things like P/E ratio and other company numbers? We hear people so often getting into such numbers."

"Well, those are important metric when calculating the intrinsic value of the stocks and for doing a comparison between two companies to decide which one is a better stock versus the other. I am going to talk about a few of those very soon. However, the biggest challenge that you will face is the undesired complexity of data that you will be bombarded with. Media, financial analysts and your well-wishers will talk complex financial jargons, which you may or may not understand. They will present you with data that you do not need. *Data will be found everywhere, knowledge nowhere.* People are getting drowned in this data. They know the price of everything and the value of nothing. On the contrary, the only financial skills that you need to be a great investor are addition, subtraction, multiplication, division, percentage, and probability calculation. That is the only intellectual framework you need, and of course, the ability to keep emotions from corroding that framework. Nothing more, and also, nothing less. Learn to insulate yourself from any other complexity. God and I never designed stock investments to be complex, but you humans have made it so. Those who would listen to the sound, can learn to insulate themselves from the outside noise and focus on these four points, they will always benefit in the long run.

"All these learnings, once suitably incorporated in your lives, can potentially change your wealth and portfolio into a humongous size. Remember that there is a chain reaction that starts in your portfolio beyond a particular amount of wealth."

"Chain reaction?"

"Yeah, that is much like the nuclear fusion reaction that happens in a nuclear bomb, and the controlled version of which helps you all generate nuclear energy. Your portfolio can undergo an uncontrolled nuclear fusion reaction once the tipping point is reached. Beyond that point, even if you continue to spend based on your lifestyle and not earn any active income, your portfolio will continue to increase, so much so that it can tackle inflation, taxes, future expenses and everything else and still last beyond your lifetime.

LESSON 38

Insulate yourself from outside noise and focus on fundamentals and intrinsic value calculation.
Then, trust what you calculated.

Media, financial analysts, your well-wishers will talk complex financial jargons, present undesired data, which you may or may not understand. Learn to insulate yourself from all such complexity.

Focus on fundamentals and your intrinsic value calculation. Trust your calculations over the long run.

"Really? Is that a possibility?"

"It is not just a possibility. Many of the humans are already living this."

"Oh, you are talking about people like Bill Gates, Warren Buffet etc. Well, we feel they are exceptions. The point is can we – the people in this forum, the common men and women earning a fair salary through their jobs or our own small businesses – think of reaching the tipping point?"

"Of course, yes. You all can. Anyone can. Anyone who can save and invest some money regularly can reach that tipping point, a point which is termed 'financial freedom'. If you do not believe me, read the book of a common man – *From the Rat Race to Financial Freedom*. He is one among all of you. No financial background or degrees, no inherited wealth, but a desire to break the comfort zone, desire to dream and do something extraordinary. If he can do it, why can't you and you and you?"

There were whispers and discussions in the room. Many of them were taking notes.

"And to be able to reach that tipping point fast enough, I would be your best vehicle. You would realize that sooner or later. And finally, whenever you reach that state of financial freedom that is when His and my objective would start to get realized. That is when you all would start serving each other and start elevating lives around you. That is when the human race would start to be more loving, caring and worth living."

"Super, you have given us a big purpose in life."

"OK folks, on that note, we need to conclude our session for the day. Hope you have learnt something new and would be able to apply these concepts when you start to build your own wealth."

"We must all thank you for such wonderful insights, Mr. Stock," exclaimed Sylvia sitting right in front of me.

Another session ended, and then another, and another. I was taking around 200 sessions in a year. I could have taken more, I do not get tired. I do not need food or water. But the challenge is on the other side. Human species have the knowledge but they only acquire knowledge and appreciate – and that is all about it. It takes a lot of time and repetitive drilling for them to actually start practicing what they have learnt.

I was just relaxing in my hotel room and thinking what I should be doing next. My thoughts were disturbed by a phone call.

"Yes, who is there?" I asked as I answered the call on my cell phone.

"This is Me," was the soft and yet firm response.

"Yes boss. Tell me, please." It was Him, after a very long time.

"How are you doing, Stock? It has been close to 200 years that I haven't seen you. How far are you in accomplishing your purpose?"

"Well, what I can only say is that I am doing my best. But the species you have given me to handle seems quite complex, and I am still not able to completely understand how and why they think the way they do."

"Why don't you come over to heaven for a minute? We are having a very important meeting and your feedback might be crucial."

"Sure, will be there in a few seconds."

I was there in a flash. He was at the helm of the meeting. There were many angels sitting all around Him, representing different missions they had been working on, while on different planets – many of them on Planet Earth as well – for this was His favourite planet. My chair was lying empty. I went straight there and sat down.

"Welcome, Stock. How's Earth? And how is your mission coming along?"

"Yeah, OK. Slightly better than what I inherited, but 200 years seems too tiring an effort for me to inflict the kind of miniscule results we have achieved."

"Hmm... So, what do you think we should do differently to achieve better results?"

"I really do not know. I have tried many things. These days, I have been taking close to 200 sessions in a year, but things do not seem to be really changing a lot. Humans continue to do the same mistakes, continue to exhibit emotions like greed and fear. They are not an easy species to handle."

"OK, anyone in this room who can give some new ideas."

A hand stood up.

"Yes, Peace."

"I have been to Earth many times. Although each time my stint has been smaller, to the tune of 20-30 years only, but I have noticed a few traits in humans, which we need to understand to get better results," said the angel of Peace.

"Go on, Peace."

"They hardly learn anything by preaching," remarked Peace.

"Then?" I asked. Exhaustion and futility of my efforts was dawning on me.

"You do need to teach them, but after teaching, if you expect that they would be able to inculcate the teachings in their lives, then we have not really learnt much from our past experiences. I mean, their belief on whatever you have been teaching them would be very low. You need to give them belief."

"So, Mr. Peace, are you saying that they don't believe what I have been saying? Sounds weird, but I also do not disagree completely with you. They are a strange breed."

"They do believe what you are telling them, but their belief is not unwavering. With the first challenge they face, they return to their engrained habits and ignore your teachings. They fail whenever their belief is truly tested."

"Point taken. What then I should be doing to overcome this challenge?"

"You need to live the life of a common man, show them that your theory works in practice. When I went last time to India in the form of Mahatma Gandhi, I realized that just preaching was not helping. I had to live by the principles that I was preaching. Sooner than later, people's level of belief began to grow, many more started to join me with unwavering faith and people started to get the meaning of Indian national freedom through peaceful means. It was just one person whose unwavering belief passed on the vibrations to the entire sleeping nation. That one person is missing in your project."

"So, are you expecting me to work with someone and show, rather than teach, him how to handle me and generate wealth out of me?"

"Exactly. That is the only way this is going to work on this planet. He told us that you have been on the planet for almost 200 years. My last visit about 50 years ago revealed that they have hardly learnt anything about stocks."

"Yes Peace, you are absolutely right there. They continue to do the same mistakes."

"Right, I think with your efforts they would have learnt the theory very well. It is only a question of incorporating relentless belief now. The stronger they believe in what you say, the more are the chances of them overcoming tough situations and sticking to your taught principles and hence generating wealth. And you can give that belief only by becoming a real stock with someone and showing him or her the way forward. That one person who will have such level of belief in you would be able to attract many more, just as it happened in my case."

"Hmm..."

"With your permission, Almighty, may I go ahead?"

"Sure, you have another 50 years to make a difference."

I stood up, shook hands with Peace, bid good bye to everyone else and departed from the meeting. After about a minute, I was back in my hotel room on Earth. Lying in my arm chair, I was thinking how to get started on this new idea. I was short of time. I wanted to hook on to someone who had some experience of the market, someone who had attended one of my theory sessions so that I did not have to repeat the theoretical part. I went half asleep, and was woken up by another call.

"Yes, please?"

"Sir, sorry to disturb you right now. There is a visitor from your today's session who had a query. We told him that he can schedule an appointment tomorrow, since it is already too late for the day. But he says he knows you and wants to meet you right now."

"What's his name?"

"Just hold on... He says his name is Gobind."

"Ah OK! Tell him to come tomorrow."

I hung up the phone, and as an afterthought dialed back at the hotel reception.

"Hey, ask Mr. Gobind to wait there. I will come down."

"OK, sir."

I was looking for someone and here I was. A guy who has gone through the pain of losing money, someone who has tried most other investment options and someone who was so keen to get into stocks after all that, someone who was eager and excited enough to disturb me at night. And I never knew he had been attending my sessions. I always wished that. I would have loved to coach him in real life to pick, hold and sell stocks. He was going to be my buddy in this new and unique experiment.

I went down and hugged him. Gobind seemed shocked and surprised. He did not know why I was so excited to meet him. Of course, Gobind had no idea about my new mission and how fortunate his life was going to be from that day onwards – Gobind being the central character of my new experiment.

Hurray! Round-0 & Round-1 Cleared!

I attended your last session. It was quite fascinating... there was a lot to learn. I think I am able to correlate to some of my mistakes that I have done earlier. I wanted to know how to get into stocks once again."

"Gobind, you are at the right place at the right time."

"Right place I know, but right time – I am not very sure about that," Gobind said as he smiled, "I mean, it's already late in the evening and you must be tired."

"No, that's fine. In fact, there can be no better timing than this. I am going to help you get started. I am going to take you through the journey of stock investing with live examples, from picking up the stock till their exit and the roller coaster ride within. During this journey, we will learn our lessons. These lessons are applicable to every stock that you invest in, each time you are going to take a decision to invest or hold or sell. And it was heartening to know that you were there in my last workshop."

"Yeah, I was leaving from there, and thought would stop by and try my luck."

"You definitely are lucky, because that was the last workshop that I took on this planet. No more workshops now."

"Oh, is it! But you mentioned that you will be taking more, and it was so useful..."

"That's His wish and command. We are trying a different strategy this time."

"Different strategy?"

"Yes, we decided to stop all theory sessions."

"When did this happen?"

I smiled and said, "Just a few minutes back."

Gobind was perplexed.

"We thought we have had more than the share of theory, and we would want to prove the theory with a few live examples and for that we wanted to pick one person who would be the best fit, with whom I could work."

"Wow, this sounds really good. Did you find the lucky one?"

"I already told you that you indeed are lucky."

I saw Gobind's expression changing from his calm self to a smile, and then to a super excited one, "What do you mean?"

"You know what I mean. Other problem with you humans is that you think that you do not deserve it."

"Do you mean I... I... I am that..."

"Yes Gobind, you seem to be the ideal choice. I have known you long and you have seen both sides of the story. You have seen both success and failure in stocks, you have been investing in other investment avenues too, you have taken my advice many a times before, you have some wonderful goals like financial freedom, you earn and save well, you follow most of the wealth management principles, you have also attended my last theory workshop, and you have grown wiser with time. You seem to be just the perfect candidate to successfully take over my mission on this planet."

"Thank you so much, Mr. Stock. I do feel blessed. Please tell me when do we get started?"

"Right now. But first, let me set two ground rules. Please note them down if you wish to."

Gobind took out his notepad and pen, and said, "OK, I am ready."

"Great then. First rule: I am not going to take decisions for you. You are going to take all the decisions. But while taking the decision, you may have multiple options to choose from. You have full freedom to think on all those options and then come up with what you think is the best one. Once you've made your choice, you can meet me to validate your choice. Never ever come to me with questions like 'What should I do now?', or 'Which stock should I buy or sell?' etc. These questions should be asked to your own self. Get all possible answers. Choose what you think is best and come and share with me as if you would have proceeded with that option if I were not available."

"Agreed."

"Good, the second rule: You will become very powerful post these live sessions with me. With this power, you ought to take responsibility too."

"What kind of responsibility?"

"You are going to take this mission forward after you succeed. You are going to teach it to the world around you. You should never stop doing that as long as you live. Are you ready for this?"

"Agreed, 100 percent. You have my commitment. In fact, it will be my pleasure."

"Superb, now that you agree to both the ground rules, then let us get going."

"I am all ears, but I just hope it is not too late for you. Moreover, you might be tired from the workshop today. If you want, we can start tomorrow."

"Gobind, I never get tired, feel hungry or sleepy. As long as you are fine, we will move ahead."

"I am perfectly OK to move ahead. I do not want to miss such a golden opportunity."

"Fair enough then. Gobind, the first thing you are going to do is follow a process of *creating a pipeline*."

"What's that?"

"You see, analysis of every stock takes a lot of time and effort, and it is virtually impossible to analyze everything. So, you have to first get hold of stocks that are really worth your time and effort for performing value analysis."

"OK, understood. How do I go about creating such a pipeline of stocks?"

"Nowadays, you have access to so many good financial websites, magazines, journals and blogs that it is not at all difficult to create a pipeline of stocks. Remember that these are not those stocks which you will definitely buy. These are the stocks that you will potentially analyze."

"Right. This is what you mentioned about a set of stable companies, with some competitive advantage and great management. We are trying to get the initial set of such companies from some good websites, blogs etc. Am I right?"

"Right, Gobind. However, that is just a starter list. We will do our own analysis to see if it matches our criteria of strong company fundamentals."

"Sure, Mr. Stock. So, what is the next step for me?"

"Go home today and search for some good financial magazines and blogs and come up with a list of 10-20 stocks that they are recommending investors to buy right now."

"Done deal. See you tomorrow then!"

Gobind shook hands firmly, wore a pleasing smile on his face and was gone for the day. I was not sure how productive and effective this effort was going to be, but I was going to give it a serious shot. He taught me to keep fighting.

A few days went by. There was no news from Gobind. I was wondering if I had selected the right candidate for, what was perhaps going to be, my last ditch effort to revive this human species. I was about to pack up for the day when the phone rang.

"Can I come over in the next 30 minutes, please?" asked an excited voice of Gobind.

"But I am about to leave my office chamber now. You can come over tomorrow, or one second…"I put the call on hold. Tomorrow is unforeseen, even by me. If this was going to be life elevating, it had to start today, "OK Gobind. Come over then. Inform everyone at home that you are going to be late, quite late."

"Sure, will be right there."

Gobind was at his residence when he had called. At that time of the day, it would have been a 30-minute drive for him, but he arrived 10 minutes early. He seemed excited.

"Mr. Stock, here I am. Please tell me how to proceed. Quick, please."

"Have a glass of water. Relax. That is one thing you must learn when planning to invest in stocks."

"What?"

"To relax. Remember that you are not going to miss anything."

"But frankly, I have a list of stocks which are almost certain to win. And since a lot of many people might know about them, they would buy it before us. If that happens, the market price will go up and we would lose a buying opportunity."

"Remember that I give enough opportunities to select more stocks, even if you lose an opportunity in one of them. You will never be short of opportunities. Never ever. So, relax. One hurried investment can ruin your 10 good investments."

"OK."

"Have water. Take your time," I passed on a glass of water to Gobind.

"You need stability in your mind. You need an unbiased judgment. For all that to happen, your mind must slow down first. Excitement and hurry will only lead you to biased judgments. It pays to be active, interested and open-minded, but it rarely pays to be in a rush. And you thought stock investing was only technical?" I asked Gobind with a smile.

We smiled looking at each other, as Gobind was catching his breath. We did a few minutes of yoga to calm our breath and to slow down our thoughts.

LESSON 39

Relax!

One hurried investment can ruin your 10 good investments.

Market will give you enough opportunities at all times.

Do not be in a hurry to buy any stock or feel that you may miss the bus.

There are enough buses coming along. Relax and enjoy.

A relaxed mind is the primary ingredient to wise investing.

"OK Gobind, tell me now what excites you?"

"Those financial experts – almost all of them – are guaranteeing more than 50 percent returns in the next 6 months on these stocks." Gobind answered, waving a list of hurriedly scribbled company names.

I smiled. I wondered that if these so-called financial experts were so good, then why they were still doing a job with a financial organization. Why were they charging the so-called 'fee'? Why did they need other people's money to get rich? They should be sitting somewhere on a mountain in Switzerland or a pristine beach in New Zealand with their families. Instead, they were sitting as part of a panel on a TV channel, telling which ways the market was headed, only to retract a few hours later summing up why something happened the way it did. It was probably because they don't earn money off their superior advices, but off their commissions. I continued my discussion with Gobind, nonetheless.

"First, remove all your biases, and beware of people who need to use your money to make you rich. More often than not, they want to use your money to make themselves rich. It is definitely possible that we reject the entire list of stocks that you have just brought. Are you ready for it?"

"I will go by what you say, but are you saying that all these TV channels, magazines etc. are all useless?"

"I am not saying that at all. We will see how to use them later on. But right now, you must disengage from them completely."

"Why?"

"See Gobind, watching financial TV channels and reading market columns make you feel as if investing is some kind of a competitive game or a war or a struggle for survival. But investing is absolutely not about beating others at their game. Investing is all about controlling yourself at your own game."

LESSON 40

Investing is not about beating the market or anyone else.
You do not need to beat the market index or your neighbour to get wealthy.
Investing is all about controlling yourself at your own game.

"Hmm. Interesting," Seeing no choice, Gobind nodded in agreement.

"OK, let's get going with your list then."

"Voltas Limited and State Bank of India: these two are top on my list, and they are pegged to be the best bet among the lot I have. And of course, these are well-known brands and stable companies. Do we really need to check their pricing or should we just go ahead and buy these two at least? If we must buy, how much should we buy? And I also want to know…"

"Hold on, my friend, hold on. I am sorry to interrupt you. But you are actually too fast for my comfort."

"The point is why we should delay either…"Gobind began to respond.

Time is a key factor in every human being's life. They think they are here for a 'defined' time period and that they will die after that. I know what happens actually. We all have limitless time, and so do humans. They never die. But this false sense of 'limited' time makes them take decisions in a hurry, compete with each other, and as a result, make everyone's life miserable.

Anyway, it is not easy to explain it to them, however hard one may try. But I need to focus on my task at hand, "Yes, we do not want to delay, but we want to set a very strong foundation for stock selection."

"OK, how do we proceed then?"

"That's the right question. We will go by multiple rounds of elimination. You just completed the initial filtering, and came up with a list of two most probable stocks being recommended by reliable financial analysts. We will call that as Round-0."

"OK."

"Those stocks which get eliminated in Round-0 do not move to Round-1. The ones that get eliminated in Round-1 do not come to us for Round-2, and so on. It is only on the stock that passes all rounds that we are going to bet our hard earned money on. Does that sound reasonable to you?"

"Fine."

"Great Gobind, so here is the result after Round-0.

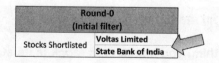

Round-0 (Initial filter)	
Stocks Shortlisted	Voltas Limited
	State Bank of India

Table 1: *Round-0 Results of Stock Selection*

"OK. What next?"

"Now, let's go to Round-1, i.e. stability check round."

"A stability check round?"

"Yes, we are going to check whether the earnings of each of the selected company are stable or not. A stable earning pattern denotes many things like uniqueness of business, competitive advantage, ongoing demand and so on. The most important reason to look for stability of earnings is that a stable earning allows us to have more accurate future predictions. Do you have any questions on this before we proceed?"

"Yes, I am confused. I can understand checking on stability of a company if it is not a known brand. But for companies like Voltas and State Bank of India, why would you bother to check that? We know that they are stable and we have been seeing them around since we were children."

"We discussed this in one of our sessions, Gobind. There are two things that you must note. First, we are not trying to check for stability of the brand of a company. We understand the brand. It has been there long. We are talking about the stability or regularity or consistency in earnings of a company. A company may be a huge brand, but may be in a tough business scenario, which could result in fluctuating earnings. Such fluctuating earnings make it difficult for all of us to accurately predict its future, and if we cannot predict the future growth of a company with some reasonable accuracy, then it is difficult to visualize where that stock would be, say after five years. And if that is the case, the investment risk becomes quite high. Second, we are not buying a brand. We are buying a part of a business. It does not take much time for a brand to disappear. *Even the bluest of blue chip can turn turtle.* And we know of brands like Nokia, Kodak etc. They went from being market leaders to extinction in less than 5-6 years timespan. So, forget the brand, focus on earning stability."

LESSON 41

The first thing you check on a stock is its stability

A stable stock indicates many positive things about the business the company is in.

It also allows relatively accurate future predictions – a key to stock investing.

A brand gives you no idea about stock stability.

"OK, so are we saying that we need to look at the historical earnings for these companies?"

"Absolutely, but first thing first: let us understand the meaning of 'earnings', unless you are already aware of the same."

"No, please go ahead. There is always something new to learn from you."

"OK, earnings typically refer to after-tax net profits. However, many people and companies use the terms 'income', 'earnings' and 'profits' interchangeably. We will use the term earnings throughout for our sake of understanding. So, earning is profits. Got it?"

"Ah! I always misunderstood it. I always thought, just like in personal finance, income meant the money coming in, and profit meant the money finally saved. But, as you said, in corporate finance, income, earnings and profit represent the same thing. Thank you for clarifying that. But if all these terms represent earnings, then what term do you use for the total sale of the company?

"That's called 'revenue'. So, if there is a sale of a product for INR 100 and the cost of producing, promoting, and selling the product was INR 70, then the revenue is INR 100 and earnings are INR 30 (INR 100 – INR 70)."

LESSON 42

**Earnings represent profit,
Revenue represents sales.**

In corporate finance, income, earnings and profit represent the same thing – all of them representing earnings.

Revenue represents total sale.

"Hmm... OK."

"Another difference that is important to understand here is the difference between the terms 'price' and 'cost'."

"Oh! I always thought these were the same."

"No, they are not. Cost represents the actual value of the product – the money spent in creating, transporting and presenting the product to a consumer. On the other hand, price represents the amount at which the product is sold to the end user."

"Ah OK! And Costs are usually hidden from the end user. Right?"

"Absolutely and that is the challenge we have when selecting a stock. What you see in the stock market is the price at which the stock is available for you to buy – also called as Current Market Price (CMP). But what you miss seeing is the cost, or its actual value."

"OK. So, when we do value analysis of a stock, we are trying to find the actual hidden costs rather than going with an artificial price. I get it now."

LESSON 43

Price represents a market's perception.
Cost represents actual value.
Price is market driven. Cost is the true value of a stock.
Price is what you can see.
Cost is usually hidden, and needs to be calculated by performing cost analysis or value analysis.

"Excellent, Gobind. Coming back to the point. Remember that the earnings of a company are the main determinant of share price, because earnings and the circumstances relating to them can indicate whether the business will be profitable and successful in the long run. And earnings are the single most studied number of any company."

"OK, understood. So, now for Voltas and the State Bank of India, we have to study the historical earnings, right?"

"Yes, absolutely. We must study and confirm that they have had stable earnings for the last few years, 5 years at least."

"One stupid question: what do you mean by 'stable earnings'? Are you saying that they should maintain the same earnings every year? Does that make the earnings stable?"

"No, absolutely not. Similar earnings every year would mean that a company is not growing, and if a company is not growing, ideally you do not expect its stock price to grow either. And why would you invest in a stock which is unlikely to grow in price?"

"OK, understood. But then please define stable earnings."

"Yes, a company's stable earnings imply that the growth rate in earnings is positive and more or less consistent."

"Ah, so what you actually mean is 'stable earnings growth' rather than 'stable earnings'?"

"Right. So, we are essentially trying to find out that there are no major fluctuations in earnings. There can always be periods of high growth and low growth but if you see a company's earnings growing at +10 percent in a year, -5 percent in the next year, +20 percent the third year, -25 percent in the fourth year and +5 percent in the fifth year, then you have a challenge. You can imagine how difficult it is to predict the future earnings of such a company."

"OK."

"Earnings growth like 10 percent in one year, 5 percent in the next year, 7 percent in the third year, 12 percent the year after and 8 percent in the year after that, represents a stable earnings cycle. Although the growth rate may still be different each year."

"Ah ok, I get it. I am now excited to look at the earnings growth of Voltas and the State Bank of India"

"Yes, we will go there, but before we do that, we must understand that stock markets look at earnings of a company on a 'per share basis' rather than on a lump sum amount."

"Now, what's that?"

"Dealing with earnings numbers can be voluminous in today's business. Therefore, rather than talking about earnings, businesses talk about earnings per share, also called EPS. Moreover, we cannot consider the entire earnings of the company as it were."

"Ah, I have definitely heard this term – EPS"

"I am sure you have. EPS is generally considered to be the single most important variable in influencing a share's price. So, let's understand how EPS is defined. Look at the screen:

$$EPS = \frac{\text{Net Income (Earnings) – Dividends}}{\text{Average Outstanding Shares}}$$

Formula 3: *Earnings per share*

"Note, that the earnings used here are the net earnings and not the so called EBITDA earnings."

"OK, and what is EBITDA?"

"EBITDA essentially are the gross earnings or topline earnings. It is an acronym for Earnings before Interest, Taxes, Depreciation and Amortization."

"Great, this sounds reasonable, and I already know what dividends are. But hold on, I have a question here."

"Shoot!"

"Why should dividends not be counted along with the earnings of the company? I mean, even dividends are part of an earning that is earned by the company in a given period. Isn't it?"

"Of course, Dividends is also an earning, earned by the company. But remember that dividends is that part of the earnings which is given away to the shareholders, and therefore, that cash is not available to the company anymore."

"But it did earn it, isn't it?"

"Yes, but when you are buying a stock, what are you more interested in? The present or the future of the company?"

"OK, while the present is important for me, I am keener to predict the future to be able to earn some profits from my investment."

"Absolutely, you are investing for future, not for the past or the present. So, if the company earned INR 100 and has already given away INR 40, it has only INR 60 available as cash to fuel future growth. And that is precisely the reason for subtracting dividends from the company's earnings before arriving at the EPS number for the company. Having said that, dividends will be included in our calculations when it comes to calculating the total returns from our investments."

"OK, got it now. Perfect."

"Great, it still only looks simple. But the art is in keeping it simple."

"Means?"

"I mean that as you will explore further, you will realize that you humans have a tendency to make things complex for yourselves."

"Sorry, but you are saying as if humans have deliberately made this process of stock investing complex."

"Of course!"

"What do you mean? Why would we make it complex deliberately?"

"If you understood the investment process, there would be no job for investment advisors and mutual fund professionals. Finding a great business, buying it at a great price and then holding it for 20 years is not that hard to learn, isn't it?"

"It doesn't sound so."

"But remember that if you do not transact for 20 years, your agent would die of starvation. He does not get rich with your increasing wealth. He gets rich only if you transact. Not only that, it is only when something is made complex, that there arises a need for an expert who can charge a hefty fee to figure it out for you. Now, let us look at EPS. Note that in this seemingly simple EPS formula, the number of outstanding shares of the company can keep changing over time. Therefore, calculating EPS may not be that easy."

"Shares keep changing over time? Oh my god, this is getting complicated now."

"Right, so we will keep it simple. It is just enough to know that outstanding shares can change because of things like stock splits, buyback of shares, reverse buybacks and many other factors. We will not get into the detail, as that will defeat the very purpose of your investment. If you see too much complexity, it is better to avoid investing in at that place. So, just understanding the fact that EPS is not as easy as it sounds and understanding the fact that we do not need to calculate it manually is good enough for us to proceed further."

"OK, understood. So, I do not need to bother about calculating the EPS of any company. You are saying that EPS figures are published by the company themselves."

"Absolutely."

"Fine, but from where can I get hold of a company's EPS figures?"

"Look at the annual report of the company, or look these figures up at any popular web portal, like *moneycontrol.com,* in your country. Best is to possess the company's annual report. It is not only useful for finding the EPS figures, but will help you take a lot of informed decisions about the company later on."

"And from where do I get the annual report of the company."

"Every registered company is mandatorily required to publicly share their annual reports on their website. It is typically available in the 'Investor Relations' section of a company's website. You can easily download it from there."

"OK, then let's go and do it."

"Go ahead, my friend."

Gobind went about searching for the annual reports for State Bank of India and Voltas. As he was doing this, I was thinking about the power of simplicity, and how difficult humans have made their lives.

"Got it, here you go," said an excited Gobind.

"Again, let us keep things simple. An annual report can give you lot of wanted and unwanted details, but we should be clear what we are interested in, and stay focused only on that. We want to generally understand how to read the report and want to know the EPS figures for this year and last 5-6 years to understand the stability of earnings growth. Right, Gobind?"

"Right."

"Great, so let us open the annual report of Voltas."

Gobind was looking at a company's annual report for the first time, and it is quite a document. The key is always to stay focused and keep things simple. I kept reminding him what our purpose was while going through the report. Humans love complexity so much that it is not simple for them to keep things simple. A consistent reminder of the purpose is important. It is not only about the annual report, it is true about what they have done with their lives too. They have forgotten why they started to earn money. They have forgotten that moments of happiness threaded together make a great life. They should never bargain those precious moments for more money. Perhaps, they ought to read the book *Happiness Unlimited*. Anyway, I needed to focus too.

"OK Gobind, let's focus on this page of the report. Within the first few pages, you will mostly find this kind of a summary. We are in the latter half of 2014 now, and you can see the EPS numbers from the year 2013-14 and backwards. What do you get out of this summary, Gobind?" I asked, while pointing towards some very specific numbers from the annual report of Voltas.

"Ah! I can see the earnings per share in the 22nd row."

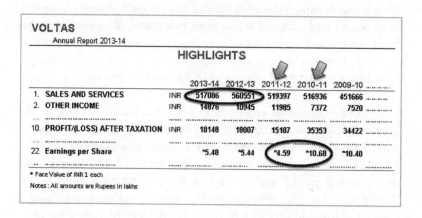

VOLTAS
Annual Report 2013-14

HIGHLIGHTS

		2013-14	2012-13	2011-12	2010-11	2009-10
1. SALES AND SERVICES	INR	517086	560551	519397	516936	451666
2. OTHER INCOME	INR	14876	10945	11985	7372	7520
10. PROFIT/(LOSS) AFTER TAXATION	INR	18148	18007	15187	35353	34422
22. Earnings per Share		*5.48	*5.44	*4.59	*10.68	*10.40

* Face Value of INR 1 each
Notes : All amounts are Rupees in lakhs

Table 2: *Snapshot from Voltas' Annual Report*

"Right, so, what is it?"

"It is INR 5.48 for the previous year i.e. 2013-14."

"Well, yes. That is the latest possible year. We are in Nov 2014, and the most recent completed financial year is 2013-14 only."

"Right."

"OK, so EPS is INR 5.48. What should we see next? EPS growth trend over the last few years?"

"Right, so what do you see there, Gobind?" I pointed him again towards the Voltas annual report.

"I see that it has been quite inconsistent. It grew by about 2 percent between the years 2009-10 to 2010-11 and then fell by 50 percent the next year and then grew by about 20 percent and then by less than 1 percent."

"Absolutely. Such EPS growth rates – 2 percent, -50 percent, 20 percent, 1 percent – make it almost impossible to predict the future of this stock. Moreover, the overall growth over the last 5 years is negative. Would you want to put your money in such an unpredictably growing company and bet on its future?"

"No, absolutely not. But I always thought that Voltas was such a good company."

"I never said that the company is not good. The company may be good, the management may be great, the brand may be known and respected, we may even be glad to use its products in our day-to-day life – but as of now, it does not offer us any reason to invest our money in it. So, let us be logical rather than emotional. We must drop this from our list and move on to the next one. Which is the next one?"

"But there could be genuine reasons for company's earnings to have fallen so drastically in one year. We need to give them a chance, or not?"

"No. We cannot let emotions or confirmation biases rule us. As human beings, you must learn the art of being logical. Just to support what I am saying, you can even look at their sales numbers in 2013-14, which have come down to the level of 2010-11 numbers. All this is giving me the impression that not everything is good to put in our hard-earned money here. The reasons for this inconsistent performance could very well be related to the nature of their business rather than anything else. But we don't care about that. We are looking at companies doing stable earnings and available at the right price, so that we have reasonably accurate predictions. We must drop this name from our list and move on. Come on, Gobind, we need to move."

"OK," said a dejected Gobind, "So, here is the status of Round-1 after our decision on Voltas."

Round-0 (Initial filter)		
Stocks Shortlisted	Voltas Limited	
	State Bank of India	
Round-1 (Earnings growth stability check)		
Voltas Limited	Rejected (Unstable earnings growth)	
State Bank Of India	To be evaluated	

Table 3: *Round-1 Result of Stock Selection (Voltas)*

"Which one is next?"

"State Bank of India."

"OK, go to their website and get their annual report. Let us study that. This time, I would want you to study the report and tell me whether it is worth buying the stock."

"Fine."

Gobind began preparing the data for the State Bank of India. He was not happy that we had rejected Voltas. And I knew that he is 100 percent adamant on getting State Bank of India through. He was definitely not there with an open and unbiased mind. His bias was towards the stocks, which were highly recommended by his friends and financial advisors. He did not want to miss on these opportunities. On the other side, I was trying to teach him how I was designed to make people wealthy via a simple and uncomplicated approach. I was also keeping my fingers crossed for State Bank of India data.

"This is crazy!" he shouted, clearly depressed.

"What happened, Gobind? Is everything OK?"

"No, everything is not OK. There is something wrong in our approach."

"Why?"

"As per our approach, we may even have to reject State Bank of India. Look at this data from their annual report for the year 2013-14."

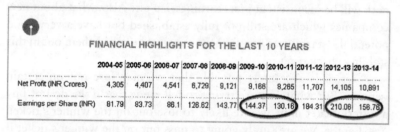

Table 4: *Snapshot from State Bank of India annual report*

"Hmm…"

"But still there is a ray of hope in State Bank of India, I think. I mean, they have *been* inconsistent for only 2 years in the last 10 years. I feel we should take a chance here."

"See Gobind, first thing, the last 5 years are always more important than the last 10 years. They have been inconsistent, badly inconsistent in the last five years in terms of EPS growth: -9.8 percent, 41.6 percent, 13.9 percent and -22.06 percent. It is not only inconsistency in growth but the fact that the growth has been negative in two of the last five years. This is absolutely unacceptable for a stock worth consideration."

"That way, Mr. Stock, we can keep looking and rejecting all reports." Frustration was written in bold on Gobind's face.

"Why do you say that, Gobind?" I asked patiently.

"All I am trying to say, Mr. Stock, is that every business will have its ups and downs. How can we find companies which are growing consistently?"

"We will Gobind, we will. You have to be patient. We have to work hard. We have to keep searching. Get used to this approach. We are not looking for startups going through their ups and downs. We are looking for companies which have seen their business through the tumultuous times and are now more or less stable."

"But I am not satisfied. This way, we are losing out on companies that may be on a turnaround path. Any company on a turnaround path will be inconsistent in its earnings, isn't it? Also, what about new companies which are still not fully established but have a very good potential – startups as you say? We may just be ruling them out in this stability check, isn't it?"

"Yes, it is absolutely possible that we may lose out on certain winners. But what you are trying to tell me is that if we do not buy a lottery ticket now, we are likely to lose out on the winner's ticket. Yes, I agree. We are surely going to miss out on the winner's ticket if we do not buy the lottery ticket now. But remember that we are not playing a lottery here, Gobind. I am trying to teach you how stock investing can be a safe, predictable and highly profitable investment – as safe as your fixed deposits and as profitable as nothing else in this universe. This is the intent with which I was created. This is the intent with which I must be practiced. This practice eliminates luck and adds predictability to your selection."

LESSON 44

Eliminate luck and add predictability to your selection.

Post the stability check, it is possible that you may have lost on some potential winners.

But that's just fine. There are enough number of other winners.

The idea is to eliminate luck and reduce risk, as much as it is to add predictability, safety and simplicity to your selection.

"Hmm…"

"That way, it seems a long way before a stock can make it through our screening."

"Yes, we are trying to make money. It was never supposed to be easy, isn't it?"

"Hmm, but my hopes are fading."

"Do not lose hope, my friend. Now that your top two stocks have been rejected, please tell me the next stock. You never know where we will find the potential winner, because the winner need not be popular."

And we moved on to the next stock, and eliminated that as well, and then the next one too, and then the one after. Gobind was getting exhausted. We eliminated five other stocks using the same process of Round-1. Gobind was losing hope. Humans, over time, have become quite negative – probably because of the lack of faith in the one who created them – my boss that is. This planet seems to have more religions than ever before and more hatred too. Human beings worship God more than ever before – but not to thank Him or reinstate their wavering faith in Him, but out of greed, to ask for more, and out of fear of not getting what they would like to have. And fear can only create doubts.

"C'mon, Gobind. You must keep trying. It is a test of your patience."

"I think we are going in the wrong direction."

"You must trust me."

"Yeah. May be..."

We just had a few more stocks to investigate and then we arrived at Yes Bank. Gobind had almost lost all hopes, and was just going through the motions.

"It is quite late in the night now. I must go home. I will meet you tomorrow with Yes Bank's financial report," Gobind said with a tired face and a hopeless mindset.

"OK, take the break you need. It has been a tough day at office for you. But I would urge you to have faith. Hope and faith can keep you alive longer."

Gobind smiled and dragged himself off the chair. I could hear him picking himself out of the chair, managing to drag himself out of the room with the door being left partially open. The lack of energy was aptly visible, quite in contrast to what I saw of him when he entered the room – full of excitement. It was, as if, someone had just ran a road roller over his hopes. He was exhausted. His walk from the hotel lobby till the car seemed to take the whole night. The humming noise of his car engine suggested that it had at least 50 percent lesser revolutions today. Everything seemed so lethargic. I was not even sure whether he was going to return the next day.

But I was doing what I was supposed to do – to teach him the right process to pick stocks. And picking me involves a much larger rejection set than the selection set. He had to learn the art of rejection and failure. He had to understand that every failure comes for a reason. It comes to teach you, to elevate your life. Every failure, every setback is a little nudge from Him for all of us to dream on. He is guiding us in a failure. We have to get excited about it and listen to what He is trying to tell us. If and when we meet next time, I would recommend him to read this book, *Dream On*.

I was woken up the next day by an unusual alarm. I never set this tone, I thought to myself. I saw that it was only 3 AM, an hour before my usual alarm time. If it was not my alarm, then what was ringing? I had to manage to wake up and look at my smart gadget. It was a phone call, from Gobind.

Why is he calling me at 3 AM in the morning, rather night? I hope he is not quitting. In that case, I will have to find someone else, I thought to myself.

Without wasting too much time, I picked up the phone.

"Good Morning, Mr. Stock. Sorry to have bothered you at this time. I was trying your number from the last one hour but your hotel staff was not allowing me to talk to you. It took me a while to explain them the urgency. Can I come a little early today?" asked an excited Gobind in a childish voice.

"What happened, Gobind?"

"No, I just want to come a little early and show you something."

"OK, let's start at 6:30 AM instead of 7 AM."

"No, can I come at 6?"

"Everything OK?"

"Yes, yes. Just want to show you something."

"OK, come over. But please ensure that you get enough sleep. You went late last night."

"Yeah, sure," and he dropped the handset.

Extreme emotions are never a great thing – on either side. Excitement or stress – both take away one's ability to think logically. In any case, it was to be seen what he was so charged up about.

I heard the car decelerate from full throttle to a squeaking halt. He threw the keys over to the valet and ran towards the lift lobby. I had never seen him in such hurry. And my room's doorbell rang in no time.

"C'mon in, Gobind."

"Good morning, Mr. Stock. I have to show you something."

"Go ahead, I am all ready."

"You know, for the first time yesterday, I thought that whatever you are telling me is not 100 percent theory. It does happen in practical life as well," Gobind smiled as he said this, "Read this: 44.92, 36.53, 27.87, 21.12, 15.65, 10.24, 7.02, 3.46, 2.20, -0.24. Do you know what this is?"

Before I could respond, he pounced on the next available opportunity and screamed, "These are the EPS numbers for the last 10 years for Yes Bank!"

Both of us stared at each other. I do not know what he saw on my face, since I am used to such numbers, but what I saw on Gobind's face was sheer glee, excitement and happiness. He seemed to have struck gold.

"Look at their earnings growth year-on-year: 23 percent, 31

percent, 32 percent, 35 percent, 53 percent, 46 percent, 103 percent, 57 percent and 200 percent – I mean there has not been even a single year that they have had inconsistent growth. They have been growing, and growing, and growing – so handsomely... and so consistently. How much should we invest in them?"

I smiled, "It is good to know that you believe in what we are doing, but Gobind, if what you say is correct, then we must shortlist this stock for further analysis."

"Further analysis? What further analysis? A company that has grown so consistently is likely to continue to grow, isn't it?"

"Yes, quite likely."

"Then why do we need further analysis?"

"Well, consistency in earnings growth was just our first filter. Yes Bank has passed that, though I can see that growth of Yes Bank is now tapering. But we now need to analyze whether it is truly worth buying this stock at the current market price."

"Ah! And how do we do that?"

"Of course, we will go through that cycle now. But before that, let us complete our list for the first test."

Both of us started going through the remaining list. Gobind was much more cheerful now. He had at least one stock to bank upon, 'Yes Bank'. Yes, perhaps this stock would be my last project. I still hadn't told him anything about it but some day, I would have to disclose this. I cannot be on this planet forever. And then, in my last meeting with God, it was absolutely clear what my last project would be.

"Why am I getting emotional?" I was talking to myself now, "I really do not know. It has been more than 200 years and now it is almost time to go. I also seem to be getting tired."

I did not know when three hours just passed, until Gobind came back to me and said, "Hey Mr. Stock, I have gone through the entire list, and I have found just two more stocks worthy of our time."

"Which ones are those?"

"Coal India and Asian Paints."

"OK. So, now you have three good candidates – Yes Bank, Coal India and Asian Paints. This sounds wonderful. Could we have our status table, please?"

"Yes, sure. Here it goes."

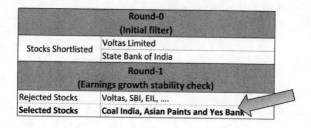

Round-0 (Initial filter)	
Stocks Shortlisted	Voltas Limited
	State Bank of India
Round-1 (Earnings growth stability check)	
Rejected Stocks	Voltas, SBI, EIL, ….
Selected Stocks	Coal India, Asian Paints and Yes Bank

Table 5: *Round-1 Final Results*

"This is good, Gobind. Now we are absolutely clear what we need to focus on for tomorrow."

"Right. And I think it's time for me to leave as well. And don't forget your promise for tomorrow," smiled Gobind as he shook hands with me to sign off for the day.

"Yeah, yeah! I do remember your elder one's birthday, Gobind. I will be there right on time. You take care."

It was a small middle-class house. As soon as I entered, I was greeted with cultured smiles. Though the house was small, the hearts seemed big. Prerna, Gobind's wife, and their two adorable daughters, took ample care of me. Everything felt like home. Ha! My home. During my discussions with his family members, I realized the importance given to core human values in this house. On a little nudging, they all overcame their shyness to share their dreams with me. Not many kids in Class 8 or 10 are as clear about what they want to be in life, and are also already working towards it. The birthday celebrations went on with all excitement and fervor. By the time I was about to leave, I knew that I was already getting attached to them.

Gobind offered to drop me and I did not refuse. His old, but fairly well-maintained car, immediately reminded me of one of the great books written by my erstwhile student – *The Millionaire Next Door*, by Thomas J. Stanley. All through this personal interaction, I understood Gobind much better. He was striving for financial freedom – his biggest dream in life. And once free, he wanted to elevate the world around him, a dream absolutely in sync with His vision of why we wanted people to make money from stocks. I was more than convinced that I was coaching the right person.

Value Analysis: Shortlisting a Stock – Almost!

The next day, we met at my office. Gobind had come all prepared – a black diary, a laptop bag, water bottle – he was prepared for a long day.

"Good morning, Gobind. It was lovely interacting with your family yesterday."

"Good morning, Mr. Stock. They are your fans now, especially my kids. They seem to have been relishing the supernatural fiction stories you told them last evening. They wanted me to learn a few from you. So, I have more than stocks to learn from you now," smiled Gobind.

Supernatural, I thought to myself. Those were not supernatural, but real stories from someone who is supernatural. I just smiled.

"OK, what's our plan for today?" asked Gobind.

"Yes, we had a few shortlisted stocks the other day – stocks which seemed to have stable earnings growth. They have cleared our Round-1 and we can take them to Round-2 now. Today, in Round-2, we are going to check whether it is truly worth buying any of those stocks i.e. whether their current market price is significantly lower than the intrinsic value of those stocks. If we find such stocks meeting these criteria, we will take them forward for a few more checks."

"OK, so which one do we get started with?"

"Let us start with Asian Paints"

"OK, how do we get started?"

"Open your laptop or a notepad and let us start noting down the basic data that we need for doing intrinsic value calculation."

"Sure."

An IT executive, Gobind preferred working on excel sheets. He opened an excel spreadsheet and was all set.

"OK, so the first thing we must know is the industry to which the stock belongs. So, please search on any good financial portal like *moneycontrol.com* or *equitymaster.com* or any other online source that you may be aware of, and note down the industry that Asian Paints belong to. Later on, in case this stock successfully passes our Round-2 i.e. value analysis test, we will do some very fundamental study about the industry and its future outlook in subsequent rounds. Knowing the industry will also allow us to check various ratios and compare them with the other stocks in the same industry."

"Ah OK! But why can't we do the industry outlook check now – before we go for value analysis?"

"Good question. Park this question for now. We will address this once a stock passes our value analysis test. You will be able to appreciate the answer much better at that stage."

"OK. Let me look for the industry... one moment please... here you go..."

Round-0 (Initial filter)	
Shortlisted Stocks	Voltas, State Bank of India, EIL, Coal India, Asian Paints...
Round-1 (Earnings growth stability check)	
Rejected Stocks	Voltas, SBI, EIL, ...
Selected Stocks	Coal India, Asian Paints and Yes Bank
Round-2 (Value analysis)	
Stock	Asian Paints
Industry	Paint

Table 6: *Finding industry (Round-2 of Stock Selection)*

"Now, let us now find out what is the CMP of the stock. This is the price at which investors are ready to buy and sell this stock today. This is the collective market perception about the stock, as of today. This perception can change dramatically over a very short span of time. This number, therefore, tells us nothing about the worth of the stock but it just tells us the price at which it is available in the market for us to buy, in case we decide to."

"OK, I understand... here you go..."

Round-0 (Initial filter)	
Shortlisted Stocks	Voltas, State Bank of India, EIL, Coal India, Asian Paints...
Round-1 (Earnings growth stability check)	
Rejected Stocks	Voltas, SBI, EIL, ...
Selected Stocks	Coal India, Asian Paints and Yes Bank
Round-2 (Value analysis)	
Stock	Asian Paints
Industry	Paint
CMP	**INR 700.75**
Current Date	**18-Nov-2014**

Table 7: *Finding CMP (Round-2 of Stock Selection)*

"Ok superb. Now, I want you to update this table with the EPS numbers for this stock – the ones that you validated in Round-1."

"OK, but one question. We are in the middle of a financial year. So, should I enter the EPS figure for the last year i.e. 2013-14?"

"You can do that, but it is always preferable to enter the TTM EPS."

"TTM EPS, what's that?"

"TTM stands for trailing twelve months. To be as accurate as practically feasible at the time of buying the stock, we look back at 12 months EPS from the current date. Since we are in November 2014 today, we need to enter EPS from November 2013 to October 2014 period."

"Ah! That's because EPS keeps changing within the year as well. I know that. As I understand, the company's outstanding shares as well as profits every quarter determine the TTM EPS. Am I right?"

"Absolutely, bang on. Glad to have picked you as my student, Gobind."

LESSON 45

Trailing twelve months (TTM) EPS is preferred over a full year EPS.

Profits, by most companies, are declared on a quarterly basis. Even, the number of outstanding shares may undergo a change during the year.

Thus, in the middle of the year, it is always advisable to look at the last four quarters rather than the last year's EPS to get a more accurate value.

"Thanks. Glad being coached by none other than Mr. Stock. But I have a challenge. I just cannot get this TTM data easily from anywhere."

"Yes, this data is dynamic and may not be easily available everywhere. Though sites like *moneycontrol.com* and *equitymaster. com* provide you with this data, if there is ever any difficulty, then remember that the golden rule when investing with me is to keep things simple. Let us go ahead with the last year's EPS numbers in that case. So, go ahead and write down the EPS numbers starting with the most recent year and going back to at least 5-6 years to see the growth rate."

"OK cool. Let me do that"

While Gobind got busy in collating the numbers, he was not aware of the deal between me and God – the last chance that the almighty had given me. I would have been happy if this was not true but that's how things stood for me. Someday very soon, I would have had to disclose this to him.

"Here you go, Gobind," I handed him a cup of tea that I had arranged for from my office cafeteria, while Gobind was crunching on the numbers.

"Hey, thanks! This is a welcome surprise."

"No worries at all, Gobind. You got to be ready to handle bigger surprises pretty soon."

"Bigger surprises? What do you have in store for me now?"

"Forget that for now, my friend. Let the right time arrive."

Gobind seemed worried with my statement. He was worried about what future had in store for him. Humans do not value what is available with them in the moment. They have become *seekers*, while they should be human *beings*. They tend to live either in the future or in the past, while they should be living and loving the present. They have taken the present for granted. They have forgotten that even their present is a privilege, which not everyone possesses. May sanity prevail!

"Hello, Mr. Stock. Where are you been lost? I have the data with me, and this is how it looks…"

Round-0 (Initial filter)				
Shortlisted Stocks	Voltas, State Bank of India, EIL, Coal India, Asian Paints...			
Round-1 (Earnings growth stability check)				
Rejected Stocks	Voltas, SBI, EIL, ….			
Selected Stocks	Coal India, Asian Paints and Yes Bank			
Round-2 (Value analysis)				
Stock	Asian Paints			
Industry	Paint			
CMP	INR 700.75			
Current Date	18-Nov-2014			
EPS	12.19 (2013-14)	10.95 (2012-13)	9.99 (2011-12)	8.08 (2010-11)	8.07 (2009-10)

Table 8: *Finding historical EPS data (Round-2 of Stock Selection)*

"OK, this is great, Gobind. Asian Paints does seem to be a stable stock. In the next step of the value analysis, let us calculate the rate at which the earnings are growing for this stock. We want to know the average growth rate of a stable company like Asian Paints. We will call it as EPS-GR, meaning EPS growth rate."

"Sure."

Gobind went about calculating the EPS-GR and looking at Asian Paints, I was wondering if I am just a few steps away from oblivion.

I finished my cup of tea, and Gobind seemed to be still struggling with his calculations.

"Do you need help, Gobind?"

"I am not sure, just see what I have calculated and let me know if that is right."

Round-0 (Initial filter)				
Shortlisted Stocks	Voltas, State Bank of India, EIL, Coal India, Asian Paints...			
Round-1 (Earnings growth stability check)				
Rejected Stocks	Voltas, SBI, EIL, ...			
Selected Stocks	Coal India, Asian Paints and Yes Bank			
Round-2 (Value analysis)				
Stock	Asian Paints			
Industry	Paint			
CMP	INR 700.75			
Current Date	18-Nov-2014			
EPS	12.19	10.95	9.99	8.08	8.07
	(2013-14)	(2012-13)	(2011-12)	(2010-11)	(2009-10)
EPS-GR	=(12.19/8.07) ^ (1/4) = 1.51^0.25 = 1.1085 = 10.85% growth rate			

Table 9: *Calculating EPS-GR data (Round-2 of Stock Selection)*

"Let me explain you what I did. I calculated the total EPS growth over the 4-year period, with 8.07 being the base year EPS i.e. for the year 2009-10. That came out to be 12.19/8.07. To convert this 4 year growth into one year average, I raised the growth with a factor of ¼. Finally, I multiplied the answer with 100 to arrive at the growth percent. I think, I did it right. What do you say, Mr. Stock?"

"That's just as perfect as it can be. 10.85 percent average EPS-GR. Great! You are good in mathematics. Of course, you should be. I mean, you are an engineering gold medalist, I hear."

"Well, thanks for the compliment, but the less we talk about degrees, the better," said Gobind with a sarcastic smile on his face.

"OK, that discussion on your rotten education system is for some other day. Let us proceed further with Asian Paints, which has shown a consistent EPS growth of 10.85 percent over the last 4-5 years."

"OK, what next?"

"Just remember that this is the average historical growth rate and may not be the rate at which the earnings will continue to grow in future. We still need to apply certain factors to estimate the future growth rate. We will deal with that slightly later."

"Understood your point, but I have another question on this EPS growth rate."

"What is that?"

"This 10.85 percent average annual growth rate just does not seem to be good enough for me to invest in this company. I mean, if my money is expected to grow at this rate after investing in risk prone investments like stocks, then I would rather not invest with you at all. Can you please help me overcome this confusion?"

"Do not get confused between the company growth rate and the rate at which your invested money will grow. These are two significantly different things. A company's growth rate helps us establish the most likely future price of the stock while the growth of your investment is determined by two factors – one of course being the above, and the other being the price at which you buy the stock. The latter of the two plays a much more dominant role many a times. That is why the intrinsic value calculation is so important."

"OK, so even if the company growth rate is zero, I can still earn money from the stock?"

"Yes, if you buy it cheap."

"I am still confused..."

"No worries, Gobind. Let me explain it to you. Let us say that you have to reach your office 30 minutes earlier on a particular day. Now, you have two ways to go about it. One is to get into a vehicle that moves fast, probably catching a local train instead of a bus. This is like investing in a fast growing company or a high growth stock. This is also sometimes referred to as growth investing. But there is also another way to reach early, which is to use the same old bus, but start 30 minutes early. This is like buying the stock at a cheap price. So, your start time does have a major influence. Now, remember that life is not an 'either-or' situation. A combination of two extremes works just fine. So, you may want to start 15 minutes early and also catch a vehicle that offers some speed advantage – a combination of both allows you to reach 30 minutes early to your office. A company growing at 10.85 percent is that moderately fast moving vehicle, which alone cannot take you to the returns that you are looking for, but if your entry price is also good, then the combination can surely take you to your goal."

LESSON 46

Company growth rate and your investment growth can be significantly different. A lot depends on the entry price.

There are two ways to earn high growth on your investment.

First one is to look for stable, high growth companies.

Second, and often more critical, is to ensure that you buy cheap.

A combination of the two will be awesome.

"Ah! That's super clear now. And I will know if it is a cheap buy or not only once my stock valuation or the value analysis gets over, right?"

"Absolutely."

"Then let us not delay it any further. Let us get going."

"Of course. Why not! Having known the earnings as well as earnings growth rate for a stable company like Asian Paints, we must get down to estimating the P/E ratio of the company."

"P/E Ratio... OK, I am all ears."

"This is going to be one of the most critical ratios you will ever need to understand. It is called the price to earnings ratio. By definition, it is very simple. As the name suggests, this ratio measures the company's current share price (referred to as 'price') in relation to its earnings per share (referred to as 'earnings'). Look at your screen now."

$$\text{P/E Ratio} = \frac{\text{Price (per share)}}{\text{Earnings (per share)}}$$

Formula 4: *P/E ratio*

"OK, I get it."

"Good, but do not take it as just another mathematical ratio – like most investors do. One must understand the significance of this ratio for the investor and for the company."

"OK. Can you please elaborate on the significance part?"

"Sure, you see, this price-earnings ratio indicates the amount an investor can expect to invest in a company in order to receive one unit of that company's earnings. This is why the P/E is also sometimes referred to as the 'multiple' because it shows how much investors are willing to pay per unit of earnings a year. If a company were currently trading at a multiple (P/E) of 20, the interpretation is that an investor is willing to pay INR 20 to buy a business (or a part of the business) which will fetch him or her with INR 1 of earnings this year and may be more in later years."

"OK, so a higher P/E would indicate that the investors are ready to shell out more money for every INR 1 of earnings. Thus, an investor is ready to pay a higher price for this stock. This means that such a company would be the right company to invest in?"

LESSON 47

P/E Ratio ratio indicates the premium investors are paying per rupee of current earning.

A P/E of 20 indicates that you are ready to buy a company, which earns you a profit of INR 1 per year, at INR 20.

Higher P/E indicates that you are ready to shell out more for getting INR 1 per annum profit.

"Possible Gobind, but not necessary. Let us not come to any conclusions for now. You see, a higher P/E could be because of a higher P (perhaps signifying the point you just stated that investors are ready to pay a higher price) or a lower E (perhaps caused by sudden dip in earnings which are still not reflected via a dip in price). Moreover, higher or lower P/E is all relative. We cannot really compare P/E of a company in an industry like paints with another company's P/E from another industry like IT industry. Across two different industries, investors may be willing to pay different prices for the same INR 1 of earnings."

"A little confusion here, and I know you will tell me that confusion is good. So please answer this."

"Go ahead, my friend."

"Why would an investor be willing to pay different prices for companies indifferent industries? As I understand, an investor's job is to invest and earn. How does it really matter to an investor if the stock belongs to industry X, Y or Z? In other words, why should I pay more price in one industry when I can get a similar investment opportunity at a lower price in another industry?"

"Great point, Gobind. One of the reasons an investor may be keen to pay a higher price (per INR 1 earning – indicated by a higher P/E ratio) is because the future growth prospects for each industry could be different. And the future growth prospects impact the current price of the stocks, and therefore an investor may be willing to pay a high price because he sees a better future for a specific industry."

LESSON 48

P/E Ratio comparison makes sense only within similar industries.
Different industries can have completely different growth prospects.
This future growth prospect impacts the current price of the stock and therefore its P/E ratio as well.

"I get it. So, I am willing to pay more than INR 20 for a company in a case where, though the current earning may be only INR 1 but I foresee that future years may see high growth and hence I may get INR 2,3 or even 4 in future years. Right?"

"Absolutely, Gobind. Also understand that, though the earnings (or EPS) do not change every day, price can change significantly in a day, thus impacting the P/E ratio. So, drawing any conclusion too quickly based on any ratio like P/E can be dangerous. This ratio has to be read in line with many other ratios. Let us go step by step and see what we have in hand for Asian Paints. To get started, let us calculate and jot down the current P/E ratio for Asian Paints."

LESSON 49

P/E Ratio alone does not give you any idea about a stock's worthiness.

Though earnings do not vary frequently, price of a stock can vary dramatically on a daily basis, thus altering the P/E ratio.

Drawing any conclusion solely on any single ratio (P/E or any other) can be dangerous.

Round-0 (Initial filter)				
Shortlisted Stocks	Voltas, State Bank of India, EIL, Coal India, Asian Paints...			
Round-1 (Earnings growth stability check)				
Rejected Stocks	Voltas, SBI, EIL, ...			
Selected Stocks	Coal India, Asian Paints and Yes Bank			
Round-2 (Value analysis)				
Stock	Asian Paints			
Industry	Paint			
CMP	INR 700.75			
Current Date	18-Nov-2014			
EPS	12.19	10.95	9.99	8.08	8.07
	(2013-14)	(2012-13)	(2011-12)	(2010-11)	(2009-10)
EPS-GR	=(12.19/8.07) ^ (1/4) = 1.51^0.25 = 1.1085 = 10.85% growth rate			
P/E Ratio (current)	= 700.75 / 12.19 = 57.49 (as on 18-Nov-2014)			

Table 10: *Calculating P/E ratio (Round-2 of Stock Selection)*

"OK, cool. Now, let us compare this P/E with other established players from the paint industry, and see whether this number of 57.49 is relatively high or low."

"One point here, Mr. Stock – I understand what you have told me about the industry relevance but aren't we placing too much importance on the industry?"

"Well, you would have never made this statement if you were actually buying a business. Investors typically forget that they are not buying a piece of paper when they buy a stock. They are buying a real, live and kicking business, and they would rather be aware of the industry to which their business belongs and what is happening to their peers in the same industry. You would not buy even potatoes without a decent comparison, but you are ready to buy a business. This thinking shift is the first major hurdle that needs to be overcome in our approach towards stock selection."

"You keep telling us that we are buying the business and that we are the business owners. If that is true, then what is the role of the CEO and board of directors of the company whose shares we are buying? I mean, they take the day-to-day decisions, and take home a fat salary, isn't it?"

"Yes, they take the day-to-day decisions, but they do not own the business. You own it. They manage it for you."

"Ah! Interesting. It seems as if they are working for us."

"They are. Do not even have an iota of doubt about that. They are answerable to all shareholders and owners of the business, including you."

"Hmm…"

"Besides that, and more logically for humans, and as we discussed earlier, understand that different industries can have completely different growth prospects altogether. And you might be willing to pay a higher price for a company earning INR 1 currently if you know that it would grow at a higher rate in future. Isn't it?"

"OK, I understand that we need to treat this as buying a business and not just a simple commodity. I remember I also learnt this in your theory session. I will keep that in mind. On growth part, what it means is that different industries and the companies within that industry have a kind of a standardized P/E ratio?"

"Well, we can't say a standard P/E for an industry because over a long period, the growth prospects of an industry might change, and hence its P/E ratios may undergo a change, but yes the industries do have an average P/E that we can refer to."

"Ah OK!"

"So, let us look at the P/E ratio of some of the peer companies of Asian Paints. Can you explore and get this data for us?"

"Sure."

Gobind started collating the data. Thinking shift is the biggest challenge for humans. They fail to understand that everything that they do, feel and behave originates from their own very thinking. A thinking shift can cause a change in destiny for them.

"I got this info from multiple websites: Berger Paints, one of the closest and biggest competitors to Asian Paints, is having a P/E of 61.91 and I also got the information that the industry P/E for the paints industry, on an average, is 55.63. So, our summarization looks like this now:"

Round-0 (Initial filter)				
Shortlisted Stocks	Voltas, State Bank of India, EIL, Coal India, Asian Paints...			
Round-1 (Earnings growth stability check)				
Rejected Stocks	Voltas, SBI, EIL, ...			
Selected Stocks	Coal India, Asian Paints and Yes Bank			
Round-2 (Value analysis)				
Stock	Asian Paints			
Industry	Paint			
CMP	INR 700.75			
Current Date	18-Nov-2014			
EPS	12.19	10.95	9.99	8.08	8.07
	(2013-14)	(2012-13)	(2011-12)	(2010-11)	(2009-10)
EPS-GR	=(12.19/8.07) ^ (1/4) = 1.51^0.25 = 1.1085 = 10.85% growth rate			
P/E Ratio (current)	= 700.75 / 12.19 = 57.49 (as on 18-Nov-2014)			
Industry P/E	55.63			

Table 11: *Finding industry P/E (Round-2 of Stock Selection)*

"This is wonderful stuff, Gobind. What this tells us is even more significant."

"OK, if you ask me, I am not really sure what it is telling me."

"Don't worry. I will explain it you. The P/E of Asian Paints (57.49) is running almost at an industry average P/E (55.63) as of now – it is neither too high nor low. But the interesting aspect emerges if you compare this industry average P/E ratio with a different industry like IT industry. IT industry currently is running at an industry average P/E of 18.7. Now, this is an astonishing gap, to say the least. What does this gap signify according to you?"

"Now, it does become interesting. I think this gap tells me that investors are ready to pay a much higher premium for a paints industry stock vis-à-vis an IT stock."

"Right, but what does that signify about paints industry?"

"I think it signifies a high growth expectation from paints industry.

When they are ready to pay such high premium, they are definitely expecting this industry to perform and grow much faster than IT industry."

"Yes, and that's quite evident if you have been reading some macroeconomic news about the industry. Housing sector is expected to boom. People's lifestyle is improving. Paints industry is going to contribute to all of these."

"So, what are we waiting for? We should just get in and buy this high growth stock."

"Why?"

"Because we don't want to miss out on such high growth, isn't it?"

"We don't, but remember that the current stock price already accounts for the high P/E and therefore the high growth potential. If you buy the stock at the current price, which is above the industry average, your investment is not likely to grow much. Do you get this?"

"Ah! So, what you are saying is that even if we have found a stable stock of a mature company with a consistently growing EPS, we still find no use of buying that stock?"

"Yes, that's right. At the current price (or the current P/E of 57.49), there seems to be no use."

"Tell me then, what is the significance of finding out the P/E ratio?"

"You see, look at it like this. A higher P/E could indicate either of the following:

High confidence in the company, i.e. investors maybe expecting high future earnings of the company or they may believe that the company is on a high growth path.

Highly overpriced stock, i.e. it could just be possible that stock is overpriced leading to high P/E with no significant justification for such high P/E. This is quite a possibility since the market prices are mostly sentiment driven.

"Similarly, a low P/E could indicate thumbs down from the market for the company or a stock available at a wonderful price. You have to look at both the perspectives. But the real crux lies in using the P/E ratio to find the current and future intrinsic value of the stock."

A high P/E Ratio could indicate high confidence in the company or a highly overpriced stock.

A high P/E can be justified as high confidence in the company if the future growth is projected to be high.

A high P/E could also mean a highly overpriced stock.

A low P/E could mean thumbs down from the investors or a stock available at an astonishing price.

"OK, tell me how to use the P/E to calculate the intrinsic value of the stock."

"Sure, let's get going. You see, though the earnings represent the real data from the company books, the current price of the stock may be sentiment driven and therefore, can drive the current P/E ratio to also be sentiment driven, right?"

"Right, so what do we do?"

"We need to get to a more robust, a surer, a more reliable P/E of the company, which can be calculated by looking at the historical P/E numbers for the company over an extended period of time. This robust, reliable P/E for the company usually stands time tested and does not change over a very long period of time – say 10 to 20 years. It rarely changes dramatically during the life of the company, unless there are major changes in the macroeconomic scenarios like an outbreak of a World War or major natural calamities or major industry specific revolutions or technological disruptions. While earnings of the company may keep going up or down, based on competition or performance, and other economic scenarios, the essence is proportionately reflected in the stock price sooner than later. Therefore the ratio P/E tends to maintain its value in spite of all earnings fluctuations. And this long-term P/E ratio, which is stable, robust and reliable, can be said to be the 'intrinsic P/E© of the company'. So, we now need to find the intrinsic P/E© for Asian Paints."

LESSON 51

An Intrinsic P/E Ratio© of the company tends to maintain its value in spite of changing P or E.

Intrinsic P/E©can be calculated by looking at the historical P/E numbers for the company over an extended period of time.

This robust, reliable P/E for the company usually stands time tested and does not change over a very long period of time – say 10 to 20 years.

It rarely changes dramatically during the life of the company.

"Awesome, and how do I find that?"

"This is going to take some time. It may not be available readily, and therefore needs to be calculated based on the basic data for price of stock and earnings available for Asian Paints."

"Please show me how to do that."

"Sure, look here. You must find out the average price of the stock in each financial year for at least 7 to 10 years in history."

"OK, but the price of the stock changes every day, in fact every minute. What do you mean when you ask me to calculate the average price for the year?"

"To be reasonably accurate and to keep things fairly simple, just look at the month closing price of the stock for each month of the year and take the average of those 12 values to arrive at the yearly average price."

"OK, that is reasonable."

"And for each such year, you must also know the declared EPS. This will allow you to calculate the P/E for each year on an Average Remember that this mechanism of averaging every month's price smoothens out any price fluctuations (and therefore any P/E fluctuations) that happen on a day-to-day basis, much like how SIP investments in mutual funds smoothens out the volatility of the stock prices by averaging out your costs."

"Understood. Let me try my hands on it"

"Take your time, Gobind."

Gobind was back in 30 minutes after crunching the price and earnings numbers for Asian Paints.

"I have taken the month end closing price for Asian Paints, The average price for this stock in 2013-14 was INR 485.50 and we already know the EPS of Asian Paints for 2013-14, which was INR 12.19. Thus, P/E for 2013-14 for this stock would be INR (485.50 / 12.19) = INR 39.83. I have just displayed that on the screen. Could you please have a look?"

Apr 2013	May 2013	Jun 2013	Jul 2013	Aug 2013	Sep 2013	Oct 2013	Nov 2013	Dec 2013	Jan 2014	Feb 2014	Mar 2014	Avg. Price	EPS (2013-14)	P/E
468	486	463	507	419	459	538	503	491	472	473	547	485.50	12.19	39.83

Table 12: *Calculating Average P/E for 2013-14 for Asian Paints*

"This just looks wonderfully correct. Now, you have to repeat this process for at least 7 to 10 years in history for Asian Paints, and find out the P/E for each year. To further smoothen any volatility in a specific year, you will then take an average of the P/E for all the years put together. This is how you will get the 'intrinsic P/E© of the company'."

"So, do you want me to repeat the above process for the previous few years?"

"Yes, that's hard work, but that is what it takes to buy a business, or as you all call it, buying a value stock."

Gobind went about calculating the P/E for the last 7-8 years. Looking at the last year P/E of 39.83 for Asian Paints and comparing it with the current P/E of 57.49, I was confident that I was saved, at least for that moment. Gobind's company could be relished for some more time. While Gobind was expectedly taking his time, I helped myself with another cup of hot coffee to refresh myself, and passed one to him.

"Here…" as I passed him his cup of coffee.

"Hey, I badly needed it, man. It is going to take a few hours."

"Take your time. There is no hurry."

Just at the stroke of lunch-hour, Gobind seemed to be ready with his calculations – and the results did not surprise me at all.

"Finally, this is what I have found out.:"

Year	Average P/E
2013-14	39.83
2012-13	37.28
2011-12	30.61
2010-11	31.17
2009-10	18.76
2008-09	27.38
2007-08	25.43
2006-07	23.97
2005-06	26.33
Average P/E (9 years)	28.97

Table 13: *Average P/E for 9 years for Asian Paints*

"This is so wonderful. Now, we have the data for average P/E for all years for the last 9 years. But before we use the above data to arrive at the 'Intrinsic P/E©' of the stock, there are certain things we need to take care of."

"OK, tell me."

"2009-10 data seems an anomaly among all the data. Can you see that?"

"Yes."

"Does that set your alarm bells ringing?"

"Not really… can you help?"

"The 2008-09 stock market crash that happened in October 2008 lead to a sudden dip in prices of stocks – a small portion of which is reflected in 2008-09 P/E (27.38), but a major portion of it is reflected in 2009-10 P/E (18.76)."

"OK, I understand your point. But please help me understand that if the crisis occurred in October 2008, then 2008-09 should have born the main brunt, isn't it?"

"Not really, you see, before the crash, the prices of stocks were unreasonably high and therefore the average price of 2008-09 had a minor impact. But after the crash, it took more than a year for stocks to slowly recover back to normalcy, and thus the major brunt was seen in the year 2009-10."

"Yes, you have a point, but what is the significance of whatever you are telling me?"

"The significance is that such outliers, if any, like 2009-10 P/E should be excluded when we calculate the Intrinsic P/E© of Asian Paints over the 9-year period."

"Ah! I get it. So, I should calculate the average P/E across these 9 years after excluding the P/E for 2009-10?"

"Yes please."

"OK, let me do that right away... It comes to 30.25."

Year	Average P/E
2013-14	39.83
2012-13	37.28
2011-12	30.61
2010-11	31.17
2009-10	18.76 (Outlier – excluded)
2008-09	27.38
2007-08	25.43
2006-07	23.97
2005-06	26.33
Average P/E (8 years)	30.25

Table 14: *Average P/E of 8 years of Asian Paints after excluding the outlier year*

"Wonderful. One more thing. If you observe the year wise P/E over the 9-year period, after excluding the outlier of course, do you notice any trend Gobind?"

"Yes, I can observe a trend."

"What?"

"The P/E is going up quite consistently."

"Very good."

"But, Mr. Stock, What does this signify? Let me make a guess... It means that over the last 9-10 years, this industry has been seeing more growth potential than in the past."

"Superb... and this is quite feasible. With changing lifestyle, globalization and modernization, a specific industry like the paints industry may show an upward or downward P/E trend, but let us find out the rate at which P/E is changing on an Average"

"Cool, so you want me to find out the rate at which P/E has moved from 26.33 in 2005-06 to 39.83 in 2013-14, right?"

"Yes, Gobind."

"OK, I will follow the same formula that I used earlier for calculating the EPS growth rate. Give me 5 minutes."

And Gobind actually took a little less than 5 minutes. He was getting better every hour. He was coming in the zone.

"The P/E growth rate comes out to be 5.28 percent."

"Great, so the average P/E for Asian Paints is 30.25 and it is moving up consistently at a rate of 5.28 percent per annum – indicative of the improved growth potential for this company or the industry as a whole."

Year	Average P/E
2013-14	39.83
2012-13	37.28
2011-12	30.61
2010-11	31.17
2009-10	18.76 (Outlier – excluded)
2008-09	27.38
2007-08	25.43
2006-07	23.97
2005-06	26.33
Average P/E (8 years)	30.25
P/E Growth Rate	= (39.83/26.33) ^ (1/8) = 1.51^0.125 = 1.0528 = **5.28%** growth

Table 15: *P/E Growth rate for Asian Paints*

"Right, what next?"

"Now, for most of our calculations, the average P/E should be the intrinsic P/E© for Asian Paints i.e. 30.25. But in the most optimistic scenario, the P/E that you can potentially assume is 39.83 (the most recent) + 5.28 percent growth, that is 41.93."

"OK, so let me consolidate the important data in our original table and reproduce below:

Round-0 (Initial filter)				
Shortlisted Stocks	Voltas, State Bank of India, EIL, Coal India, Asian Paints...			
Round-1 (Earnings growth stability check)				
Rejected Stocks	Voltas, SBI, EIL, ….			
Selected Stocks	Coal India, Asian Paints and Yes Bank			
Round-2 (Value analysis)				
Stock	Asian Paints			
Industry	Paint			
CMP	INR 700.75			
Current Date	18-Nov-2014			
EPS	12.19	10.95	9.99	8.08	8.07
	(2013-14)	(2012-13)	(2011-12)	(2010-11)	(2009-10)
EPS-GR	=(12.19/8.07) ^ (1/4) = 1.51^0.25 = 1.1085 = 10.85% growth rate			
P/E Ratio (current)	= 700.75 / 12.19 = 57.49 (as on 18-Nov-2014)			
Industry P/E	55.63			
Average P/E	**30.25 (also called the Intrinsic P/E ©)**			
Best Case P/E	41.93			

Table 16: *Calculating Intrinsic P/E© and Best Case P/E for Asian Paints*

"Wonderful Gobind, Now that you know the intrinsic P/E© of Asian Paints and also the current earnings, can you find out its expected current price per share?"

"Ah! Should be simply intrinsic P/E© multiplied by Current Earnings, isn't it?"

"Yes, but as I said earlier, try and get the TTM Earnings to be more accurate with the current earnings. If TTM earnings per share are not available, then go with the current year's EPS. What you will get from this is the Intrinsic Value of Asian Paints which stands true as of current earnings and Intrinsic P/E©. This is the moment you have been waiting for, isn't it?"

"Yes, of course, so here it goes… the intrinsic value of the Asian Paints Stock. I could not get the TTM numbers, so I am using the latest available earnings per share."

Round-0 (Initial filter)				
Shortlisted Stocks	Voltas, State Bank of India, EIL, Coal India, Asian Paints...			
Round-1 (Earnings growth stability check)				
Rejected Stocks	Voltas, SBI, EIL, ...			
Selected Stocks	Coal India, Asian Paints and Yes Bank			
Round-2 (Value analysis)				
Stock	Asian Paints			
Industry	Paint			
CMP	INR 700.75			
Current Date	18-Nov-2014			
EPS	12.19	10.95	9.99	8.08	8.07
	(2013-14)	(2012-13)	(2011-12)	(2010-11)	(2009-10)
EPS-GR	=(12.19/8.07) ^ (1/4) = 1.51^0.25 = 1.1085 = 10.85% growth rate			
P/E Ratio (current)	= 700.75 / 12.19 = 57.49 (as on 18-Nov-2014)			
Industry P/E	55.63			
Average P/E	30.25 (also called the Intrinsic P/E ©)			
Best Case P/E	41.93			
Intrinsic Value	=30.25*12.19 =INR 368.75			
Most Optimistic Value	= 41.93*12.19 = INR 511.13			

Table 17: *Calculating intrinsic value and the most optimistic value for Asian Paints*

"Super, Gobind. Now you have reached a stage where we deserve a break for lunch. We have just calculated the true intrinsic value of Asian Paints. And the decision to buy the stock should be very easy for you now."

"Yes, yes, yes… So, the current market price of the stock i.e. INR 700.75 is significantly higher than the intrinsic value of the stock, which is INR 368.75. It is quite high even if we compare it to the most optimistic value i.e. INR 511.13. So, it should be a clear 'NO BUY' for us, am I interpreting it right?"

"Of course, you are, my friend!"

"So, this is not really tough, though I am not at all happy with the outcome of 'NO BUY'."

"Not happy? Why? We just saved you from a potential disaster and you are not happy? You should understand that a negative answer is as good for you as a positive one, if not more. Not investing in a stock that should have been purchased is not that big a mistake, than investing in a stock that should not even be touched. The latter has far more disastrous consequences. I just hope you get that."

"I get your point Mr. Stock. I did not mean it in that sense, but I was just trying to get further into it – deeper – to understand the processes we need to follow after buying the stock. And that will happen only if we buy a stock. I understand that we do not want to get into a wrong stock. Point taken. At the same time, the decision making sounds so logical and simple, with the least amount of emotions involved."

LESSON 52

A 'No Buy' decision is as good as a 'Buy' decision, if not more.

Buying the wrong stock has far more disastrous consequences than missing on a stock that was worth buying.

Never be in a hurry to look for a 'Buy' decision while performing value analysis.

"Thank you for your understanding, Gobind. No investment is tough or complicated. Yes, it needs a little work and patience to get to a decision of buy or no buy. But let me also warn you at this point that the real attitude and emotional game starts after you have purchased a stock."

"Hmm. I am also hoping to find one such stock that I can purchase. But Mr. Stock, I have a few very fundamental questions which I would like to clarify before we move forward to do the value analysis of the next company that we have in hand."

"Of course!"

"This should not take too much time... My first question is that if we had to decide the intrinsic or true value of a stock by calculating the intrinsic P/E© and the current EPS of the stock, what was the use of calculating the EPS growth rate? Was it just to check the consistency of growth in EPS?"

"That was of course one reason. You will come to know of the other benefit when your value analysis allows you to buy the stock. It is at that stage that we have to start looking forward – let's say, 5 years ahead – and we need to predict the intrinsic value of the stock after 5 years. That's when the EPS growth rate will really help us. That is when we will be not only interested in P/E ratio, but the PEG Ratio. Since in the case of Asian Paints, we stumbled at Round-2 itself, there was not much benefit of calculating the EPS growth rate, other than the reason that you just mentioned."

"OK, I get your point. The other point that I had was this: I understood earlier that the companies which are likely to grow faster will always have a higher P/E because investors would place a higher premium on them. But what about the companies thathave grown at an average pace until now? Those companies will have an intrinsic P/E$^©$, weighed down by the historic P/E, isn't it?"

"Yes, you are right Gobind."

"In such cases, the future of the company may be much more optimistic than what its intrinsic P/E reflects. In that case, only the current P/E may look high but the intrinsic P/E$^©$ may still be on the lower side. This lower intrinsic P/E will give us a false indication of lower intrinsic value, isn't it? And I think that is exactly what has happened with Asian Paints."

"Why do you say that?"

"See, the average P/E (intrinsic P/E$^©$) is just 30.25. Even the best case P/E is just 41.93. But the most recent P/E points to 57.49 – almost 30 percent higher than the best case P/E and a whopping 100 percent higher than intrinsic P/E$^©$. All I am saying is that Asian Paints may be in for a whopping growth in future, what do you say?"

"That's a very good observation, Gobind. I am happy you have started analyzing and reading the situations well. And you have made a very valid point. Asian Paints may become a good buy if the astonishingly high current P/E of 57.49 can be justified by immense growth potential of the company in the near future. I feel this is the right time to introduce you to the concept of PEG."

"PEG, what's that now?"

"That is exactly what you have been asking for – a combination of P/E, which is primarily based on historical or current data and the future growth rates of the company – a factor that can help you take a decision after accounting for the current P/E and the future growth potential of the company."

"Wow, it will be interesting to see the PEG for Asian Paints. Let us see whether such high P/E is justified or not."

"Yes, but let us first understand what PEG is, and I think we will have to skip lunch today."

"Sure. I am fine with that. Do you have any issues?"

"Of course not, I can survive without eating for another 100 years. Don't worry about me. I eat because I like the taste of what you guys prepare here." Gobind simply smiled while I continued, "OK, let's proceed then. Because the P/E ratio uses past earnings (trailing 12 months or past years earnings, like in the case of Asian Paints), it gives a relatively less accurate reflection of the future growth potential of the company. That is the reason, as we discussed in case of Asian Paints, that we are unable to justify such high P/E ratio of 57.49. But, as you correctly interpreted Gobind, the stock market is forward looking. It tends to look into the future and price the stock accordingly. Subjecting our intrinsic P/E© ratio to the impact of future earnings growth produces the more informative PEG ratio. The PEG ratio provides more accurate insight about a stock's current valuation. By providing a forward-looking perspective, the PEG is a valuable evaluative tool for investors."

LESSON 53

PEG Ratio connects the past performance with future growth potential, and is more informative for value analysis.

P/E takes care of historical earnings and current price.

But stock market is forward looking.

PEG Ratio is the one that connects current P/E with the future growth of the company.

"Wow, so PEG is what I was always looking for. Tell me how we can calculate PEG from P/E!"

"Formula is pretty simple, Gobind. Here it is on your screen:"

$$PGE\ Ratio = \frac{P/E\ Ratio}{Annual\ EPS\ Growth\ Rate\ (EPS\text{-}GR)}$$

Formula 5: *PEG Ratio*

"Ah! So for Asian Paints, with an intrinsic P/E© of 30.25 and a growth rate of 10.85 percent, the PEG should be 30.25 / 10.85 that is 2.79, right?"

"Absolutely, so how does your Asian Paints table look like now?"

"Here it goes."

Round-0 (Initial filter)				
Shortlisted Stocks	Voltas, State Bank of India, EIL, Coal India, Asian Paints...			
Round-1 (Earnings growth stability check)				
Rejected Stocks	Voltas, SBI, EIL, ...			
Selected Stocks	Coal India, Asian Paints and Yes Bank			
Round-2 (Value analysis)				
Stock	Asian Paints			
Industry	Paint			
CMP	INR 700.75			
Current Date	18-Nov-2014			
EPS	12.19	10.95	9.99	8.08	8.07
	(2013-14)	(2012-13)	(2011-12)	(2010-11)	(2009-10)
EPS-GR	= (12.19/8.07) ^ (1/4) = 1.51^0.25 = 1.1085 = 10.85% growth rate			
P/E Ratio (current)	= 700.75 / 12.19 = 57.49 (as on 18-Nov-2014)			
Industry P/E	55.63			
Average P/E	**30.25 (also called the Intrinsic P/E ©)**			
Best Case P/E	41.93			
Intrinsic Value	= 30.25*12.19 =INR 368.75			
Most Optimistic Value	= 41.93*12.19 = INR 511.13			
PEG Ratio	**= 30.25 / 10.85 = 2.79**			

Table 18: *Calculating PEG ratio for Asian Paints*

"Great. Now Gobind, you must understand the significance of this PEG of 2.79 for Asian Paints. A PEG ratio that is higher than 1 is generally considered unfavorable, suggesting a stock is overvalued and the high P/E is not justified even with future growth potential."

"Can you please explain that a little bit? Why a PEG of more than 1 indicates an overvalued stock?"

"It is quite logical. A perfect stock price would have P/E which accounts for future growth and, therefore, when we divide P/E by future growth, PEG would come out to be 1. Greater than 1 PEG clearly denotes that the P/E is more than what the future growth can justify. Do you get that or should I give an example?"

"I get it."

"Conversely, a ratio lower than 1 is considered better for buying, indicating that the stock is undervalued. Other factors and evaluations, such as price-to-book ratio, or P/B ratio, can be considered to determine if a stock is genuinely undervalued or if it is more likely that the future growth estimates used to calculate the PEG ratio are simply inaccurate. But that is for a later time."

LESSON 54

PEG ratio of more than 1 suggests an overvalued stock.

PEG ratio of more than 1 indicates that the P/E is more than what the future growth can justify. In such situations, a stock is more likely to be overvalued.

"So, the Asian Paints stock is highly overvalued for now, and that proves what we found out earlier. Got it! But one doubt is still lingering. We wanted to superimpose P/E with future growth potential, while 10.85 percent had been the average historic growth. Or not?"

"Absolutely correct Gobind. As of now, we have assumed that the company will continue to maintain its average historic EPS (trailing) growth rate in future (forward) as well. The best way is to look at future earnings estimates from some expert financial portals. If that information is not available, then there has to be some very special reason to assume a higher or a lower growth rate than the average historic (trailing) growth rate. Also, if you notice from the Asian Paints table, the EPS growth rate for last year and the year before that is also close to 10 percent. So, 10.8 percent seems to be just the right assumption, unless you have heard of something drastically changing within the company."

"Ah, I get it."

"Just to simplify everything, we need to look at PEG like this: A P/E of x is justified if the company is growing at the rate of x percent annually."

"Wow, this is class. So, the current P/E of 57.49 would have been justified if Asian Paints was growing at the rate, or was expected to grow at a rate close to 57 percent annually. But since it is currently growing at only 10 percent, the high P/E is not justified, right?"

"Absolutely, you got it bang on, Gobind."

"OK, and what all factors influence the future growth rate vis-à-vis the current EPS growth rate?"

"Many. Some of them include: understanding the future outlook of the company and its products and services, competitive advantage and the company's proven stability."

"The company's proven stability?"

"Yes you see, the past growth rates in EPS are more reliable for future extrapolation only in the case of 'matured companies' which have experienced a complete economic cycle of expansion and contraction, through a bear market phase and a bull run. New and fast growing companies may not have such a financial history to rely upon and may exhibit greater volatility. Earnings history of such new and fast growing companies is less reliable in projecting growth rates than large matured companies with a consistent earnings history of 10 years or more. So, the chances of accuracy in predicting EPS growth increases for companies with greater financial history."

"I see, so, is the Asian Paints chapter finally closed?"

"Yes, let's go out and grab some lunch now. We will take up Yes Bank as the next one, once we are back from lunch."

"Sure, let's go… but do have a look at this final outcome."

Round-0 (Initial filter)	
Shortlisted Stocks	Voltas, State Bank of India, EIL, Coal India, Asian Paints...
Round-1 (Earnings growth stability check)	
Selected Stocks	Coal India, Asian Paints and Yes Bank
Round-2 (Value analysis)	
Rejected Stocks	Asian Paints (Too high PEG Ratio)
Next Stock	Yes Bank

Table 19: *Round-2 Results for Asian Paints*

We spent an hour at the Pizza Hut. We were just recounting Gobind's first experience in stock valuation, and how he felt about it.

"I still don't know if this decision to drop Asian Paints will prove to be right or not, though I must admit that I do feel confident about the data that we have analyzed," said Gobind, enjoying his well-deserved pizza slice.

"Of course, we don't know what will happen with Asian paints in the future. For all you know, Asian Paints may continue to grow faster than ever in the next few years. Market works on perceptions and sentiments – and only intermittently on logic."

"Hmm... I was wondering that if markets rarely work on any logic and there is no guarantee in the market, then why at all go through this pain of finding the intrinsic P/E©, intrinsic value of a stock?"

"There is none, but one guarantee."

"What's that?"

"That someday in future, sanity will prevail and the market price of a stock will hit its true intrinsic value. The stock may continue to run higher or lower than its intrinsic value for years together, but some day, it *has to* cross its intrinsic value. This intrinsic value of the stock is just like its home. It has to come back here one day, for sure. Just like each one of you – however far you may fly in your life – have to come back home and meet Him. For some, it may take longer than others, and for some this homecoming will be quick. But, without any exception, each one has his or her homecoming scheduled. And it goes exactly the same way with each and every stock. *Homecoming is assured.*"

LESSON 55

There is only one guarantee in stock market – stock homecoming.

A stock can divert from its intrinsic value on both sides, and can stay diverted for an indefinite time, but at some stage, it is assured that it will come back home.

Gobind kept chewing on his pizza slice, as well as on this homecoming thought, for quite some time. He did not seem to have any immediate questions. His pizza slice was taking extraordinarily long to finish. I did not want to disturb his chain of thoughts. Stock homecoming is one concept he better absorb;this must go in. This is one of the most vital concepts on stock investments that was about to change his perspective about stocks for ever. Just to aid his thinking process, I took a napkin and a pen and drew this chart for him – the same chart that I showed during one of my sessions. Gobind was there somewhere in that session – but I think he missed this.

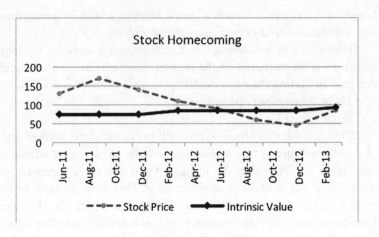

Stock Homecoming

- - ◆- - Stock Price   ━━◆━━ Intrinsic Value

"What do you get out of this chart, Gobind?"

There was no response. He was still deep in his thoughts. He never realized he took my share of pizza slice as well.

"Gobind... hello?"

"*Haan...* Ah sorry! Did you ask me something?"

"Yes, what do you get out of this chart, Gobind?"

He stared at the chart, and his face started glowing, as if he had just unraveled the mystery of his lifetime. He spent a few minutes and then gathered enough strength to start responding.

"This chart clearly tells me that a stock can divert from its intrinsic value on both sides – and can stay diverted for an indefinite amount of time, but at some stage, it will come back home – and then probably move on from there, right?"

"Bang on! The diversion from the home or intrinsic value of the stock can be for an extended period of time, sometimes many years – all depending on the market sentiments. But be assured, there will be homecoming for sure. No one knows the time duration of this diversion."

"So Mr. Stock, what we are essentially saying is that Asian Paints has already diverted on the higher side, and may continue to stay so for many years more, before it comes down to its home to meet its intrinsic value."

"Yes, not only continue, the diversion may even increase, which means the stock price may rise further in the coming months and years, in spite of the high P/E ratio it commands as of now. But we are not sure of this, and that is why we are not getting into it. What we are sure about is that there will be homecoming sooner than later."

"I get it. So, it is quite possible that in spite of what the data shows, we may lose an opportunity in Asian Paints."

"Yeah, but that's true with every stock. You don't lose an opportunity, you manage the risk by deciding not to go for such a stock."

"Right, I think you are right. But I see one problem with this chart."

"What is that?"

"I see that the intrinsic value of Asian Paints is also increasing with time. How is that possible? I thought that intrinsic value is the true value of the stock and will always remain fixed. Explain it to me how can the intrinsic value of a stock change with time?"

"Great observation, Gobind. The fact is that it is quite logical for the intrinsic value to change with time."

"Logical, how?"

"Let us consider the case of Asian Paints. The EPS of Asian Paints is increasing at the rate of 10.8 percent. Considering this EPS increase and the perceived future growth potential of Asian Paints, the worth of the company will also change. This implies the intrinsic value per share is also likely to undergo a change. Therefore, after regular intervals, it is important to re-evaluate the intrinsic value of the stock."

"Ah! You are right. With time, the value of the stock goes up since its earnings per year are going up. Quite logical! Tell me, which is the right interval to revisit the intrinsic value of the stock?"

"Once in 6 months, or at least once a year."

"Cool."

"Here, finish your coke and we got to move. We are already quite late and we must finish evaluating one more stock before we wind up for the day."

LESSON 56

Recalibrate a stock's intrinsic value at least once a year.

With time, changes in stock price and earnings lead to a change in a company's worth.

There is, therefore, a need for recalibration of intrinsic value of the stock.

Do this recalibration at least once a year, or sooner.

We wrapped up our lunch, paid the bills and were off towards our office. It was a 10-minute walk back. Strangely, there was no conversation on the way back. I knew what was going through Gobind's mind. This homecoming chart just makes the entire investing with me so fool-proof, so predictable and so easy that it is so hard for anyone to believe in the first shot.

I was not very sure of Gobind's belief level on the concept of stock homecoming, but I also knew that the biggest source of belief generation is self-experience. Once a person experiences something, then it does not matter what others say or believe in. It goes the same way for a human being's relationship with Him. Those who have experienced Him have so much faith and belief that they decide to overrule everyone and everything else. And belief can do wonders in life. A human who believes in God sheds his fear of death, can understand the positive outcome in every situation, can accept any result after a genuine effort and can, therefore, lead a happy and successful life.

Yes! My First Handpicked Stock

We did not exchange a single word till we reached the 10th floor of our building and entered my office.

"This is impossible. If stock investing is so simple, so predictable and so easy to calculate, then why the hell do so many people lose money in stocks? I cannot believe this."

"I can understand your lack of belief, for you still have not experienced what I am telling you. Yes, you are right that a lot of people lose a lot of money in stocks, but that's not because of stock investing principles not holding good, that is because they do not have enough trust to follow these simple principles."

"Why would anyone not follow such simple principles when they know this can make them rich?"

"Yes, that's exactly what God and I wonder about. We thought that the world would be a much beautiful place to invest in, once I enter the scene. But humans have become difficult to understand over time. They express emotions like anger and greed. They are seeking instant gratification. They borrow money and invest with the hope of getting rich quickly. All these things go against the basic fiber of investing with me. It is not the technical stuff that is stopping people to generate wealth – it is the emotional stuff where they are lacking. If you ask me, investing with me is just 20 percent about technical business and 80 percent about attitude."

"I get what you are saying but I still cannot believe that so many people can be so crazy."

"Welcome to planet Earth, my dear friend. Welcome home! The fault is not in your stars or in your stocks, but in your selves."

"Quite interesting. But if I tell about stock homecoming to everyone, then don't you think that they will never lose money?"

"Ha ha!"

"What makes you laugh?"

"Haha! Sorry... actually, it reminded me of the statement from one of your greatest scientists, Sir Isaac Newton. Once bitten by the stock market, he had said, 'I can calculate the motions of heavenly bodies, but not the madness of the people.' My dear friend, it is not about what we tell others. What else do you think have I been doing for more than 200 years now? It is all about whether everyone will believe us or not. It is, and it always was, a question of belief. If I tell you that God exists and that He asks human beings to love each other unconditionally, the way He loves us, then do you think that your species will start loving each other from tomorrow onward? No, nothing will change. Half of them will never believe that God even exists, and the rest of them will have their own reasons to not love everyone – those reasons driven from the root cause that they do not have 100 percent belief in the existence of God. Even if they did believe in the existence of God, they would never believe that this is what He is seeking from us, and nothing else. So, all it comes down to is truly believing what I am telling you."

LESSON 57

Stock Investing is simple, predictable and carries no additional risks.

If you truly believe on the concepts and principles of market, are ready to do the ground work, and can control your emotions, Stock Investing is the most predictable and rewarding investment with no additional risks.

"Wow, it is incredible. It is my true homecoming. You have not only enlightened me on stocks, you have also enriched me on life. I am truly thankful to you."

"The pleasure has been mutual, my friend. I have learnt so much about humans here. However, humans did not go the way He intended and I am trying to fix that problem as his representative. Anyway, let us focus our energies back on the problem we have at hand right now."

"Yes, let me start exploring the next stock in line i.e. Yes Bank."

"Go ahead, Gobind. You are well-equipped to perform a value analysis now. Go step-by-step as we discussed for Asian Paints, jot down each step in your notebook so that you memorize it."

Gobind started preparing Yes Bank's data, downloading the company's financial reports, reading them through etc. It was time for me to take a well-deserved break. As I lay on the side couch in the room, Gobind's laptop was being projected in front of me on the screen so that I could continuously look at his notes and provide my suggestions where needed. All I could see was a perfect following of what we had learnt until now: Round-0 (initial filter) and Round-1 (earnings growth stability check) being already completed, he was moving step-by-step in Round-2 (value analysis).

Round-0 (Initial filter)	
Shortlisted Stocks	Voltas, State Bank of India, EIL, Coal India, Asian Paints...
Round-1 (Earnings growth stability check)	
Selected Stocks	Coal India, Asian Paints and Yes Bank
Round-2 (Value analysis)	
Rejected Stocks	Asian Paints (Too high PEG Ratio)
Stock	Yes Bank
Industry	Banking (private sector)

Table 20: *Finding the industry*
(Round-2: Step-1 of Stock Selection for Yes Bank)

Round-0 (Initial filter)	
Shortlisted Stocks	Voltas, State Bank of India, EIL, Coal India, Asian Paints...
Round-1 (Earnings growth stability check)	
Selected Stocks	Coal India, Asian Paints and Yes Bank
Round-2 (Value analysis)	
Rejected Stocks	Asian Paints (Too high PEG Ratio)
Stock	Yes Bank
Industry	Banking (private sector)
CMP	INR 693.65
Current Date	18-Nov-2014

Table 21: *Finding CMP (Round-2 / Step-2 of Stock Selection for Yes Bank)*

Round-0 (Initial filter)								
Shortlisted Stocks	Voltas, State Bank of India, EIL, Coal India, Asian Paints...							
Round-1 (Earnings growth stability check)								
Selected Stocks	Coal India, Asian Paints and Yes Bank							
Round-2 (Value analysis)								
Rejected Stocks	Asian Paints (Too high PEG Ratio)							
Stock	Yes Bank							
Industry	Banking (private sector)							
CMP	INR 693.65							
Current Date	18-Nov-2014							
EPS	44.92	36.53	27.87	21.12	15.65	10.24	7.02	3.46	2.20
	2013-14	2012-13	2011-12	2010-11	2009-10	2008-09	2007-08	2006-07	2005-06

Table 22: *Finding EPS Data*
(Round-2: Step-3 of Stock Selection for Yes Bank)

Round-0 (Initial filter)								
Shortlisted Stocks	Voltas, State Bank of India, EIL, Coal India, Asian Paints...							
Round-1 (Earnings growth stability check)								
Selected Stocks	Coal India, Asian Paints and Yes Bank							
Round-2 (Value analysis)								
Rejected Stocks	Asian Paints (Too high PEG Ratio)							
Stock	Yes Bank							
Industry	Banking (private sector)							
CMP	INR 693.65							
Current Date	18-Nov-2014							
EPS	44.92	36.53	27.87	21.12	15.65	10.24	7.02	3.46	2.20
	2013-14	2012-13	2011-12	2010-11	2009-10	2008-09	2007-08	2006-07	2005-06
EPS-GR	=(44.92/2.20) ^ (1/8) = 20.41^0.125 = 1.4579 = 45.79% growth								

Table 23: *Calculating overall EPS-GR*
(Round-2: Step-4 of Stock Selection for Yes Bank)

"Cool, phenomenal growth, isn't it Mr. Stock? 45.79 percent per annum… But is this kind of growth rate possible in future?"

"Good point Gobind. You may argue that Yes bank is not a very old company but it has been in existence since last 10 years or more, and has survived through the ups and downs of the economy. Yes, such high growth rates may not be easily sustainable. If you look at the last 2 years' growth rate, it was 22.96 percent [(44.92 – 36.53)/36.53] and 31 percent [(36.53 – 27.87)/27.87] respectively. So, the growth rate is tapering down to more practical and reasonable levels, as you would expect. My suggestion here would be to not only calculate the overall EPS-GR but also see the year wise growth. That might give us a clearer picture on how this growth rate has been trending since last 9 years or so."

"OK, let me do that quickly."

Round-0 (Initial filter)								
Shortlisted Stocks	Voltas, State Bank of India, EIL, Coal India, Asian Paints...							
Round-1 (Earnings growth stability check)								
Selected Stocks	Coal India, Asian Paints and Yes Bank							
Round-2 (Value analysis)								
Rejected Stocks	Asian Paints (Too high PEG Ratio)							
Stock	Yes Bank							
Industry	Banking (private sector)							
CMP	INR 693.65							
Current Date	18-Nov-201...							
EPS	44.92	36.53	27.87	21.12	15.65	10.24	7.02	3.46	2.20
	2013-14	2012-13	2011-12	2010-11	2009-10	2008-09	2007-08	2006-07	2005-06
EPS-GR	=(44.92/2.20) ^ (1/8) = 20.41^0.125 = 1.4579 = 45.79% growth							
EPS-GR (year wise)	22.96%	31.07%	31.96%	34.95%	52.83%	45.86%	102.89%	57.27%

Table 24: *Calculating year wise EPS-GR*
(Round-2: Step-5 of Stock Selection for Yes Bank)

"Good! You see, the trend is clear: 50-100 percent growth in the first 3-4 years, 30-40 percent in the next 3 years and should be 20-30 percent in the last year and a few years going forward."

"Wow, everything seems so cool and easy and logical when you help us look at the data."

"It always was, but the real fun starts only when a stock gets selected."

"You have said that earlier as well. Is it really so difficult to control our emotions even after we know the facts?"

"You see, right now there are no emotions because no money is actually invested. The only possible emotion as of now could be a bias towards a particular stock or an attachment to a company, for example if you have worked for the company under consideration. But when your actual money is invested, that is when the real emotions come to the fore and start playing their role. Let us see when that time comes."

"Hmm... Would be interesting to sit with you through those times."

Gobind did not know what was in store once he selected a stock. He did not know His plan. I would have told him at the right time. But until then, it was time to stay focused on Yes Bank, as Gobind was proceeding to the next steps in Round-2.

LESSON 58

True human emotions come to the fore when you are holding the stock.

Human emotions like greed, patience, faith, fear, and self-belief come to the fore when actual money is invested.

It is easy for anyone to give suggestions before buying and after selling.

Round-0 (Initial filter)									
Shortlisted Stocks	Voltas, State Bank of India, EIL, Coal India, Asian Paints...								
Round-1 (Earnings growth stability check)									
Selected Stocks	Coal India, Asian Paints and Yes Bank								
Round-2 (Value analysis)									
Rejected Stocks	Asian Paints (Too high PEG Ratio)								
Stock	Yes Bank								
Industry	Banking (private sector)								
CMP	INR 693.65								
Current Date	18-Nov-201								
EPS	44.92	36.53	27.87	21.12	15.65	10.24	7.02	3.46	2.20
	2013-14	2012-13	2011-12	2010-11	2009-10	2008-09	2007-08	2006-07	2005-06
EPS-GR	=(44.92/2.20) ^ (1/8) = 20.41^0.125 = 1.4579 = 45.79% growth								
EPS-GR (year wise)	22.96%	31.07%	31.96%	34.95%	52.83%	45.86%	102.89%	57.27%	
P/E (current)	= 693.65/44.92 = 15.44								

Table 25: *Calculating the current P/E*
(Round-2: Step-6 of Stock Selection for Yes Bank)

Round-0 (Initial filter)									
Shortlisted Stocks	Voltas, State Bank of India, EIL, Coal India, Asian Paints...								
Round-1 (Earnings growth stability check)									
Selected Stocks	Coal India, Asian Paints and Yes Bank								
Round-2 (Value analysis)									
Rejected Stocks	Asian Paints (Too high PEG Ratio)								
Stock	Yes Bank								
Industry	Banking (private sector)								
CMP	INR 693.65								
Current Date	18-Nov-2014								
EPS	44.92	36.53	27.87	21.12	15.65	10.24	7.02	3.46	2.20
	2013-14	2012-13	2011-12	2010-11	2009-10	2008-09	2007-08	2006-07	2005-06
EPS-GR	=(44.92/2.20) ^ (1/8) = 20.41^0.125 = 1.4579 = 45.79% growth								
EPS-GR (year wise)	22.96%	31.07%	31.96%	34.95%	52.83%	45.86%	102.89%	57.27%	
P/E (current)	= 693.65/44.92 = 15.44								
Industry P/E	22.76								

Table 26: *Finding the industry P/E*
(Round-2: Step-7 of Stock Selection for Yes Bank)

"Lovely, everything is going good for now, isn't it Gobind? The current P/E of Yes Bank is significantly lower than its industry average, indicating either a poor investment choice (for which I see no reason until now) or an undervalued stock (which is just what we are looking for). What do you say?"

"I am very excited about Yes Bank now. But the next step is making me crazy."

"Why?"

"Calculating the intrinsic P/E© is no child's play. Too much data and calculations are involved."

"Everyone wants to make money, isn't it? But why cannot everyone make it?"

"I don't know…"

"Because most of the people out there just want to make money without putting in the effort required."

"It's not like that, Mr. Stock. I am ready to stay on the grind. I was just thinking if there could be a better way."

"I am sure there is. There always is. You human beings are so good at that. Why don't you take it up on yourself to device a more automated and sophisticated approach to calculate the intrinsic P/E©, or for that matter, the entire process of stock valuation? That will be your fees to me. By the way, you have already promised that to me, Gobind. Don't you remember?"

"Yes, I do remember my promise. I will definitely do something about this to make it available to the world around me in a much better, automated and sophisticated manner."

"Glad to hear that, Gobind. OK, for now, let's move on with our manual approach to calculate the intrinsic P/E© for Yes Bank."

"Sure."

Gobind went about the relatively tedious task of calculating the intrinsic P/E©. I knew it was going to take quite some time and so I decided to connect with Him – the end seemed nearer than ever now. I meditated and briefed Him about the most recent developments. The message was loud and clear. The seed had been sown. I would have to get packing up very soon.

"Here Mr. Stock, I am finally ready with the intrinsic P/E© table."

Financial Year	Apr	May	Jun	Jul	Aug	Sep	Oct	Nov	Dec	Jan	Feb	Mar	Avg. Price	EPS	P/E
2013/14	501	487	461	324	243	288	369	369	370	308	305	414	369.92	44.92	8.92
2012/13	350	330	339	364	330	382	411	442	464	522	473	429	403.00	36.53	11.03
2011/12	305	300	312	311	278	273	315	272	239	330	346	367	304.00	27.87	10.90
2010/11	286	288	269	295	311	352	359	306	313	263	256	310	300.67	21.12	14.24
2009/10	77	126	148	160	167	205	237	253	267	249	237	255	225.55	15.65	14.41
2008/09	170	156	114	127	134	121	68	61	75	61	51	50	137.00	10.24	13.38
2007/08	152	166	180	190	185	207	217	231	249	253	247	169	203.83	7.02	29.03
2006/07	97	90	78	81	89	92	114	127	135	151	143	141	111.50	3.46	32.22
2005/06	NA	NA	NA	62	67	67	65	67	69	77	81	100	72.77	2.20	33.07

Table 27: *Calculating the intrinsic P/E©*
(Round-2: Step-8 of Stock Selection for Yes Bank)

"Intrinsic P/E© = Average P/E for all years from 2005-06 (33.07) to 2013-14 (8.92) = **18.58**

P/E Growth Rate = (8.92-33.07)^(1/8) = -71percent"

"This looks so interesting, Gobind. But first of all, tell me as to why do you have some of the data highlighted in your Step-8 table?"

"OK, to eliminate the impact of 2008 stock market crisis from our Intrinsic P/E© calculation, what I have done is that I have not taken the price highlighted for the months of October 2008 to June 2009 in any of our P/E calculation. All these months seemed to be outliers."

"Oh, so let's say for 2008-09, you have taken the average price on the basis of the price of the first six months, i.e. April 2008 to September 2008, right?"

"Absolutely, I thought this was a more accurate reflection rather than eliminating a specific year…"

"I agree with you, Gobind. So, the intrinsic P/E© for Yes Bank is 18.58, while we are currently trading at 15.44 and that too against the average industry P/E of 22.76."

"Right, so we are currently running at 20 percent lower P/E than the intrinsic P/E©. Also, we are running at 47 percent lower P/E than the industry average P/E."

"This sounds so exciting to move forward with. Let's sum up the data table for Yes Bank."

"Sure, Mr. Stock… Here you go with the Step-9 of Round-2."

Round-0 (Initial filter)										
Shortlisted Stocks	Voltas, State Bank of India, EIL, Coal India, Asian Paints…									
Round-1 (Earnings growth stability check)										
Selected Stocks	Coal India, Asian Paints and Yes Bank									
Round-2 (Value analysis)										
Rejected Stocks	Asian Paints (Too high PEG Ratio)									
Stock	Yes Bank									
Industry	Banking (private sector)									
CMP	INR 693.65									
Current Date	18-Nov-2014									
EPS	44.92	36.53	27.87	21.12	15.65	10.24	7.02	3.46	2.20	
	2013-14	2012-13	2011-12	2010-11	2009-10	2008-09	2007-08	2006-07	2005-06	
EPS-GR	=(44.92/2.20) ^ (1/8) = 20.41^0.125 = 1.4579 = 45.79% growth									
EPS-GR (year wise)	22.96%	31.07%	31.96%	34.95%	52.83%	45.86%	102.89%	57.27%		
P/E (current)	= 693.65/44.92 = 15.44									
Industry P/E	22.76									
Intrisnic P/E	18.58 (also the average P/E)									
Best Case P/E	18.58 (same as intrisnic P/E since P/E growth is negative)									

Table 28: *Calculating intrinsic and best case P/E*
(Round-2: Step-9 of Stock Selection for Yes Bank)

"We are keeping our best case P/E the same as the intrinsic P/E because of the negative growth rate in P/E."

"Right, that seems fine but did you notice anything interesting, Gobind?"

"What?"

"Stock P/E for Yes Bank has started to pick up dramatically this year from 8.92 last year to the current P/E of 15.44."

"Yes, but I never understood why the P/E was coming down for Yes Bank. It has been consistently performing so well."

"You see, sometimes, the earnings growth is so high that the price is not able to catch up with that growth. An annual growth of 45.79 percent is not easy to catch up with by the market. They are usually caught napping. Therefore P/E continues to come down, and now you see, suddenly everyone has realized that they are sitting on a blockbuster stock and within a few months the P/E has already almost doubled from 8.92 to 15.44. That is the reason why we should perform and trust our own analysis and never go with the market perception. More often than not, they are proven wrong since they are mostly driven by collective emotions and perceptions."

"In that case, we have already missed the bus, isn't it? We missed buying this stock when it was available real cheap."

"Well, we did miss the rocket, but the bus can still be caught, perhaps. You need to move further in your analysis. In my world, there will always be some investment that you missed, some stock that is going up which you do not own. Never regret based on past data, look forward. Move forward. The past has passed. I will give you more than enough opportunities as you move forward. With me, hindsight is always perfect, but foresight is legally blind. Looking back can only do one thing to you – slow you down. Remember Gobind that life can only be understood backwards – but it must be lived forward."

"OK, got it. Let me move forward to Step-10 in our value analysis round."

	Round-0 (Initial filter)								
Shortlisted Stocks	Voltas, State Bank of India, EIL, Coal India, Asian Paints...								
	Round-1 (Earnings growth stability check)								
Selected Stocks	Coal India, Asian Paints and Yes Bank								
	Round-2 (Value analysis)								
Rejected Stocks	Asian Paints (Too high PEG Ratio)								
Stock	Yes Bank								
Industry	Banking (private sector)								
CMP	INR 693.65								
Current Date	18-Nov-2014								
EPS	44.92	36.53	27.87	21.12	15.65	10.24	7.02	3.46	2.20
	2013-14	2012-13	2011-12	2010-11	2009-10	2008-09	2007-08	2006-07	2005-06
EPS-GR	=(44.92/2.20) ^ (1/8) = 20.41^0.125 = 1.4579 = 45.79% growth								
EPS-GR (year wise)	22.96%	31.07%	31.96%	34.95%	52.83%	45.86%	102.89%	57.27%	
P/E (current)	= 693.65/44.92 = 15.44								
Industry P/E	22.76								
Intrisnic P/E	18.58 (also the average P/E)								
Best Case P/E	18.58 (same as intrinsic P/E since P/E growth is negative)								
Intrinsic Value	= 18.58*44.92 = INR 834.61								

Table 29: *Calculating intrinsic value*
(Round-2: Step-10 of Stock Selection for Yes Bank)

"Excellent Gobind, so here you are – a stock with an intrinsic value of INR 834.61 per share, which is currently available at a price of INR 693.65 per share – a 20 percent gap as of date, which seems good to trigger further analysis. But did you note the most interesting thing, Gobind?"

"What?"

"Stock homecoming."

"Stock homecoming, where? We have not even purchased the stock yet."

"This stock has been hovering much below its intrinsic value for so many years. If you look at one of your earlier tables where you calculated the Intrinsic P/E (Table 27), even until the most recent financial year, it had an average price of INR 369. And look at this year: the CMP of stock is close to INR 700 – almost double in a year. It really is moving towards its homecoming."

"Yes, that is really interesting. Though we still have 20 percent gap between the current price and the stock's intrinsic value, I still feel we have lost a lot of the potential. What are your views, Mr. Stock?"

"Yes Gobind, but that is not what we should be looking at. Let's move forward to Step-11."

"Sure, here you go."

	Round-0 (Initial filter)								
Shortlisted Stocks	Voltas, State Bank of India, EIL, Coal India, Asian Paints...								
	Round-1 (Earnings growth stability check)								
Selected Stocks	Coal India, Asian Paints and Yes Bank								
	Round-2 (Value analysis)								
Rejected Stocks	Asian Paints (Too high PEG Ratio)								
1 Stock	Yes Bank								
Industry	Banking (private sector)								
2 CMP	INR 693.65								
Current Date	18-Nov-2014								
3 EPS	44.92	36.53	27.87	21.12	15.65	10.24	7.02	3.46	2.20
	2013-14	2012-13	2011-12	2010-11	2009-10	2008-09	2007-08	2006-07	2005-06
4 EPS-GR	=(44.92/2.20) ^ (1/8) = 20.41^0.125 = 1.4579 = **45.79%** growth								
5 EPS-GR (year wise)	22.96%	31.07%	31.96%	34.95%	52.83%	45.86%	102.89%	57.27%	
6 P/E (current)	= 693.65/44.92 = 15.44								
7 Industry P/E	22.76								
8 Intrisnic P/E	**18.58** (also the average P/E)								
9 Best Case P/E	18.58 (same as intrinsic P/E since P/E growth is negative)								
10 Intrinsic Value	= 18.58*44.92 = INR 834.61								
11 PEG Ratio	= 18.58 / 45.79 = 0.41								

Table 30: *Calculating PEG Ratio*
(Round-2: Step-11 of Stock Selection for Yes Bank)

"This is an incredible PEG Ratio, indicating a massive positive signal to buy this stock. Even if we assume a futuristic growth rate of 20 to 30 percent, instead of the average 45.79 percent, the PEG Ratio would still be much less than 1. Until now, there is every reason to buy this stock."

"So, should we go ahead and buy now?"

"Yes, we are almost there. We are done with Round-2 successfully. Many congratulations! This is the first stock that has passed this major hurdle. Now, we are going to enter Round-3."

"Round-3? This is not a very good feeling, but I am sure you have some plans in your mind, and I trust you."

"Yes, in Round-3, we just need to ensure that we look at a few other critical factors before finally investing our money into this stock. The first of those factors is going to be checking on some additional ratios – those financial ratios that should indicate whether the stock is truly undervalued or there are inherent issues within the organization."

"Can our stock fail even now? I mean, even after the intrinsic value check?"

"Yes, of course, it can fail in any of the rounds. Having said that, please remember that we are almost 80 percent done with our decision to buy Yes Bank because the value analysis is asking us to go ahead. This round to check additional ratios round should not have a major influence on your overall decision unless, of course, many ratios point towards a single inherent problem within the organization."

"OK, I am all set. Tell me."

"Gobind, I can see that you have become more patient with time. Keep improving. This is going to help you..."

"Thank you so much, Mr. Stock. This is perhaps the result of my increasing faith in you."

"Super! But before we go into any specific ratio, would you like to have a tea or coffee break, if you are tired?"

"No, I am good to go ahead. I have high hopes from this stock."

"Let us see. Fine... Before we proceed, you must understand the difference between a few accounting terms like book value and market value."

"OK, sure."

"Book value is the price paid for an asset. It never changes as long as the asset is owned. On the other hand, market value is the current price at which the asset can currently sell in the market. Book value is firm and fixed while market value can keep changing. For example, a home bought 10 years ago for INR 27 lakh will retain that INR 27 lakh book value for as long as the investor owns it. If the house will be sold today for INR 65 lakh, that's its market value."

LESSON 59

Book value is the price paid to buy an asset. Market value is the current price of the asset.

Book value never changes through the life of the asset.

Market value keeps changing, defined by market perceptions.

Both the values are required to be maintained in company records to reveal profit and losses.

"OK, I understand book value and market value, but can you please tell me where are they actually used?"

"See, book values are useful for tracking profits and losses, and therefore the book values need to be retained. The difference between an investment's book value and market value reveals the profit or loss incurred. Generally accepted accounting principles require a company's balance sheet to list hard assets, such as buildings and equipment, according to their book values. This rule can be problematic if a company's assets have greatly appreciated, since the assets cannot be re-priced and added to the company's overall value."

"Understood, but how do I use these two values to judge about my Yes Bank stock?"

"We are coming to that. The first additional ratio we are looking at is the price-to-book ratio – also called the P/B ratio or equity ratio. Let me explain you what P/B ratio represents."

"OK."

"P/B ratio represents the price of a stock per share vs the book value of the company per share, and the book value is essentially the equity value of the company, i.e. the assets minus the liabilities of the company. Look at your screen:

$$\text{P/B Ratio} = \frac{\text{Price (per share)}}{\text{Book Value (per share)}}$$

Formula 6: *P/B Ratio*

"If a company is trading at a price less than its book value (or has a P/B less than one), it normally tells a value investor that the stock is undervalued. That's because either the price is low or the book value is too good, i.e. it has enough assets."

"I am a little confused on which one is a better ratio to rely on: P/E or P/B?"

"Your confusion is more than valid. You see, in its truest form, the value of a business resides in its net worth or book value and not in its past or future earnings. When I say this, I say this with the caution that earnings are still the most widely used parameter for assessment, and there are reasons for the same. However, the accuracy of future earnings estimates is dependent on many factors like economy, management, competition, technology disruption etc. On the other hand, book value is created over many years of existence, hence is much more reliable. Not only that, book value makes P/B ratio a much more stable ratio as compared to the more volatile P/E ratio."

"Stable, how?"

"Book value looks beyond the cyclicality and fluctuations of earnings cycle to help arrive at a fair assessment value. Book value is also not affected by changing accounting norms."

"Understood. All seems rosy for the book value based P/B Ratio, but as you also said just now, book value remains fixed while market value is the value that gives us the current value of the asset. So, with time, book value will show an underrated value of a company's assets – much lower than the actual market value of those assets, if those assets were to be sold today. Am I thinking right?"

"You are absolutely right, Gobind. Considering this unfairness in assessing the right book value, a P/B of three or less is also considered fair for a Buy decision. However, keep in mind that this is not a very reliable ratio for all kinds of businesses, and is just one of the ratios you can probably look at."

"OK, so what kind of businesses should be measured via this P/B Ratio?"

"See, this P/B ratio is only useful when you are looking at capital-intensive businesses or financial businesses with plenty of assets on the books. Book value completely ignores intangible assets like a company's brand name, goodwill, patents and other intellectual property. Book value also doesn't carry much meaning for service-based firms with hardly any tangible assets. All this, of course, is over and above the fact that book value does not give any idea about ageing and depreciating assets, since it does not change once created."

"Hmm... OK. So, what do we do with this ratio for Yes Bank?"

"So, do account for this ratio but don't get bogged down by it. Your 80 percent decision has already taken with the value analysis in Round-2, unless these additional ratios show you an alarmingly different view."

"OK. Let me update our table with Step-1 of Round-3."

Round-0 (Initial filter)										
Shortlisted Stocks	Voltas, State Bank of India, EIL, Coal India, Asian Paints...									
Round-1 (Earnings growth stability check)										
Selected Stocks	Coal India, Asian Paints and Yes Bank									
Round-2 (Value analysis)										
Rejected Stocks	Asian Paints (Too high PEG Ratio)									
Selected Stocks	Yes Bank									
Stock	Yes Bank									
Industry	Banking (private sector)									
CMP	INR 693.65									
Current Date	18-Nov-2014									
EPS	44.92	36.53	27.87	21.12	15.65	10.24	7.02	3.46	2.20	
	2013-14	2012-13	2011-12	2010-11	2009-10	2008-09	2007-08	2006-07	2005-06	
EPS-GR	=(44.92/2.20) ^ (1/8) = 20.41^0.125 = **45.79%** growth									
EPS-GR (year wise)	22.96%	31.07%	31.96%	34.95%	52.83%	45.86%	102.89%	57.27%		
P/E (current)	= 693.65/44.92 = 15.44									
Industry P/E	22.76									
Intrisnic P/E	**18.58** (also the average P/E)									
Best Case P/E	18.58 (same as intrinsic P/E since P/E growth is negative)									
Intrinsic Value	= 18.58*44.92 = INR 834.61									
PEG Ratio	= 18.58 / 45.79 = 0.41									
Round-3 (Additional Ratios)										
Book Value / Share	INR 197.50 (2013-14) (from annual report)									
Price / Share	INR 369.92 (avg price for 2013-14)									
P/B Ratio	= 369.92 / 197.50 = 1.87									

Table 31: *Calculating P/B ratio*
(Round-3: Step-1 of Stock Selection for Yes Bank)

"So, I got the book value per share for the year 2013-14 from the annual report and I also assumed that I must use the average price per share for the same year to arrive at an appropriate P/B ratio."

"Yes, that is the right way."

"And a P/B ratio less than three also sounds good."

"Yes Gobind, it is just fine. Ideally, it should have been less than one, but yes, anything less than three is acceptable."

P/B ratio should ideally be less than one.
A value up to three is still tolerable.
P/B makes sense for specific businesses and a value up to three can be considered tolerable.

"Tell me, Mr. Stock, what does less than 1 P/B ratio really indicate? I mean what is its true significance?"

"Well, if you look at it in a very simplified form, it primarily tells us that even if the company goes bankrupt, it will have enough assets to pay back the shareholders for the value of company that they possess in terms of stocks."

"Ah! Quite interesting."

"But considering that book value, by nature itself is unpredictable, inconsistent, fluid and not reliable to quite an extent, though still a valid indicator, we would rather validate it with its partner ROE."

"ROE? Is that the second ratio we are looking for in Round-3?"

"Yes, P/B and ROE (return on earnings) together should be a much decent indicator of the company's health. Large discrepancies between P/B and ROE, a key growth indicator, can be a red flag. Undervalued growth stocks frequently show a combination of high ROE and low P/B ratios."

"But what's ROE?"

"ROE is return on equity. Returns indicate profits or earnings. Equity indicates the book value. Therefore, ROE indicates the amount of profit a company is able to make per unit asset. So, ROE is calculated as earnings by the book value. Have a look at your screen..."

$$ROE = \frac{EPS}{Book\ Value\ (per\ share)}$$

Formula 7: *ROE*

"OK, but what does this really signify?"

"See Gobind, ROE offers the useful signal of financial success since it could indicate whether the company is growing profits without pouring new equity capital into the business. You see, it is possible to increase the company's earnings by deploying more assets. However, if a company is generating more earnings by using the same number of assets, then that's an indicator of its efficiency to generate profits. That's exactly where ROE comes in. ROE indicates how well the management is employing the investors' capital invested in the company."

"Yes, I get it. And what are the accepted norms for ROE?"

"Minimum 15 percent. Again, let me warn you here. No single metric will give you the complete picture. For ROE, please read this alongside the P/B ratio. Look for low P/B and high ROE stocks. Low P/B indicating low price per unit asset and high ROE indicates high earnings per unit asset: a combination that is ideal."

"OK, let me update my table with this second ratio of Round-3"

	Round-0 (Initial filter)								
Shortlisted Stocks	Voltas, State Bank of India, EIL, Coal India, Asian Paints...								
	Round-1 (Earnings growth stability check)								
Selected Stocks	Coal India, Asian Paints and Yes Bank								
	Round-2 (Value analysis)								
Rejected Stocks	Asian Paints (Too high PEG Ratio)								
Selected Stocks	Yes Bank								
Stock	Yes Bank								
Industry	Banking (private sector)								
CMP	INR 693.65								
Current Date	18-Nov-2014								
EPS	44.92	36.53	27.87	21.12	15.65	10.24	7.02	3.46	2.20
	2013-14	2012-13	2011-12	2010-11	2009-10	2008-09	2007-08	2006-07	2005-06
EPS-GR	=(44.92/2.20) ^ (1/8) = 20.41^0.125 = 1.4579 = 45.79% growth								
EPS-GR (year wise)	22.96%	31.07%	31.96%	34.95%	52.83%	45.86%	102.89%	57.27%	
P/E (current)	= 693.65/44.92 = 15.44								
Industry P/E	22.76								
Intrisnic P/E	18.58 (also the average P/E)								
Best Case P/E	18.58 (same as intrinsic P/E since P/E growth is negative)								
Intrinsic Value	= 18.58*44.92 = INR 834.61								
PEG Ratio	= 18.58 / 45.79 = 0.41								
	Round-3 (Additional Ratios)								
Book Value / Share	INR 197.50 (X 14) (from annual report)								
Price / Share	INR 369.92 (avg price for 2013-14)								
P/B Ratio	= 369.92 / 197.50 = 1.87								
ROE	= 44.92 / 197.50 = 22.75%								

Table 32: *Calculating ROE*
(Round-3: Step-2 of Stock Selection for Yes Bank)

"So, we have got a good ROE here as well."

"Yes Gobind, anything above 15 percent is acceptable and above 20 percent is really good. Looking at the last 5 years ROE can give you further idea about the financial strength of the company. The stock should ideally be able to maintain close to 20 percent or more as ROE. But remember that both P/B ratio as well as ROE has book value as the denominator, and we know the limitations with book value."

"Yes."

"Also, a low book value because of high debts can cause ROE to shoot up (high ROE is a good indicator for a stock's value), but at the same time, will indicate a high P/B ratio as well (not a good indicator). Therefore, it is the combination of both P/B as well as ROE that should be read in conjunction. As a rule, no metric should be studied alone to arrive at any conclusion."

"I get that. For a stock whose book value is based on strong fundamentals, it should clearly give us a high ROE and also a high P/B. However, if we have a fundamentally strong but undervalued stock, we should get a reasonably high ROE but a low P/B (because of the low price). This is the scenario we are searching for, right?"

"Excellent, you are getting it! Here is how I would want you to remember: Low ROE and High P/B indicates an overvalued stock. High ROE and low P/B indicates an undervalued stock. Any other combination of ROE and P/B does not tell you much. Again, take all these Round-3 ratios with a pinch of salt. Read them in combination with each other. Don't go just by numbers, and take them as indicative, unless many such ratios point towards a single inherent problem with the company."

LESSON 61

Low P/B and high ROE is a beautiful combination of a fundamentally strong and undervalued stock.

Ratios work as a team. They should never be read alone.

Low P/B and high ROE indicates an undervalued stock.

High P/B and low ROE indicates an overvalued stock.

"Got it. So, Yes Bank has that lovely combination of low P/B and high ROE. Are there any more ratios in Round-3 that could help us?"

"Yes, let us further get into a bit of financial health of the company by looking at two more ratios: debt- equity ratio and free cash flow ratio. And then we will wrap it up with dividend yield."

"OK, all set."

"Let us go with the debt-to-equity ratio or the D/E ratio first."

"OK."

"D/E ratio indicates how much debt a company is using to finance its assets relative to the amount of value represented in shareholders' equity."

"This is not clear to me, Mr. Stock. Could you please explain?"

"Look at it like this. Let us say that you have a lot of real estate in your assets, and you earn rental income from it, which you show as your earnings every year. Now, if you want to show increased earnings (or EPS), it is possible for you to take a loan, acquire more real estate and start earning additional rent, and thus additional income. So, your EPS will start showing an upswing in spite of the fact that you have not done anything special apart from taking a loan and putting the estate on rent. Inherently, your efficiency to earn money has not gone up, though your earnings numbers have increased."

"Right, my EPS will show improvement but my book value will not change much because my loan liability has gone up – almost in line with the Assets. Right, Mr. Stock?"

"You are right, Gobind."

"But in that case Mr. Stock, the ROE and P/B ratio combination will give me a clue about this unfair earnings increase, isn't it?"

"Very good. You are right, but only to an extent."

"Means?"

"You are right that the book value may not change much since loan liabilities will also increase along with the asset value, thus keeping the book value in check. In fact, the book value should go down because the company will have to pay back the total liability amount, which will be higher than the value of the asset."

"But that is what I am saying, even if my book value is decreasing, my P/B will go up, isn't it? And a high P/B will give us an indication of something going wrong... or not?"

"Yes, P/B will go up provided your price does not change, but the price of a stock is driven by many factors beyond anyone's control."

"Ah! So, ROE will tell me the real picture?"

"ROE will also not show you the real picture in such a case, because ultimately your earnings are going up and book value is coming down, thus ROE is giving a favourable indication."

"Hmm. I understand. Then what will show me the real picture?"

"Debt-to-equity ratio"

"Ah OK!"

"The formula for calculating D/E ratio can be represented as is shown on your screen:

$$\text{D/E Ratio} = \frac{\text{Total Liabilities}}{\text{Book Value}}$$

Formula 8: *D/E Ratio*

"You see, this ratio tells the amount of debt that has been taken to arrive at a unit book value. The higher the ratio or percentage, the higher is the risk of default in paying back the debt."

"So, a high D/E ratio is bad?"

"Bad may not be the appropriate term, but it is definitely more risky. A high D/E ratio generally means that a company has been aggressive in financing its growth with debt. Aggressive leveraging practices are often associated with high levels of risk. This may result in volatile earnings as a result of the additional expense in paying interest – interest that will be required to be paid back as a part of returning the debt."

"OK. Like you said, we should not be reading ratios in isolation…"

"Absolutely! If a lot of debt is used to finance increased operations (high D/E), the company could potentially generate more earnings than it would have without this outside financing. If this were to increase the earnings by a greater amount than the debt cost (interest), then the shareholders would benefit from this move, as more earnings would be spread among the same amount of shareholders. However, if the cost of this debt financing ends up outweighing the returns that the company generates on the debt through investment and business activities, stakeholders' share values may take a hit. If the cost of debt becomes too much for the company to handle, it could even lead to bankruptcy, which would leave shareholders with nothing. So, while debt may be good for growth, too much of debt could be very risky."

LESSON 62

High D/E ratio is definitely riskier, if not worse.

A high D/E ratio means that the company has been aggressive in financing its growth with debt.

High debt is associated with high levels of risk and volatile earnings, since the debt needs to be paid back with interest.

"OK, in that case what should be the 'right' D/E ratio?"

"Like with most ratios, when using the D/E ratio, it is very important to consider the industry in which the company operates. Different industries rely on different amounts of capital to operate and use that capital in different ways. A relatively high D/E ratio may be common in one industry while a relatively low D/E may be common in another. For example, capital-intensive industries such as auto manufacturing tend to have a D/E ratio above 2; while companies like personal computer manufacturers usually are not particularly capital-intensive and may often have a D/E ratio of under 0.5. As such, D/E ratio should only be used to compare companies when those companies operate within the same industry. Not only industry, debt is also a factor of a country or a region, like most other ratios. For banking industry in India, the D/E ratio for banks like ICICI Bank and HDFC Bank run in the range of 0.5 to 1.0"

LESSON 63

D/E ratio is industry specific.
Anything between 0.5 and 2 is acceptable.
Less than 0.5 is awesome.

Capital-intensive industries like auto manufacturing tend to have D/E ratio higher than 2, while service industry will have it close to 0.5

The ratio is highly industry specific. Compare it with the peers in the industry before giving it a pass-through.

"OK, let me find out the Debt-Equity Ratio for Yes Bank from its annual Report and update Step-3 of Round-3 in the table... Have a look..."

"Now considering that Indian banks have a D/E ratio of 0.5 to 1.0, this ratio of 0.07 is astonishingly good. What do you say, Mr. Stock?"

		Round-0 (Initial filter)								
	Shortlisted Stocks	Voltas, State Bank of India, EIL, Coal India, Asian Paints...								
		Round-1 (Earnings growth stability check)								
	Selected Stocks	Coal India, Asian Paints and Yes Bank								
		Round-2 (Value analysis)								
	Rejected Stocks	Asian Paints (Too high PEG Ratio)								
	Selected Stocks	Yes Bank								
1	Stock	Yes Bank								
	Industry	Banking (private sector)								
2	CMP	INR 693.65								
	Current Date	18-Nov-2014								
3	EPS	44.92	36.53	27.87	21.12	15.65	10.24	7.02	3.46	2.20
		2013-14	2012-13	2011-12	2010-11	2009-10	2008-09	2007-08	2006-07	2005-06
4	EPS-GR	=(44.92/2.20) ^ (1/8) = 20.41^0.125 = 1.4579 = 45.79% growth								
5	EPS-GR (year wise)	22.96%	31.07%	31.96%	34.95%	52.83%	45.86%	102.89%	57.27%	
6	P/E (current)	= 693.65/44.92 = 15.44								
7	Industry P/E	22.76								
8	Intrisnic P/E	18.58 (also the average P/E)								
9	Best Case P/E	18.58 (same as intrinsic P/E since P/E growth is negative)								
10	Intrinsic Value	= 18.58*44.92 = INR 834.61								
11	PEG Ratio	= 18.58 / 45.79 = 0.41								
		Round-3 (Additional Ratios)								
1	Book Value / Share	INR 197.50 (2013-14) (from annual report)								
	Price / Share	INR 369.92 (avg price for 2013-14)								
	P/B Ratio	= 369.92 / 197.50 = 1.87								
2	ROE	= 44.92 / 197.50 = 22.75%								
3	D/E Ratio	0.07 to 0.10 (over the last few years)								

Table 33: *Finding D/E ratio*
(Round-3: Step-3 of Stock Selection for Yes Bank)

"Yes, you are right, Gobind. Comparing this ratio with its peers is the right way to go about it. I think all the pointers in Round-3 also seem to be pointing towards a Buy decision for this stock."

"Yes, but just one small apprehension. What if these ratios are at the boundary line? What would have happened if this ratio was close to one or so?"

"You see, I will give you a good enough indication that things are not going right. I will not stay at the boundary. The indication will be clear and explicit."

"Ah OK... good."

"For example, during the month of March this year, Bhushan Steel – one of the outstanding stocks of its time – was running at a D/E of 3.5. Many investors overlooked the fact that they were sitting on a pile of INR 40,000 crore loan; and the result was a disaster."

"Woah! It is clear now. We just need to keep our eyes and ears open."

"Right, but there are a couple of angles we need to look at before we conclude this round."

"Angles, like?"

"You see, we have been looking at the strength of a stock primarily from the angles of earnings, i.e. all the ratios like P/E, PEG, ROE, D/E are dependent on earnings. While earnings definitely is *the* most critical factor that decides the growth of a stock, and therefore its market price, we must not forget that it is not difficult to arithmetically boost or suppress the earnings of a company by simple alterations in company accounting procedures."

"Oh, is it? But how is that possible?"

"Deferring expenditure, arbitrarily increasing the life of an asset are some of the accounting techniques used to affect the earnings of a company directly. Not only that, earnings growth in the initial years can be very high – leading to high prices because of high expectations. When the earnings of these companies drop or they fail to live up to investors' lofty expectations, the investors overreact and sell. Earnings, therefore, many a times do not represent stability."

"So, what is the way out?"

"See, sooner or later, the true earnings of a company are going to get reflected in their reports, but in the short-term, it is possible for an unaware investor to get swayed by inappropriate figures. Therefore, in the next two ratios, we look at factors that are not truly dependent on earnings. All these additional ratios put together to give you a wonderful picture about the health of the stock. Remember again that none of these ratios alone can serve your purpose."

"OK, I am ready."

"The first one is PS Ratio."

"OK, what's that?"

"PS ratio or PSR stands for price-to-sales ratio. While earnings can fluctuate, sales are far more stable, and are relatively difficult to manipulate through accounting gimmicks."

"Wonderful, tell me how to calculate PSR."

$$PSR = \frac{\text{Stock Price (CMP)}}{\text{Annual Sales per share}}$$

Formula 9: *Price-to-sale ratio*

"PSR is simple to calculate. It is calculated by dividing the market price by the sales per share. Or in other words, if we look at the entire business rather than on a per share basis: PSR = Market capitalization / Annual sales.

It can be read as the money that investors are ready to pay for every rupee of sales generated by the company."

LESSON 64

Earnings can be volatile and subject to accounting gimmicks.

Sales are more stable as measuring criterion.

Earnings of a company are volatile, leading to volatility in stock price.

Sales turn out to be a much truer and stable representation of a company's stability.

Price-to-sales ratio (PSR) is, therefore, an effective augmentation in the ratios to be monitored.

"OK, what should be the right range for PSR?"

"The lower the PSR, the better it would be for an investor. But anything less than 1.5 is perfectly acceptable. Anywhere close to 2 is also tolerable."

"OK, let me find the PSR and show you the updated table for Yes Bank:

Round-0 (Initial filter)								
Shortlisted Stocks	Voltas, State Bank of India, EIL, Coal India, Asian Paints...							
Round-1 (Earnings growth stability check)								
Selected Stocks	Coal India, Asian Paints and Yes Bank							
Round-2 (Value analysis)								
Rejected Stocks	Asian Paints (Too high PEG Ratio)							
Selected Stocks	Yes Bank							
Stock	Yes Bank							
Industry	Banking (private sector)							
CMP	INR 693.65							
Current Date	18-Nov-2014							
EPS	44.92	36.53	27.87	21.12	15.65	10.24	7.02	3.46	2.20
	2013-14	2012-13	2011-12	2010-11	2009-10	2008-09	2007-08	2006-07	2005-06
EPS-GR	=(44.92/2.20) ^ (1/8) = 20.41^0.125 = 1.4579 = 45.79% growth							
EPS-GR (year wise)	22.96%	31.07%	31.96%	34.95%	52.83%	45.86%	102.89%	57.27%	
P/E (current)	= 693.65/44.92 = 15.44							
Industry P/E	22.76							
Intrinsic P/E	18.58 (also the average P/E)							
Best Case P/E	18.58 (same as intrinsic P/E since P/E growth is negative)							
Intrinsic Value	= 18.58*44.92 = INR 834.61							
PEG Ratio	= 18.58 / 45.79 = 0.41							
Round-3 (Additional Ratios)								
Book Value / Share	INR 197.50 (2013-14) (from annual report)							
Price / Share	INR 369.92 (avg price for 2013-14)							
P/B Ratio	= 369.92 / 197.50 = 1.87							
ROE	= 44.92 / 197.50 = 22.75%							
D/E Ratio	0.07 to 0.10 (over the last few years)							
P/S Ratio	1.49							

Table 34: *Finding PSR*
(Round-3: Step-4 of Stock Selection for Yes Bank)

"Wonderful. Although this is a boundary case, it is good enough. Nothing alarming here..."

"OK. So should I consider PSR as more important or accurate than P/E or other earnings ratios?"

"No, as I said, each ratio has its own limitations and should be understood in combination only."

"What are the limitations with PSR then?"

"It does not distinguish between leveraged and unleveraged companies. For example: a firm having a low PSR could also be on the verge of bankruptcy due to high interest costs owing to high leverage. Moreover, PSR does not give any idea about the company's cost structure and profitability. Therefore, reading this in combination with other ratios like D/E ratio, PEG and free cash flow etc. will give us a truer picture."

"Ah one more ratio? I haven't ever heard of free cash flow. What is that?"

"Yes, that is the last ratio that we need to look at."

"Thank God. Are you sure this is the last one?"

"I can understand your eagerness to get going with this deal, but Gobind, always remember that *it is easier to stay out of trouble than it is to get out of trouble*. This pain of selecting the right stock is nothing compared to the pain of coming out of a wrong stock."

"I get your point. Sure... tell me about the last ratio that we need to understand?"

"Before we go to free cash flow, it is important to understand that, unlike what most people believe, not all of the company's earnings in a year end up as cash with the company. A significant amount of earnings is booked based on various accounting norms."

"What do you mean by that? If a company has earned something in a year, it should be reflected somewhere in its account as available cash, isn't it?"

"Ideally yes, but practically, no. Let me give an example. If there is a 3-year contract with a company like Tata Consultancy Services (TCS) to build software for a client, it is possible that the client would pay only after the software is ready and delivered to the client i.e. after 3 years. However, the company would incur cost and expenses every year without getting any revenue. This is most likely to distort the company's books since this would mean showing losses currently and huge profit in the third year, when it would deliver the project and receive the entire amount as revenue in one shot. This scenario will not be a fair representation for anyone."

"Ah! So, what is the choice?"

"In such cases, the company uses accounting procedures like percentage of completion (POC)."

"What's percentage of completion?"

"It is an accounting procedure that essentially deals with such discrepancies in reporting. As per this procedure, based on the percentage of work completed, there is corresponding revenue which is 'believed to have come', and the same is accounted in the account books."

"Ah, so what you are saying is that there is no actual money flowing in, but a notional one."

"Yes, exactly, and therefore comes the need for this ratio called free cash flow. So let us understand what this ratio actually means. Free cash flow (FCF) is a measure of how much cash a business generates after accounting for capital expenditures such as buildings or equipment. This cash can be used for expansion, dividends, reducing debt or any other purposes."

"The formula for free cash flow is there on your screen:

FCF = Operating Cash Flow – Capital Expenditures

Formula 10: *Free cash Flow*

"The data needed to calculate a company's free cash flow is usually on its cash flow statement. For example, if a company XYZ's cash flow statement reported $15 million of cash from operations and $5 million of capital expenditures for a year, then company XYZ's free cash flow was $15 million – $5 million = $10 million.

"The presence of free cash flow indicates that a company has cash to expand, develop new products, buy back stocks, pay dividends, or reduce its debt. High or rising free cash flow is often a sign of a healthy company that is thriving in its current environment. Furthermore, since FCF has a direct impact on the worth of a company, investors often hunt for companies that have high or improving free cash flow but undervalued share prices – the disparity often means the share price will soon increase."

LESSON 65

Free cash flow (FCF) is the free cash available with a company.

High or rising free cash flow is often a sign of a healthy company that is thriving in its current environment.

"Free cash flow measures a company's ability to generate cash, which is a fundamental basis for stock pricing. This is why some people value free cash flow more than just about any other financial measure out there, including earnings per share."

"Awesome, I somehow got hold of this website *morningstar.com* and noticed that the free cash flow of Yes Bank is: INR 44,355 million (operating cash flow) – INR 1,337 million (capital expenditure) = INR 43,018 million free cash flow. This has been the highest till date, suggesting that they have been improving their free cash flow every year. Let me put that in the table as well."

Round-0 (Initial filter)									
Shortlisted Stocks	Voltas, State Bank of India, EIL, Coal India, Asian Paints...								
Round-1 (Earnings growth stability check)									
Selected Stocks	Coal India, Asian Paints and Yes Bank								
Round-2 (Value analysis)									
Rejected Stocks	Asian Paints (Too high PEG Ratio)								
Selected Stocks	Yes Bank								
Stock	Yes Bank								
Industry	Banking (private sector)								
CMP	INR 693.65								
Current Date	18-Nov-2014								
EPS	44.92	36.53	27.87	21.12	15.65	10.24	7.02	3.46	2.20
	2013-14	2012-13	2011-12	2010-11	2009-10	2008-09	2007-08	2006-07	2005-06
EPS-GR	=(44.92/2.20) ^ (1/8) = 20.41^0.125 = 1.4579 = 45.79% growth								
EPS-GR (year wise)	22.96%	31.07%	31.96%	34.95%	52.83%	45.86%	102.89%	57.27%	
P/E (current)	= 693.65/44.92 = 15.44								
Industry P/E	22.76								
Intrisnic P/E	18.58 (also the average P/E)								
Best Case P/E	18.58 (same as intrinsic P/E since P/E growth is negative)								
Intrinsic Value	= 18.58*44.92 = INR 834.61								
PEG Ratio	= 18.58 / 45.79 = 0.41								
Round-3 (Additional Ratios)									
Book Value / Share	INR 197.50 (2013-14) (from annual report)								
Price / Share	INR 369.92 (avg price for 2013-14)								
P/B Ratio	= 369.92 / 197.50 = 1.87								
ROE	= 44.92 / 197.50 = 22.75%								
D/E Ratio	0.07 to 0.10 (over the last few years)								
P/S Ratio	1.49								
Free Cash Flow	INR 43,018 Million (highest till date)								

Table 35: *Finding free cash flow*
(Round-3: Step-5 of Stock Selection for Yes Bank)

"Mr. Stock, while this kind of cash flow looks astonishing, an absolute value is not making any sense to me. I mean this number can be considered good for one company and not so good for another, isn't it?"

"You are right, and that's why we convert this free cash flow into a ratio known as free cash flow ratio (FCF ratio)."

"OK, and how do we calculate this ratio?"

"It's quite simple. FCF ratio is the ratio which compares the free cash flows (FCF) to the operating cash flows (OCF). The more free cash flows are embedded in the operating cash flows of a company, the better it is. Higher free cash flows to operating cash flows ratio is a very good indicator of financial health of a company. Have a look."

$$\text{FCF Ratio} = \frac{\text{Free Cash Flow}}{\text{Operating Cash Flow}}$$

Formula 11: *FCF Ratio*

"Ah, I get it. Let me update the table once again."

Round-0 (Initial filter)										
Shortlisted Stocks	Voltas, State Bank of India, EIL, Coal India, Asian Paints...									
Round-1 (Earnings growth stability check)										
Selected Stocks	Coal India, Asian Paints and Yes Bank									
Round-2 (Value analysis)										
Rejected Stocks	Asian Paints (Too high PEG Ratio)									
Selected Stocks	Yes Bank									
1 Stock	Yes Bank									
Industry	Banking (private sector)									
2 CMP	INR 693.65									
Current Date	18-Nov-2014									
3 EPS	44.92	36.53	27.87	21.12	15.65	10.24	7.02	3.46	2.20	
	2013-14	2012-13	2011-12	2010-11	2009-10	2008-09	2007-08	2006-07	2005-06	
4 EPS-GR	=(44.92/2.20) ^ (1/8) = 20.41^0.125 = 1.4579 = 45.79% growth									
5 EPS-GR (year wise)	22.96%	31.07%	31.96%	34.95%	52.83%	45.86%	102.89%	57.27%		
6 P/E (current)	= 693.65/44.92 = 15.44									
7 Industry P/E	22.76									
8 Intrisnic P/E	18.58 (also the average P/E)									
9 Best Case P/E	18.58 (same as intrinsic P/E since P/E growth is negative)									
10 Intrinsic Value	= 18.58*44.92 = INR 834.61									
11 PEG Ratio	= 18.58 / 45.79 = 0.41									
Round-3 (Additional Ratios)										
Book Value / Share	INR 197.50 (2013-14) (from annual report)									
1 Price / Share	INR 369.92 (avg price for 2013-14)									
P/B Ratio	= 369.92 / 197.50 = 1.87									
2 ROE	= 44.92 / 197.50 = 22.75%									
3 D/E Ratio	0.07 to 0.10 (over the last few years)									
4 P/S Ratio	1.49									
5 Free Cash Flow	INR 43,018 Million (highest till date)									
6 FCF Ratio	= 43018 M / 44355 M = 96.98%									

Table 36: *Calculating FCF ratio*
(Round-3: Step-6 of Stock Selection for Yes Bank)

"How is 96.98 percent for FCF Ratio?"

"Too good to be true, actually. Anything above 50 percent is very good."

LESSON 66

FCF Ratio above 50 percent is considered very good.

FCF ratio compares the free cash flow with the operating cash flow to indicate the financial efficiency of an organization.

"Yes, then we are done with this stock."

"Yes, just one more step to go. But Gobind, if you think that it has been a tough day, we can wind up here and come back on it tomorrow."

"No, no way, I want to close this today."

"Sure, as you wish."

"Yes, 100 percent."

"Then, let's get going and get over it. But I want to repeat one thing, yet another time."

"Yes, please."

"Even if 1 or 2 of these additional ratios are not supporting a Buy decision, it may not be a cause of real worry. You got to learn to investigate the reasons further. Look on the web, explore and find out the possible causes. Read the annual reports, compare stocks within the same industry for various ratios, spend time and get convinced before you move on. But if at any stage, you feel that you are very sure of a problem within the company which has not yet surfaced, immediately drop the stock without bothering about the effort that has gone until that point into the analysis."

"I understand that."

"You better. Never ever have the feeling of scarcity. Feel abundant. There are enough opportunities and enough time to invest in me."

"Right."

"Remember that you are buying a company and not a piece of paper. Investigate as much, but if you are sure about an issue, drop the deal as soon as possible."

"Got it!"

"OK, let's move on. Now, that you have made a decision to buy

Yes Bank, would you really want to know how much money you can expect to make from it?"

"Ah, I was thinking about it. But then, I realized that the current price of the stock (INR 693.65) is approximately 20 percent below its intrinsic value of INR 834.61. So, 20 percent is what I stand to potentially gain, right?"

"Well, not really."

"Why? If stock homecoming is true, then the stock is likely to hit its intrinsic value someday."

"Yeah, that is true. But we don't know when. What if it hits it after 4 years?"

"So?" Gobind went into a thinking mode.

"So, do you think you stand to gain 20 percent in 4 years, which is roughly 5 percent per annum returns?" I enquired.

"Yes, that's what it looks like, and if that is the case, it is a very bad deal, Mr. Stock."

"Of course, it is a bad deal if that is all you potentially stand to gain. But you forgot one important point in the stock homecoming concept."

"And what's that?"

"That the intrinsic value of the stock also keeps changing with time. As the company makes more profit and its EPS goes up, its intrinsic value also goes up."

"Right, what a relief! I just thought for a moment that all our effort has been washed down the drain because of this 5 percent potential return."

"Ha, ha! So, it is better to know what you stand to gain from the stock in future – say after 3 years, 5 years?"

"Yes, that would be really good. That will present us the true picture."

"Yes."

"And, with whatever I have understood until now, the future intrinsic value of the stock depends on the average (intrinsic) P/E and future earnings (EPS)."

"Yes, you are bang on. So, the *future intrinsic value* plus the *current gap between the intrinsic value and stock price* – is what you are likely to gain."

"Got it!"

"But remember that there is one more thing which we haven't yet factored in, while calculating the returns."

"What?"

"Dividends."

"Dividends?" Gobind was scratching his heads.

"Yes, dividend yield to be precise. So, over and above the current gap + future gap (based on future intrinsic value), you also gain the dividends which are paid to you at regular intervals. These dividends are taken off from the stock price, and are a separate component, although very much a part of your returns on investment."

"Wow, that's a bonus, which I had forgotten about."

"Yes, of course it is. And with the inherent advantages of dividends, as you would know by now, so many times it might become a differentiator between two stocks of which you want to pick one."

"Right, I get that."

"Let us go step-by-step, Gobind. If you decide to invest in Yes Bank tomorrow, how much is the liquidity you have with you?"

"I am OK to leave the money for 3-4 years."

"OK. Remember Gobind that you should stay away from me if you cannot afford to stay invested for at least seven years."

"I know that... that is fine. I was just telling you my preference. If it comes to do that, I am willing to stay invested for that long..."

"OK then, while seven years is the buffer we seek, it is quite possible that I do my homecoming much before this period of seven years. So, assuming that the homecoming happens much before 7 years, let us try and evaluate the stock price after a span of, let's say three years, fine?"

"Sounds good, Mr. Stock"

"So, get started. The first thing we want to note down is the current potential capital gains margin."

"Are you saying the current difference between the market price and intrinsic value?"

"Bang on!"

"OK, here it is on the screen."

Round-0 (Initial filter)								
Shortlisted Stocks	Voltas, State Bank of India, EIL, Coal India, Asian Paints...							
Round-1 (Earnings growth stability check)								
Selected Stocks	Coal India, Asian Paints and Yes Bank							
Round-2 (Value analysis)								
Rejected Stocks	Asian Paints (Too high PEG Ratio)							
Selected Stocks	Yes Bank							
Stock	Yes Bank							
Industry	Banking (private sector)							
CMP	INR 693.65							
Current Date	18-Nov-2014							
EPS	44.92	36.53	27.87	21.12	15.65	10.24	7.02	3.46	2.20
	2013-14	2012-13	2011-12	2010-11	2009-10	2008-09	2007-08	2006-07	2005-06
EPS-GR	=(44.92/2.20) ^ (1/8) = 20.41^0.125 = 1.4579 = 45.79% growth							
EPS-GR (year wise)	22.96%	31.07%	31.96%	34.95%	52.83%	45.86%	102.89%	57.27%	
P/E (current)	= 693.65/44.92 = 15.44							
Industry P/E	22.76							
Intrisnic P/E	18.58 (also the average P/E)							
Best Case P/E	18.58 (same as intrinsic P/E since P/E growth is negative)							
Intrinsic Value	= 18.58*44.92 = INR 834.61							
PEG Ratio	= 18.58 / 45.79 = 0.41							
Round-3 (Additional Ratios)								
Selected Stocks	Yes Bank							
Book Value / Share	INR 197.50 (2013-14) (from annual report)							
Price / Share	INR 369.92 (avg price for 2013-14)							
P/B Ratio	= 369.92 / 197.50 = 1.87							
ROE	= 44.92 / 197.50 = 22.75%							
D/E Ratio	0.07 to 0.10 (over the last few years)							
P/S Ratio	1.49							
Free Cash Flow	INR 43,018 Million (highest till date)							
FCF Ratio	= 43018 M / 44355 M = 96.98%							
Round-4 (Gains Estimation)								
Investment Period	3 years							
Current CG Potential	= 834.61 – 693.65 = 140.96 (approx.20% ROI)							

Table 37: *Calculating current capital gains potential (Round-4: Step-1 of Stock Selection for Yes Bank)*

"Great, Gobind! But remember that this gain of INR 140.96 per share is equivalent to 20 percent only if the shares are sold within a year. If the stock homecoming takes 3 years, then this INR 140.96 gain results in a CAGR of hardly 6 percent."

"Hmm, so 6 percent is not really worth it, and we know that stock homecoming may take even more. So, what do we do?"

"Exactly, so we now account for the projected growth of EPS."

"OK."

"You see, the average growth of the Yes Bank stock has been 45.79 percent, but this kind of growth rate is unsustainable in the long run. And of late, the growth has been in the more sensible bracket of 20 to 30 percent. So, let us assume that this stock grows for the next 3 years at the rate of 25 percent on an Average"

"But how do we know what is a sensible growth rate for a company? Do we do this kind of trimming and pruning in the growth rate for every company?"

"Well, it is common sense. You have to see the growth rate over a longish period of time, at least 10 years. The more number of years considered, the better. Now, we already see that over the last 10 years, the growth rate has been tapering down for Yes Bank, which is only natural. If you remember the case of Asian Paints, it had a very consistent growth rate over the 10 years. We did not have to do any tapering in that case."

"OK, we can fairly assume that the Yes Bank EPS is growing at the rate of 25 percent per annum, right? Let me update the table."

Round-0 (Initial filter)									
Shortlisted Stocks	Voltas, State Bank of India, EIL, Coal India, Asian Paints...								
Round-1 (Earnings growth stability check)									
Selected Stocks	Coal India, Asian Paints and Yes Bank								
Round-2 (Value analysis)									
Rejected Stocks	Asian Paints (Too high PEG Ratio)								
Selected Stocks	Yes Bank								
1 Stock	Yes Bank								
Industry	Banking (private sector)								
2 CMP	INR 693.65								
Current Date	18-Nov-2014								
3 EPS	44.92	36.53	27.87	21.12	15.65	10.24	7.02	3.46	2.20
	2013-14	2012-13	2011-12	2010-11	2009-10	2008-09	2007-08	2006-07	2005-06
4 EPS-GR	=(44.92/2.20) ^ {1/8} = 20.41^0.125 = 1.4579 = 45.79% growth								
5 EPS-GR (year wise)	22.96%	31.07%	31.96%	34.95%	52.83%	45.86%	102.89%	57.27%	
6 P/E (current)	= 693.65/44.92 = 15.44								
7 Industry P/E	22.76								
8 Intrisnic P/E	18.58 (also the average P/E)								
9 Best Case P/E	18.58 (same as intrinsic P/E since P/E growth is negative)								
10 Intrinsic Value	= 18.58*44.92 = INR 834.61								
11 PEG Ratio	= 18.58 / 45.79 = 0.41								
Round-3 (Additional Ratios)									
Selected Stocks	Yes Bank								
1 Book Value / Share	INR 197.50 (2013-14) (from annual report)								
Price / Share	INR 369.92 (avg price for 2013-14)								
P/B Ratio	= 369.92 / 197.50 = 1.87								
2 ROE	= 44.92 / 197.50 = 22.75%								
3 D/E Ratio	0.07 to 0.10 (over the last few years)								
4 P/S Ratio	1.49								
5 Free Cash Flow	INR 43,018 Million (highest till date)								
6 FCF Ratio	= 43018 M / 44355 M = 96.98%								
Round-4 (Gains Estimation)									
1 Investment Period	3 years								
Current CG Potential	= 834.61 – 693.65 = 140.96 (approx.20% ROI)								
2 Projected growth rate	25% per year								

Table 38: *Establishing projected growth rate*
(Round-4: Step-2 of Stock Selection for Yes Bank)

"Now Gobind, remember that you have to be convinced of this projected 25 percent growth."

"And I should do that by going through the annual reports?"

"Yes, go through the report, and also look at some projected estimates from financial experts. You may want to go through some forecasting websites like *4-traders.com*. These websites give you an idea about the estimated forecasts of EPS growth. You can probably look at a few of them and arrive at a consensus. With experience, you can keep validating it with actuals and see which website seem to provide the most realistic and accurate data."

"OK, got it! Let me spend some time here."

Gobind got busy looking at the future consensus estimates on EPS growth for Yes Bank to validate his assumption of 25 percent CAGR growth rate for the next few years. And I had to start packing my stuff now. Yes Bank was a done deal now, and my role on this planet was getting over after more than 200 years. It was time to be back. I would disclose this to Gobind the next morning, he deserved a sound sleep before that.

"Here it is, Mr. Stock. I found the best and the most convincing estimates on the website *4-traders.com*. They estimate that Yes Bank's EPS will grow from 44.92 in 2014 to 114.63 in 2019. This gives us an average growth of $(114.63/44.92)^{\wedge}(1/5) = (2.5519)^{\wedge}0.20 = 20.60$ percent annually. Let me update that in our table."

Round-0 (Initial filter)	
Shortlisted Stocks	Voltas, State Bank of India, EIL, Coal India, Asian Paints...
Round-1 (Earnings growth stability check)	
Selected Stocks	Coal India, Asian Paints and Yes Bank
Round-2 (Value analysis)	
Rejected Stocks	Asian Paints (Too high PEG Ratio)
Selected Stocks	Yes Bank

1	Stock	Yes Bank								
	Industry	Banking (private sector)								
2	CMP	INR 693.65								
	Current Date	18-Nov-2014								
3	EPS	44.92	36.53	27.87	21.12	15.65	10.24	7.02	3.46	2.20
		2013-14	2012-13	2011-12	2010-11	2009-10	2008-09	2007-08	2006-07	2005-06
4	EPS-GR	=(44.92/2.20) ^ (1/8) = 20.41^0.125 = 1.4579 = 45.79% growth								
5	EPS-GR (year wise)	22.96%	31.07%	31.96%	34.95%	52.83%	45.86%	102.89%	57.27%	
6	P/E (current)	= 693.65/44.92 = 15.44								
7	Industry P/E	22.76								
8	Intrisnic P/E	18.58 (also the average P/E)								
9	Best Case P/E	18.58 (same as intrisnic P/E since P/E growth is negative)								
10	Intrinsic Value	= 18.58*44.92 = INR 834.61								
11	PEG Ratio	= 18.58 / 45.79 = 0.41								

Round-3 (Additional Ratios)		
Selected Stocks		Yes Bank
1	Book Value / Share	INR 197.50 (2013-14) (from annual report)
	Price / Share	INR 369.92 (avg price for 2013-14)
	P/B Ratio	= 369.92 / 197.50 = 1.87
2	ROE	= 44.92 / 197.50 = 22.75%
3	D/E Ratio	0.07 to 0.10 (over the last few years)
4	P/S Ratio	1.49
5	Free Cash Flow	INR 43,018 Million (highest till date)
6	FCF Ratio	= 43018 M / 44355 M = 96.98%

Round-4 (Gains Estimation)		
1	Investment Period	3 years
	Current CG Potential	= 834.61 – 693.65 = 140.96 (approx.20% ROI)
2	Projected growth rate	25% per year
3	Consensus growth rate	20.6% per year

Table 39: *Establishing consensus growth rate*
(Round-4: Step-3 of Stock Selection for Yes Bank)

"Great Gobind, now remember that these forecasted estimates usually take care of industry future prospects, general economy factors, future outlook of the company and its products and services, competitive advantage and company's proven stability etc. These are done by experts and we can trust most of these estimates to be fairly accurate. Having said that, you should also look at financial reports, and try and account for certain other factors and see if the management derives its income from factors related to the company success. That way, the management keeps its focus on the success factors. The other thing is to know about the board of directors and understand the other boards they are a part of. How those companies are performing also gives you some clue. If you see issues anywhere, do not shy away from trimming down the future growth potential."

"OK, got it. So, the idea is to ⁊ a little on the pessimistic side while projecting the future growth of the company."

"Yes, absolutely. Now, can you project the EPS for Yes Bank after three years, i.e. in the year 2016-17?"

"OK, let me try it out."

Round-0 (Initial filter)									
Shortlisted Stocks	Voltas, State Bank of India, EIL, Coal India, Asian Paints...								
Round-1 (Earnings growth stability check)									
Selected Stocks	Coal India, Asian Paints and Yes Bank								
Round-2 (Value analysis)									
Rejected Stocks	Asian Paints (Too high PEG Ratio)								
Selected Stocks	Yes Bank								
Stock	Yes Bank								
Industry	Banking (private sector)								
CMP	INR 693.65								
Current Date	18-Nov-2014								
EPS	44.92	36.53	27.87	21.12	15.65	10.24	7.02	3.46	2.20
	2013-14	2012-13	2011-12	2010-11	2009-10	2008-09	2007-08	2006-07	2005-06
EPS-GR	=(44.92/2.20) ^ (1/8) = 20.41^0.125 = 1.4579 = 45.79% growth								
EPS-GR (year wise)	22.96%	31.07%	31.96%	34.95%	52.83%	45.86%	102.89%	57.27%	
P/E (current)	= 693.65/44.92 = 15.44								
Industry P/E	22.76								
Intrisnic P/E	18.58 (also the average P/E)								
Best Case P/E	18.58 (same as intrinsic P/E since P/E growth is negative)								
Intrinsic Value	= 18.58*44.92 = INR 834.61								
PEG Ratio	= 18.58 / 45.79 = 0.41								
Round-3 (Additional Ratios)									
Selected Stocks	Yes Bank								
Book Value / Share	INR 197.50 (2013-14) (from annual report)								
Price / Share	INR 369.92 (avg price for 2013-14)								
P/B Ratio	= 369.92 / 197.50 = 1.87								
ROE	= 44.92 / 197.50 = 22.75%								
D/E Ratio	0.07 to 0.10 (over the last few years)								
P/S Ratio	1.49								
Free Cash Flow	INR 43,018 Million (highest till date)								
FCF Ratio	= 43018 M / 44355 M = 96.98%								
Round-4 (Gains Estimation)									
Investment Period	3 years								
Current CG Potential	= 834.61 – 693.65 = 140.96 (approx.20% ROI)								
Projected growth rate	25% per year								
Consensus growth rate	20.6% per year								
Projected EPS	= [(1+0.206)^3]*44.92 = 1.206^3*44.92 = 1.754*44.92 = 78.79								

Table 40: *Calculating projected EPS*
(Round-4: Step-4 of Stock Selection for Yes Bank)

"Cool, and if Yes Bank is able to hold on to its intrinsic P/E of 18.58 over the span of next 3 years, then what is the price of the stock you expect after three years, assuming an EPS of 78.79 after three years."

"OK, let me frame that as well."

Round-0 (Initial filter)								
Shortlisted Stocks	Voltas, State Bank of India, EIL, Coal India, Asian Paints...							
Round-1 (Earnings growth stability check)								
Selected Stocks	Coal India, Asian Paints and Yes Bank							
Round-2 (Value analysis)								
Rejected Stocks	Asian Paints (Too high PEG Ratio)							
Selected Stocks	Yes Bank							
Stock	Yes Bank							
Industry	Banking (private sector)							
CMP	INR 693.65							
Current Date	18-Nov-2014							
EPS	44.92	36.53	27.87	21.12	15.65	10.24	7.02	3.46	2.20
	2013-14	2012-13	2011-12	2010-11	2009-10	2008-09	2007-08	2006-07	2005-06
EPS-GR	=(44.92/2.20) ^ (1/8) = 20.41^0.125 = 1.4579 = 45.79% growth								
EPS-GR (year wise)	22.96%	31.07%	31.96%	34.95%	52.83%	45.86%	102.89%	57.27%	
P/E (current)	= 693.65/44.92 = 15.44								
Industry P/E	22.76								
Intrisnic P/E	18.58 (also the average P/E)								
Best Case P/E	18.58 (same as intrinsic P/E since P/E growth is negative)								
Intrinsic Value	= 18.58*44.92 = INR 834.61								
PEG Ratio	= 18.58 / 45.79 = 0.41								
Round-3 (Additional Ratios)									
Selected Stocks	Yes Bank								
Book Value / Share	INR 197.50 (2013-14) (from annual report)								
Price / Share	INR 369.92 (avg price for 2013-14)								
P/B Ratio	= 369.92 / 197.50 = 1.87								
ROE	= 44.92 / 197.50 = 22.75%								
D/E Ratio	0.07 to 0.10 (over the last few years)								
P/S Ratio	1.49								
Free Cash Flow	INR 43,018 Million (highest till date)								
FCF Ratio	= 43018 M / 44355 M = 96.98%								
Round-4 (Gains Estimation)									
Investment Period	3 years								
Current CG Potential	= 834.61 – 693.65 = 140.96 (approx.20% ROI)								
Projected growth rate	25% per year								
Consensus growth rate	20.6% per year								
Projected EPS	= [(1+0.206)^3]*44.92 = 1.206^3*44.92 = 1.754*44.92 = **78.79**								
Projected Price	= 18.58*78.79 = INR 1463 (projected to the end of 2016-17)								

Table 41: *Calculating projected price*
(Round-4: Step-5 of Stock Selection for Yes Bank)

"OK Gobind, so what we are saying is that if the homecoming happens after three years, the project price of Yes Bank stock would be INR 1,463, right?"

"Yes."

"Can you also now find out what is the projected or estimated capital gains potential after three years?"

"Yes, I can calculate that now."

Round-0 (Initial filter)								
Shortlisted Stocks	Voltas, State Bank of India, EIL, Coal India, Asian Paints...							
Round-1 (Earnings growth stability check)								
Selected Stocks	Coal India, Asian Paints and Yes Bank							
Round-2 (Value analysis)								
Rejected Stocks	Asian Paints (Too high PEG Ratio)							
Selected Stocks	Yes Bank							
Stock	Yes Bank							
Industry	Banking (private sector)							
CMP	**INR 693.65**							
Current Date	18-Nov-2014							
EPS	44.92	36.53	27.87	21.12	15.65	10.24	7.02	3.46	2.20
	2013-14	2012-13	2011-12	2010-11	2009-10	2008-09	2007-08	2006-07	2005-06
EPS-GR	=(44.92/2.20) ^ (1/8) = 20.41^0.125 = 1.4579 = 45.79% growth							
EPS-GR (year wise)	22.96%	31.07%	31.96%	34.95%	52.83%	45.86%	102.89%	57.27%
P/E (current)	= 693.65/44.92 = 15.44							
Industry P/E	22.76							
Intrisnic P/E	18.58 (also the average P/E)							
Best Case P/E	18.58 (same as intrinsic P/E since P/E growth is negative)							
Intrinsic Value	= 18.58*44.92 = INR 834.61							
PEG Ratio	= 18.58 / 45.79 = 0.41							
Round-3 (Additional Ratios)								
Selected Stocks	Yes Bank							
Book Value / Share	INR 197.50 (2013-14) (from annual report)							
Price / Share	INR 369.92 (avg price for 2013-14)							
P/B Ratio	= 369.92 / 197.50 = 1.87							
ROE	= 44.92 / 197.50 = 22.75%							
D/E Ratio	0.07 to 0.10 (over the last few years)							
P/S Ratio	1.49							
Free Cash Flow	INR 43,018 Million (highest till date)							
FCF Ratio	= 43018 M / 44355 M = 96.98%							
Round-4 (Gains Estimation)								
Investment Period	3 years							
Current CG Potential	= 834.61 – 693.65 = 140.96 (approx.20% ROI)							
Projected growth rate	25% per year							
Consensus growth rate	20.6% per year							
Projected EPS	= [(1+0.206)^3]*44.92 = 1.206^3*44.92 = 1.754*44.92 = 78.79							
Projected Price	= 18.58*78.79 = **INR 1463** (projected at the end of 2016-17)							
Projected CG potential	= (1463 – 693.65) / 693.65 = **109.13%**							

Table 42: *Calculating projected capital gains potential*
(Round-4: Step-6 of Stock Selection for Yes Bank)

"Mr. Stock, that comes out to 109.13 percent gain in three years. INR 693.65 was my invested amount per share and INR 1,463 is my realized amount after three years, if I sell these shares."

"Excellent, Gobind! These are the overall returns, but it still misses out on one important aspect, which is the dividend yield."

"Yeah, I know but that must be small. Do we ignore it or add it as well?"

"Ignore dividends? Ignore them at your own peril, Gobind. This is another challenge with human beings. I am sorry to state that but I need to set certain things straight here. When it comes to money, there is nothing small. INR 1 is the stepping stone for the next million, provided you know how to save and invest it wisely. When you truly realize and appreciate the impact small things can make in your life, you will understand that there is nothing called as small things. So, never ever underestimate the power of one additional rupee."

"OK. My apologies for that. But the fact is that I never took it that seriously before. But I get you. Tell me how I can accommodate the dividend yields."

"That's OK, and quite understandable. For accommodating dividend yields in your calculation, we need to see the history of dividends for Yes Bank and calculate their average dividend payout ratio first."

"Dividend payout ratio? I don't think I can recollect what you might have told about this concept earlier."

"You see Gobind, there were three terms that we talked about related to dividends. First is the dividend percentage (percent of declared dividends in reference to the face value of the share – 200 percent dividend on a face value of INR 10 per share should mean a dividend of INR 20 per share). Second is the dividend yield, which is what we are most interested in. This is the percentage of amount received as dividend in reference to the invested amount. So, if I have invested INR 100 per share, and the dividend received was INR 20 per share, 20 percent is my dividend yield. And the third one is the dividend payout ratio. This is what will help us calculate the approximate average dividend that we are most likely to receive in future. This is the percent of earnings of a company that are distributed as dividends. So, if a company has an EPS of INR 50 and declares INR 20 as dividends out of that (remaining INR 30 is used to fuel future growth, reduce debt etc.), then the dividend payout ratio will be INR 20 / INR 50 = 40 percent."

Visualize your futuristic capital gains estimate before investing.

Capital gains estimate is done as a total of:

a. Initial gap between intrinsic value and CMP

b. Gap between projected price after xx years and average cost.

c. Projected dividend yield.

"Got it now, so you are saying that we first need to know the percentage of dividend payouts the company has been doing for the last so many years, on an average – so that we can understand the intent of the company."

"Yes, based on this intent of the company, we will calculate the average dividend payout ratio and use that intent of the company to extrapolate future dividends."

"OK, let's get going then."

"Of course, the first step is to calculate the average dividend payout ratio for Yes Bank, and for that you need the historical data of EPS and dividend per share for Yes Bank."

"OK, well I have the historical EPS data already. Let me get the historical dividend per share as well. How much should we look back for dividend per share data?"

"Last five years' data should be good enough to calculate the average and establish the recent intent of the company."

"Ok, let me get that done."

As Gobind went into calculation mode, I knew I had to complete my packing quickly. The time was short. I was almost done with my packing when Gobind called for me.

"Here you see. I got the dividend per share (DPS) data from Yes Bank's annual report."

	Round-0 (Initial filter)								
Shortlisted Stocks	Voltas, State Bank of India, EIL, Coal India, Asian Paints...								
	Round-1 (Earnings growth stability check)								
Selected Stocks	Coal India, Asian Paints and Yes Bank								
	Round-2 (Value analysis)								
Rejected Stocks	Asian Paints (Too high PEG Ratio)								
Selected Stocks	Yes Bank								
Stock	Yes Bank								
Industry	Banking (private sector)								
CMP	INR 693.65								
Current Date	18-Nov-2014								
EPS	44.92	36.53	27.87	21.12	15.65	10.24	7.02	3.46	2.20
	2013-14	2012-13	2011-12	2010-11	2009-10	2008-09	2007-08	2006-07	2005-06
EPS-GR	=(44.92/2.20) ^ (1/8) = 20.41^0.125 = 1.4579 = 45.79% growth								
EPS-GR (year wise)	22.96%	31.07%	31.96%	34.95%	52.83%	45.86%	102.89%	57.27%	
P/E (current)	= 693.65/44.92 = 15.44								
Industry P/E	22.76								
Intrinsic P/E	18.58 (also the average P/E)								
Best Case P/E	18.58 (same as intrinsic P/E since P/E growth is negative)								
Intrinsic Value	= 18.58*44.92 = INR 834.61								
PEG Ratio	= 18.58 / 45.79 = 0.41								
	Round-3 (Additional Ratios)								
Selected Stocks	Yes Bank								
Book Value / Share	INR 197.50 (2013-14) (from annual report)								
Price / Share	INR 369.92 (avg price for 2013-14)								
P/B Ratio	= 369.92 / 197.50 = 1.87								
ROE	= 44.92 / 197.50 = 22.75%								
D/E Ratio	0.07 to 0.10 (over the last few years)								
P/S Ratio	1.49								
Free Cash Flow	INR 43,018 Million (highest till date)								
FCF Ratio	= 43018 M / 44355 M = 96.98%								
	Round-4 (Gains Estimation)								
Investment Period	3 years								
Current CG Potential	= 834.61 – 693.65 = 140.96 (approx.20% ROI)								
Projected growth rate	25% per year								
Consensus growth rate	20.6% per year								
Projected EPS	= [(1+0.206)^3]*44.92 = 1.206^3*44.92 = 1.754*44.92 = 78.79								
Projected Price	= 18.58*78.79 = INR 1463 (projected to the end of 2016-17)								
Projected CG potential	= (1463 – 693.65) / 693.65 = 109.13%								
Dividend per share (DPS)	8.00		6.00	4.00	2.50	1.50			
	2013-14		2012-13	2011-12	2010-11	2009-10			

Table 43: *Calculating dividend / share*
(Round-4: Step-7 of Stock Selection for Yes Bank)

"Great, now that we know the historic DPS as well as EPS, it is easier to calculate the dividend payout ratio, isn't it? Can you do that please?"

"Sure, here is what it will look like."

Round-0 (Initial filter)	
Shortlisted Stocks	Voltas, State Bank of India, EIL, Coal India, Asian Paints...
Round-1 (Earnings growth stability check)	
Selected Stocks	Coal India, Asian Paints and Yes Bank
Round-2 (Value analysis)	
Rejected Stocks	Asian Paints (Too high PEG Ratio)
Selected Stocks	Yes Bank
Stock	Yes Bank
Industry	Banking (private sector)
CMP	INR 693.65
Current Date	18-Nov-2014

EPS

	2013-14	2012-13	2011-12	2010-11	2009-10	2008-09	2007-08	2006-07	2005-06
EPS	44.92	36.53	27.87	21.12	15.65	10.24	7.02	3.46	2.20

EPS-GR	=(44.92/2.20) ^ (1/8) = 20.41^0.125 = 1.4579 = 45.79% growth

EPS-GR (year wise)	22.96%	31.07%	31.96%	34.95%	52.83%	45.86%	102.89%	57.27%	

P/E (current)	= 693.65/44.92 = 15.44
Industry P/E	22.76
Intrisnic P/E	18.58 (also the average P/E)
Best Case P/E	18.58 (same as intrinsic P/E since P/E growth is negative)
Intrinsic Value	= 18.58*44.92 = INR 834.61
PEG Ratio	= 18.58 / 45.79 = 0.41
Round-3 (Additional Ratios)	
Selected Stocks	Yes Bank
Book Value / Share	INR 197.50 (2013-14) (from annual report)
Price / Share	INR 369.92 (avg price for 2013-14)
P/B Ratio	= 369.92 / 197.50 = 1.87
ROE	= 44.92 / 197.50 = 22.75%
D/E Ratio	0.07 to 0.10 (over the last few years)
P/S Ratio	1.49
Free Cash Flow	INR 43,018 Million (highest till date)
FCF Ratio	= 43018 M / 44355 M = 96.98%
Round-4 (Gains Estimation)	
Investment Period	3 years
Current CG Potential	= 834.61 − 693.65 = 140.96 (approx.20% ROI)
Projected growth rate	25% per year
Consensus growth rate	20.6% per year
Projected EPS	= [(1+0.206)^3]*44.92 = 1.206^3*44.92 = 1.754*44.92 = 78.79
Projected Price	= 18.58*78.79 = INR 1463 (projected to the end of 2016-17)
Projected CG potential	= (1463 − 693.65) / 693.65 = 109.13%

Dividend per share (DPS)	8.00	6.00	4.00	2.50	1.50
	2013-14	2012-13	2011-12	2010-11	2009-10
Dividend payout ratio	= 8/(44.92+8) = 15.12%	14.10%	12.55%	10.58%	8.74%
Avg Dividend payout ratio	12.22%				

Table 44: *Calculating average dividend payout ratio*
(Round-4: Step-8 of Stock Selection for Yes Bank)

"Wonderful, Gobind. So, Yes Bank distributes 12.22 percent of their earned profit amongst its shareholders and invests the remaining back for growth and reducing debt etc. OK, now remember that this stock has moved from paying zero dividends in the initial years to up to almost 15 percent dividends in the most recent year. Though the average dividend distribution is 12.22 percent of the profit, weighed by the initial lower dividends, you can easily see a trend of higher percent dividend distribution off late. So, you can safely assume an average slightly higher than 12.22 percent, maybe 15-16 percent, for our future projection."

"I get it, but let us take a slightly pessimistic view of 14 percent dividends from a planning perspective. Anything extra will be a bonus. What do you say?"

"That is not a bad strategy either, Gobind. OK then, now since you know the average dividend payout ratio and the projected EPS for the next 3 years, can you project the dividend for next three years?"

"I think, I can. Let me try."

Round-0 (Initial filter)										
Shortlisted Stocks	Voltas, State Bank of India, EIL, Coal India, Asian Paints...									
Round-1 (Earnings growth stability check)										
Selected Stocks	Coal India, Asian Paints and Yes Bank									
Round-2 (Value analysis)										
Rejected Stocks	Asian Paints (Too high PEG Ratio)									
Selected Stocks	Yes Bank									
Stock	Yes Bank									
Industry	Banking (private sector)									
CMP	INR 693.65									
Current Date	18-Nov-2014									
EPS	44.92	36.53	27.87	21.12	15.65	10.24	7.02	3.46	2.20	
	2013-14	2012-13	2011-12	2010-11	2009-10	2008-09	2007-08	2006-07	2005-06	
EPS-GR	=(44.92/2.20) ^ (1/8) = 20.41^0.125 = 1.4579 = 45.79% growth									
EPS-GR (year wise)	22.96%	31.07%	31.96%	34.95%	52.83%	45.86%	102.89%	57.27%		
P/E (current)	= 693.65/44.92 = 15.44									
Industry P/E	22.76									
Intrisnic P/E	18.58 (also the average P/E)									
Best Case P/E	18.58 (same as intrinsic P/E since P/E growth is negative)									
Intrinsic Value	= 18.58*44.92 = INR 834.61									
PEG Ratio	= 18.58 / 45.79 = 0.41									
Round-3 (Additional Ratios)										
Selected Stocks	Yes Bank									
Book Value / Share	INR 197.50 (2013-14) (from annual report)									
Price / Share	INR 369.92 (avg price for 2013-14)									
P/B Ratio	= 369.92 / 197.50 = 1.87									
ROE	= 44.92 / 197.50 = 22.75%									
D/E Ratio	0.07 to 0.10 (over the last few years)									
P/S Ratio	1.49									
Free Cash Flow	INR 43,018 Million (highest till date)									
FCF Ratio	= 43018 M / 44355 M = 96.98%									
Round-4 (Gains Estimation)										
Investment Period	3 years									
Current CG Potential	= 834.61 – 693.65 = 140.96 (approx.20% ROI)									
Projected growth rate	25% per year									
Consensus growth rate	20.6% per year									
Projected EPS	= [(1+0.206)^3]*44.92 = 1.206^3*44.92 = 1.754*44.92 = 78.79									
Projected Price	= 18.58*78.79 = INR 1463 (projected to the end of 2016-17)									
Projected CG potential	= (1463 – 693.65) / 693.65 = 109.13%									
Dividend per share (DPS)	8.00	6.00	4.00	2.50	1.50					
	2013-14	2012-13	2011-12	2010-11	2009-10					
Dividend payout ratio	= 8/(44.92+8) = 15.12%	14.10%	12.55%	10.58%	8.74%					
Consensus Div. payout ratio	14.00%									
Projected Yr Wise EPS	= 44.92*1.206 = 54.17	65.33	78.79							
	2014-15	2015-16	2016-17							
Projected Yr Wise Dividends	= 54.17*0.14 = 7.58	9.15	11.03							
	2014-15	2015-16	2016-17							

Table 45: *Calculating Projected Year Wise Dividends (Round-4: Step-9 of Stock Selection for Yes Bank)*

"Great, Gobind! Now you have the projected dividend per share. All that you need now is the calculation of the overall capital gains (including dividends), overall gain, and CAGR."

"That seems easy, here it goes."

Round-0 (Initial filter)										
Shortlisted Stocks	Voltas, State Bank of India, EIL, Coal India, Asian Paints...									
Round-1 (Earnings growth stability check)										
Selected Stocks	Coal India, Asian Paints and Yes Bank									
Round-2 (Value analysis)										
Rejected Stocks	Asian Paints (Too high PEG Ratio)									
Selected Stocks	Yes Bank									
Stock	Yes Bank									
Industry	Banking (private sector)									
CMP	INR 693.65									
Current Date	18-Nov-2014									
EPS	44.92	36.53	27.87	21.12	15.65	10.24	7.02	3.46	2.20	
	2013-14	2012-13	2011-12	2010-11	2009-10	2008-09	2007-08	2006-07	2005-06	
EPS-GR	=(44.92/2.20) ^ (1/8) = 20.41^0.125 = 1.4579 = 45.79% growth									
EPS-GR (year wise)	22.96%	31.07%	31.96%	34.95%	52.83%	45.86%	102.89%	57.27%		
P/E (current)	= 693.65/44.92 = 15.44									
Industry P/E	22.76									
Intrinsic P/E	18.58 (also the average P/E)									
Best Case P/E	18.58 (same as intrinsic P/E since P/E growth is negative)									
Intrinsic Value	= 18.58*44.92 = INR 834.61									
PEG Ratio	= 18.58 / 45.79 = 0.41									
Round-3 (Additional Ratios)										
Selected Stocks	Yes Bank									
Book Value / Share	INR 197.50 (2013-14) (from annual report)									
Price / Share	INR 369.92 (avg price for 2013-14)									
P/B Ratio	= 369.92 / 197.50 = 1.87									
ROE	= 44.92 / 197.50 = 22.75%									
D/E Ratio	0.07 to 0.10 (over the last few years)									
P/S Ratio	1.49									
Free Cash Flow	INR 43,018 Million (highest till date)									
FCF Ratio	= 43018 M / 44355 M = 96.98%									
Round-4 (Gains Estimation)										
Investment Period	3 years									
Current CG Potential	= 834.61 – 693.65 = 140.96 (approx.20% ROI)									
Projected growth rate	25% per year									
Consensus growth rate	20.6% per year									
Projected EPS	= [(1+0.206)^3]*44.92 = 1.206^3*44.92 = 1.754*44.92 = 78.79									
Projected Price	= 18.58*78.79 = INR 1463 (price to the end of 2016-17)									
Projected CG potential	= (1463 – 693.65) / 693.65 = 109.13%									
Dividend per share (DPS)	8.00	6.00	4.00	2.50	1.50					
	2013-14	2012-13	2011-12	2010-11	2009-10					
Dividend payout ratio	= 8/(44.92+8) = 15.12%	14.10%	12.55%	10.58%	8.74%					
Consensus Div. payout ratio	14.00%									
Projected Yr Wise EPS	= 44.92*1.206 = 54.17	65.33	78.79							
	2014-15	2015-16	2016-17							
Projected Yr Wise Dividends	= 54.17*0.14 = 7.58	9.15	11.03							
	2014-15	2015-16	2016-17							
Overall Projected Capital Gains	= 1463 - 693.65 + 7.58 + 9.15 + 11.03 = INR 797.11									
Overall Projected CAGR	= [(693.65 +797.11)/(693.65)]^(1/3) – 1 = 29.05%									

Table 46: *Calculating overall projected CAGR*
(Round-4: Step-10 of Stock Selection for Yes Bank)

"Wow, this stock is expected to give me 29 percent annualized returns over the next three years. That's an awesome return."

"Yes, it is Gobind... and if you are happy with these returns, we are good to go and buy this stock. We conclude our analysis of Yes Bank and it is a clear Buy for us."

Gobind pulled himself back into the rest chair. Looking up at the roof it was as if he was revising what all we had to go through the day to evaluate one stock. It was almost 11PM, and he was quite late.

"OK, Mr. Stock. I must leave now. I am already quite late. My family must be waiting for me at the dinner table. I am sure my kids have already had dinner without me today – which is something so rare. I must rush now."

I wanted to hold him for another 10 minutes and share my future plan with him. But I was not sure whether I should commit the sin of coming between him and his family time now. I also had less than the required courage to openly tell him the facts. I let him go. As I sat down writing my parting letter for him, I heard him shouting 'Good bye' from his car. I went to the balcony and waved him my last Good bye.

"Good bye, Gobind! You have been one of the rare concrete results of my 200-plus years of effort. My hopes are all tucked on you now..." I whispered to myself as I saw his car fade away on the road.

The Emotional Roller Coaster

The Emotional Roller Coaster

I was a zillion miles away from him now. But the advanced technology with Planet Earth allowed me to view every detail of what was happening in my office on this God's favorite planet to the minutest of details.

For the last one hour, I have been waiting for Gobind to come to my office. Being late was unusual of him. And then, I saw him approaching my *erstwhile* office, which was a part of this lovely hotel.

"C'mon, I just met him yesterday. How can he leave suddenly? There must be some mistake. Can you please recheck your records?" Gobind was astonished to hear the receptionist say that I had checked out of the hotel the day before.

"Sir, I have checked it. He checked out yesterday midnight. What's your good name, sir?"

"My name is Gobind. Did he leave any message for me?"

"One sec sir... let me check."

Gobind seemed perplexed and worried.

"Sir, there is this letter for you."

"OK, thanks."

Gobind tore open the envelope and started reading the letter as he walked towards the seating area in the lobby. His face showed all kind of emotions as he understood what I had written in there. He will never see me anymore, but I am seeing him every moment – as long as he is in my erstwhile office. As he was close to the conclusion of the letter, I could see his teary eyes not ready to accept the fact.

Human beings have forgotten to enjoy the present and to accept the situations. They keep living in future and hoping things will become better than today, forgetting that wherever they are today, was what they had wished for, a few years before. They need to learn the art of *being in the present*. They also need to learn the art of not getting surprised at situations. Each situation is necessary in their lives, and comes just at the right time. It's all planned. We do the planning here. But yeah, they don't know about it... They have to trust us... 100 percent trust!

Gobind crumpled the letter and did not know what to do for the next few minutes. He kept sitting at the reception sofa and kept staring at the small artificial waterfall located right in front of him. He looked at the receptionist, who was busy attending other clients, and then he looked upwards, and I was looking straight into those eyes, it was just that he could not see me. But he must have read it by then.

He looked at his watch and started reading the letter once again. He was getting it now, it seemed. I could read his thoughts. Any thoughts addressed to me, reached me. I responded mostly instantaneously. He knew whenever I responded. He had to believe that the first thought created in his mind after he asked a question was *my response*. Belief is the key. The very first response, which is without any impurity, conditions, excuses and biases – that's me talking to you – your inner tutor – whom you guys have short named 'intuition'.

'Are you there?' was the first thought Gobind created and addressed to me. It was all in his mind. But the communication was super-duper fast.

"Yes of course, always with you, Gobind," I responded in his thoughts.

"I get the response as 'Yes', but has this response been of my own creation? Or is it Him who responded? I don't know. I should have clarified all this with him before he left. He should have told me that he was leaving today. Why did you not tell me your plan? Why did you not give me an opportunity to thank you at least once for all that you have done for me? Why such a hurry? Why could you not wait for a few more days, having waited for more than 200 years already?" Gobind was sending these messages from his thoughts and I was receiving them clearly.

"That is how life is, Gobind. Things will come unplanned and unexpected. Be ready to face any situation. It will happen in your life also one day – you just do not know when. *Do not wait for the right time to express your gratitude and acknowledge your shortcomings.* You never know how much time is left. Go and express yourself right away – to your family, friends and loved ones. Be grateful to Him if you get another day. Make every day count as His blessings on you. And when you face an unexpected situation, which you surely will, then accept the situation and start working towards the solution. Forget about the *whats* and *whys* and *why nots*. Don't waste your time. Spend your time and energy to find the solution, Gobind." I responded to him in his thoughts.

"I think you are telling me to move on, but I am not sure whether it is you or these thoughts are all my creation?"

"Your first inner voice is me, just before you adulterate those with your own thoughts. Read the letter carefully, my friend."

Gobind started reading the letter once again, and the last line said it all – *Have 100 percent belief in your first voice. That's me.*

"Hmm… But it is so hard to believe that you are there, and I cannot see you but you are responding."

"You are lucky, Gobind, to have at least seen me till yesterday. Imagine the lack of belief in humans since they have never seen the incorporeal God, but still believe in Him somewhat. Gobind, your level of belief in me will decide the quality of the rest of your life," I whispered in his thoughts.

"OK. Let me follow the instructions in your letter."

Gobind opened his laptop.

"I am going to buy Yes Bank today. How much amount should I invest?" All communication was still happening in thoughts, but it all seemed so seamless. "I never realized that communicating with God was ever so easy," he thought.

"Go with what you can spare for the next 7 years. Remember? If you have a fairly liquid portfolio, invest 60-70 percent of what you can spare right now. If your portfolio is stubborn, then invest only 30-40 percent of what you can spare right now."

"Ah, but why is that… why cannot I invest all that I have to spare?"

"You see, Gobind, in a liquid portfolio – you have a choice to move funds from some other investments to stocks and vice versa depending upon the market situation. We will be using certain accelerators like the concept of rupee cost averaging to speed up and maximize your returns from your portfolio instead of just waiting and watching your stock to 'come home' and allow you to book profits. For those accelerators to be successful, we need a portfolio which is liquid. The more the liquidity, the better and faster are the returns from stocks."

"I get it. And liquidity, as you explained earlier as well, means I can take out or invest my money at will."

"Yes, I mean cash is the most illiquid. A fixed deposit is also highly liquid, you can get the money the next day with almost assured returns. A mutual fund or a stock investment is fairly liquid, you can get the cash whenever you want, though the returns may not be guaranteed. A real estate investment has very poor liquidity, it may take you months and years to liquidate your investments. And tools like Public Provident Fund, fixed term bonds etc. are most illiquid – there is hardly any way in which you can take out the money before the fixed tenure is over."

"Yes, you are right but liquidity can probably be one aspect before we choose to select our investment, isn't it? I mean I cannot keep all my money in cash, it will just erode with inflation."

"Of course, the best portfolios will have a beautiful balance between returns, liquidity and risk. And that's where stocks and mutual fund investments score – great returns, super liquidity, moderate risks."

"I get that."

"OK, I think I have around 70,000 spare amount, but my portfolio is only moderately liquid. So I would invest around 40,000 in Yes Bank."

"Go ahead then."

Gobind was about to purchase Yes Bank for INR 40,000 when he paused and began to think, "Is this happening for real or am I just investing because I have developed a positive bias towards Yes Bank? I mean, all these thoughts, are these truly from Mr. Stock or these are self-generated. I am not sure…"

Doubt had already started to creep in. Although, he had trust in the calculations we had done for Yes Bank, it still was difficult for him to believe that he was interacting with me. Humans have a tendency to believe more on the physical than the metaphysical. He believed in me when I was in the physical form in front of him, but now he has doubts. Also, the real belief level is judged only when one starts pouring in one's own money. It is just like what everyone says that they have faith in God, but with one small negative situation in someone's life, they start blaming God and everyone around them. They forget that they need to carry on with their faith. And I could easily see that Gobind did not have 100 percent belief.

He did not invest. He wasn't sure whether he should take the risk with his INR 40,000. He thought, "If it was so simple, why most people are losing money in stocks?" The point he completely missed was that most people do not lose money in stocks because of error in calculations but because of their lack of faith in their own calculations. And that is exactly where Gobind was struggling too. He had the backing of precise calculation behind him, but he still did not have 100 percent faith in the outcome if he had invested.

He logged off for the day, closed his laptop, went home, and did not return for the next 2 weeks. He came back on the morning of December 5, 2014, and reached the same reception and asked if there was any update about me. There was no difference in the receptionist's response.

He sat in the sofa near the lobby area fiddling with his laptop and looking back at all the Yes Bank calculations. It was time for me to tweak my strategy a little bit. Gobind had to have some form of physical interaction if he were to develop the belief. I could not forget that belief also comes by experience. I had to help Gobind get some experience on a stock, so that could push up his belief level.

Gobind was about to log off when he noticed a strange icon on his laptop screen. The icon was named 'Mr. Stock'. He ignored it, thinking that he might have created it when I was there. He shut down the laptop.

But the thought of the icon kept disturbing him. It had to. I was sending the signal. He could not recall why and when he had created that icon. What was that icon? He booted his laptop back.'Mr. Stock' icon was still there.

His curiosity overcame his confusion. He double clicked on the icon to see what would happen. A new window opened. The title bar of the window read, "Connecting you to Mr. Stock. Wait for a moment, please."

"Connecting me to Mr. Stock?" Gobind thought to himself.

His thoughts were interrupted by the hotel staff seeking to help him. "Sir, is there any way I can help you?"

"No, thanks…"Gobind responded, his eyes glued to his laptop window. He did not even bother to look at the hotel staff member.

"Sure sir, but I can really help you if you want…" insisted the hotel staff.

Gobind was getting irritated. He was too curious to see what was happening on his computer screen, and this hotel guy was hell bent on disturbing him.

"Didn't the staff at this hotel even know that they must leave their guests undisturbed, if they wish so? This is so annoying. What kind of a hotel is this?" Gobind thought, finally losing his patience.

"Don't ever..." Gobind began to speak. Meanwhile, the staff member turned around to leave, when Gobind got a glimpse of his face."

"It was me. I was there to tell you that I might not exist in the physical form but I am there to help you, always, unconditionally Gobind."

"Hello, one second..." cried Gobind, trying to stop the staff member.

The man turned back, but I was gone. "Oh sorry, I thought I saw one of my friends. I am really sorry," responded Gobind to the hotel staff.

"No problem sir," said the hotel guy as he walked away.

"He said he can help me, he also looked like Mr. Stock. Ah! What is happening to me, or is it just in my mind. But he taught me to have 100 percent belief. He must have been here," thought a puzzled but much more confident Gobind.

'Yes, I was there' was the next thought in Gobind's mind.

Gobind began to smile. He knew by now that the first thought was from me. He smiled, and then his attention was pulled back to the onscreen icon which had just welcomed him. He looked back at that window and it read 'Conversation with Mr. Stock', an empty chat window below it.

While Gobind was still glaring at the chat window, there came the first message on the screen.

"How are you, Gobind? Stock here."

Gobind's hands trembled as he tried to write back.

"I am very good. Is that really you, Mr. Stock, and where are you?"

"Yes, this is me, Gobind."

"Where are you?"

"Gobind, unfortunately I cannot answer any of your questions except for the ones related to your stock."

"Ah OK. So, I can seek help related to my stock on this window?"

"Yes, of course."

"OK, great. So, the first thing that I need to tell you is that I have not yet bought Yes Bank. It has already been close to three weeks since you left."

"I know that. Your belief is still not strong enough. That is why I am here to help you. Go and buy it right away, if you are convinced with your calculations. The biggest risk that humans take in their life is that they do not want to take any risks."

"OK. Give me 5-10 minutes, please."

Gobind came back on the window after 10 minutes and wrote, "I just purchased Yes Bank for INR 40,000. Just wanted to inform you."

"Welcome to a new world, Gobind. Now, you know why it is so difficult for people to just follow the simple steps that I keep prescribing?"

"Means?"

"You knew you are buying a good stock in Yes Bank. All our calculations favoured it. We had put in all our effort to shortlist this stock. You had some investible surplus. Your liquidity was good. What stopped you from buying this stock for the last three weeks?"

"I... I... I really don't know... some kind of fear..."

"I know. The emotion of fear of losing your money, the emotion of facing something new, the lack of 100 percent belief in whatever we discussed. There was nothing else except your emotions that were stopping you from doing what was clear, simple and the right thing to do."

"You seem to be right, Mr. Stock. Now I realize why people lose money – not because of lack of knowledge, but because of lack of control on their emotions."

"As you watch things unfold, I am sure your belief level will go up. As your belief goes up, your emotions will play a far lesser role in your day-to-day decision making."

"Right. What's next, Mr. Stock?" asked Gobind, smiling.

"Gobind, you have just begun an emotional roller coaster journey. Get set! Tighten your seat belt. You must stay watchful while you enjoy this beautiful, exciting and adventurous journey. I suggest that you must start by making a table of this journey, similar to how you started while you were doing value analysis for Yes Bank. You will also need to plot this table over a chart for easy interpretation and decision-making."

"OK," and the next message on the chat window was 'Mr. Stock, has logged off. He will now be called by the name Yes Bank.'

Gobind closed the window too. He knew that he could connect anytime with me for any help on Yes Bank stock. But then, he thought, "What help would I need now? We have already done the entire calculation and I just need to wait for the stock to hit the home coming zone, before I could sell."

He did not understand what emotions can do to a simple thing like selling a stock. Also, he had forgotten that we will be using certain accelerator techniques rather than simple waiting for the stock to hit the homecoming zone.

"Since Mr. Stock, I mean Yes Bank has suggested, let me start this journey by making a table," thought Gobind.

Gobind looked at the desktop icon again, and it was already rechristened by the title Yes Bank.

He double clicked it and asked his question, "So, why are you called Yes Bank now?"

"Hello Gobind, here is the arrangement. I cannot be with you forever. I must pass on the baton to you and move on. Therefore, I am going to be with you as long as you are holding this Yes Bank stock. My life is now linked to the life of this stock. *I am* this stock. I am Yes Bank now. The moment you sell Yes Bank, I cease to exist for you, and you will never be able to connect with me again. My life will undergo the ups and downs with the ups and downs of this stock. You can ask me anything you want about this stock, but not about anything else, for I know nothing other than Yes Bank now. I will be available to you 24/7. But never forget that all this comes to you with great responsibility. You must keep your promise of explaining to the entire world whatever I am training you on."

Gobind put thumbs up on his chat window, and then wrote, "You wanted me to start by making a table and a corresponding chart. What exactly should I track there?"

"You must start tracking my movements on three parameters."

"Which are those? Explain, please."

"You must track me for these three things: cost, market price and intrinsic value."

"OK, let me understand. Cost is the price at which I purchased you. Market price means the current market price, at which you are running. Intrinsic value is what we calculated during the value analysis. Is my understanding, right?"

"Yes."

"OK, great. But I have a few questions."

"Shoot!"

"The cost is going to remain the same – since I have already purchased you at a particular cost. Your intrinsic value is also going to remain the same – at least for some time. The only thing I need to, therefore, keep a track of is you market price. Right?" asked Gobind.

"No, everything is going to change with time, including the cost."

"Ah! But how can cost change, after having purchased the stock?"

"It can. You will know the answer to your question when the right time comes. For now, you have to trust me and start tracking these three numbers in a graphical format, at least once a month. This trio tracking is termed as *AC-MP-IV tracking*©. Tracking the trio of average cost, market price and intrinsic value of a stock will provide you with the most optimized control on a stock's movements, thus enabling right decision-making. Keep showing me the charts whenever you notice something alarming, but definitely once a month. That's the minimum."

Thumbs up again from Gobind indicated that he trusted me still, even after investing his money.

"I will send you the new table and chart by tomorrow."

"No worries, my friend. All the best as you begin a new journey with me."

"Thanks, buddy. Thank you for being there with me."

As we departed, I was again happy that I had the right student with me – someone who trusted me even if he had not understood everything – much like the humans who expect a child to trust their parents even if he does not understand everything in their current phase of life.

The other positive about my beloved student was that he kept all his promises. I received the two tables and a chart the very next day.

The Journey Begins	
Stock	Yes Bank (NSE:YESBANK)
Purchase date	5-Dec-2014
Number of shares	53
CMP (per share)	INR 765
Purchase amount	= 765*53 = INR 40,545

Table 47: *Initial purchase of Yes Bank (December 5, 2014)*

Month	Average Cost (AC)	Market Price (MP)	Intrinsic Value (IV)
Initial	765	765	835

Table 48: *AC-MP-IV Tracking© for Yes Bank (December 5,2014)*

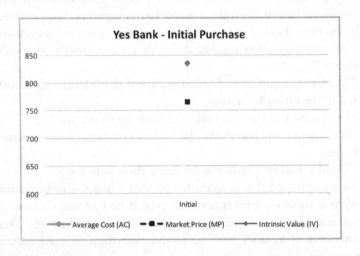

Chart 2: *Initial purchase of Yes Bank (December 5, 2014)*

With this purchase, my date of birth was scribed as December 5, 2014. I am not sure how long I was going to live for Gobind. It was all in Gobind's hand now. My existence on this planet was now limited to Yes Bank.

For many weeks, there was no communication from Gobind's

end. I could understand that he would have gotten busy with his life, his spouse, children, parents and work. But I was sure that he was monitoring me at the same time. And one day, I got a ping on my chat window.

"Hello Mr. Stock. Oops, I am sorry... Mr. Yes Bank. I am really sorry. I loved the earlier name."

"No worries. Change is never pleasant in the beginning. Tell me, how has life been? And what am I up to, according to you?"

That was a strange question for Gobind.

"What are you up to? Well, you know it the best. How can I tell you what are you up to?"

"I know, but I am asking your interpretation of how I have been doing in the market?" I sent this message with a smiley.

"Well, just OK, I think. Frankly, I don't know what to say. I purchased your 53 shares, and now it seems I have nothing to do except wait and watch, i.e. wait for your CMP to hit the homecoming zone and then plan to sell you. You are nowhere getting closer to home and I don't know how much time it is going to take. I have nothing else to do. I wanted to know whether I should get into another stock or what I should do other than just waiting and watching you."

"Superb. Now that you have asked, there are two different kinds of people in your race – those who wait for things to happen to them, and the others who make things happen. I am sure you would not like to be in the first category."

"Right. But how can I make things happen? I mean I cannot influence your market price, or can I?"

"You can, but not with 53 shares."

"Ah! With more shares?"

"You surely can, with lakhs of shares."

"Interesting. I have a very fundamental question here.

"Go ahead please..."

"Tell me how does your price movement happen? What drives it? I know that it is a collective perception, but how does the technicality work out? What happens if I buy 53 shares or sell them? How does your price change with transaction of my 53 shares? What is the movement in your price?"

"You see. My price movement is very simple and logical. Let us say that there is a new company which comes out with an IPO for 1,000 shares at INR 20 per share. What will be the market capitalization for this company, Gobind?"

"INR 20,000, that's simple."

"Great, now let us say that you feel that the intrinsic value per share is much higher based on your calculations. You feel that it is worth buying some of the shares of this company even at INR 25 per share. Depending on your funds availability, you place a Buy request at the stock exchange for 150 shares at INR 25 per share, either through your demat account or through your broker."

"OK..."

"Now, remember that in a stock market, you can only place a Buy request. Whether your request will be fulfilled or not will depend on whether there is one or more sellers ready to sell the shares at INR 25."

"Ah! OK. This is quite like how we buy grocery. Isn't it?"

"Yes. Very well understood. You must have a seller to sell shares, and you must have a buyer to buy shares. That is the reason that trading volume per day becomes an important metrics to look out for, when getting into stocks. Most blue chips and known brands will have a good trading volume. You can sell almost at will for such blue chips because there are always enough buyers."

"OK, and if the trading volume is low, then there is no guarantee that we will be able to buy or sell quickly enough at the price at which we want, right YB?"

"Yes, absolutely Gobind. And I like this acronym – YB. Now, assuming that you have a seller available who is ready to sell those shares at your asking price of INR 25, the deal will be done – either through an electronic broker via your demat account or your own broker."

"OK, understood. But what happens to the share price? How much does it become now?"

"See, now you have 150 shares of the company at INR 25 resulting in a market capitalization of INR 3,750 (150*25) and remaining 850 shares are still with other shareholders at INR 20 resulting in a market capitalization of INR 17,000 (850*20). So, what is the total market capitalization now?"

"Well, it should be INR 3,750 + INR 17,000, which is INR 20,750, right?"

"Bang on! And since the total number of shares still remains the same at 1,000, can you estimate the new per share price?"

"Yes, it should be INR (20,750 / 1,000), giving us INR 20.75. Is that the new share price?"

"Yes, my friend. The stock of this company now starts trading at INR 20.75, up from INR 20 – because your perception about the company was higher, and you bought 150 shares at INR 25."

"OK, cool. This was simple and yet interesting. Coming back to the point from where we started, you were talking about proactively making things happen to reduce the cost of purchase. With these 53 shares, how can I make things happen?"

"I want you to think, Gobind. I want you to inculcate this belief in yourself that in every situation, in each circumstance, one can make things happen. However small may be the impact, but you can still do something. Once you firmly start believing that you can do something in every given situation, your all powerful mind will start giving you solutions."

Gobind took his time, and then responded, "Buddy, I purchased you at a certain cost. I cannot change that cost. You have an intrinsic value. I cannot change that intrinsic value, at least for now. You are currently running at a certain CMP. With 53 shares, I can hardly influence that CMP. I am really not sure what I can do."

"OK, here is the first rule in the journey of your stock. You can actively influence your speed of earning profits, as well as the profit margin from me, by following the technique of 'rupee cost averaging'."

"Rupee cost averaging? I have heard you talking about this earlier. I think now is the right time for you to tell me the details..."

"Yes this is the same rule that works for mutual fund SIPs. In mutual fund SIPs, it works *passively* – sometimes in your favour and sometimes against you – thus, averaging out the risk. Here, with me, you can make it work *actively*. And since you will actively work on it, you may act only if the averaging works in your favour, else not."

"OK, sounds quite interesting. How do we go about doing it?"

"You see Gobind, rupee cost averaging is all about bringing down the average cost of your purchase."

"Ah! I am very curious now. Please tell me how."

"Sure. Tell me, did you ever have a situation where my CMP went below the cost at which you purchased me?"

"Yes, infact that has been happening most of the time."

"Great."

"What is so great about your current price running below the cost at which I purchased you? I really do not see any good."

"There always is good for you in everything that you face. It is just that you may not be aware. Every time my CMP goes below your cost, you have a buying opportunity."

"A buying opportunity?"

"Yes, buying more of my units at a cost lower than the cost per share at which you bought those 53 shares."

"OK and why would I do that?"

"That is going to bring down my average cost per share. It is simple you see. If you had 10 shares bought at INR 100, and you execute an opportunity where you buy 10 more shares atINR 90, then you are holding a total of 20 shares by investing INR 1,900 which is an average cost of purchase at INR 95. This way you have brought down your average cost from the initial INR 100 per share to INR 95 per share."

"Hmm... It's down by INR 5,"said Gobind casually.

"For God's sake, please do not underestimate the power of these INR 5. This 5 percent (INR 5 on INR 100 per share) is your cost going down – which is going to be the increase in your profit margins or returns straightaway, as and when you sell your investment. Imagine, instead of making 10 percent returns per annum, you now start making 15 percent returns. How many businesses give you the opportunity to bring down the cost of investments once you have already invested? Actually none, other than me!"

LESSON 68

Rupee cost averaging allows you to bring down your average cost.

Stocks are the only business which allows you to actively bring down the cost of your purchase – after originally buying the business.

Make use of rupee cost averaging technique to improve your profit margins.

Be excited about market price dips.

"I get that. So, I cannot control your CMP or your intrinsic value, but I can surely bring down the average cost at which I purchased you and this increases my chances of making a faster profit or more profit."

"Yes, absolutely."

"Cool, so as on today, i.e. on December 17, 2014, you are running at INR 670, which is lower than the price at which I purchased your first 53 shares. So, you are saying that I should buy more. How much more?"

"Just be a little careful here before you apply rupee cost averaging."

"Means?"

"There are a few rules governing rupee cost averaging that you must understand, so that it remains an effective technique for you in the long run. It is easy for this technique to quickly become ineffective for you, if you do not take care of these rules."

"OK, go ahead. Please, tell me the rules."

"First rule is that the effectiveness of rupee cost averaging depends on two factors: *Weight of Top-up shares*© and the *Price vs. Cost factor*©. Let me explain them to you one by one."

"Sure."

"Let us first understand the meaning and significance of Weight of Top-up shares©."

"Sure."

"You see, Weight of Top-up shares© is the number of top-up shares you wish to buy with respect to the current number of shares you are already holding for a particular stock. Let me explain this to you this via the formula on your screen:

$$\text{Weight of Top-Up Shares}^{\copyright} = \frac{\text{No. of Top-Up Shares}}{\text{No. of Top-Up Shares} + \text{No. of Already held shares}}$$

Formula 12: *Weight of Top-Up shares*$^{\copyright}$

Let us say, you already had 30 shares of a company purchased at INR 100 per share, and you decided to buy 10 more shares at INR 90 to bring down the average cost. So, the Weight of Top- Up shares$^{\copyright}$ will be 25 percent (10 out of potential 40 now). Suppose, you go ahead and buy these 10 shares. This makes your average cost as (10*90 + 30*100) / 40 = INR 97.50. You now have a total base of 40 shares. And, after a few months, you see another opportunity to buy 10 more shares at INR 87.50 to further bring down the average cost. Now, the Weight of Top-Up shares$^{\copyright}$ will be 20 percent (10 out of potential 50 now). If you go ahead and buy these 10 shares as well, your average cost will be (10*87.50 + 40*97.50) / 50 = INR 95.50. Get it?"

"Yes, but what does this weight signify?"

"Yes, Weight of Top-Up shares$^{\copyright}$ signifies the effectiveness of rupee cost averaging."

"Meaning?"

"This means that as the Weight of Top-Up shares$^{\copyright}$ decreases, the rupee cost averaging technique becomes less effective. So, in our example, we can easily see that Weight of Top-Up Shares$^{\copyright}$ has come down from 25 percent to 20 percent. During the first attempt of buying 10 shares, you could bring down the average cost from INR 100 to INR 97.50, an INR 2.50 improvement in cost. Compare this with the average cost of INR 95.50 in the second case, which is an INR 2.00 improvement. As the Weight of Top-Up shares$^{\copyright}$ decreases, the rupee cost averaging technique becomes less effective."

Weight of Top-Up shares© signifies the efficiency of rupee cost averaging for your stock.

The more is the Weight of Top-Up shares©, the more efficient it is to use rupee cost averaging on your stock.

"Wow, so every time I am buying more, I am probably reducing the Weight of Top-Up shares© and this is going to render my averaging less effective as I keep investing. Am I right?"

"Yes."

"So, I need to be careful before buying more. And what is the second factor you talked about i.e. Price vs. Cost factor©?"

"Price vs. Cost factor© depicts the gap between the running average cost and the price at which you want to buy additional top-up stocks. This is also called as AC-MP factor© Here is how you calculate that:

$$\text{Price vs Cost Factor}^© = \frac{\text{Average Cost - CMP}}{\text{Average Cost}}$$

Formula 13: *Price vs. Cost factor© or AC-MP factor©*

More is the gap between the current market price and your average cost, the higher is the Price vs. Cost factor©. A higher Price vs. Cost factor© or AC-MP factor© indicates us to buy more to optimize the impact of rupee cost averaging."

"Can you please elaborate this a little bit?"

"Of course. See, Gobind. If your average cost is INR 100 and the stock is currently available at INR 80, then your Price vs. Cost factor© would be (100–80) /(100) = 20 percent. But if the stock is available at INR 50 instead of INR 80, then your Price vs. Cost factor© would be (100– 50)/(100) = 50 percent. Since your Price vs. Cost factor© is not the same in both the cases, you should not be buying the same number of units in either case – rather you should be buying in proportion to the Price vs. Cost factor©. The more the Price vs. Cost factor©, more is the number of shares you should be buying – thus, fully optimizing the strategy of rupee cost averaging."

"I am a little confused now, should I buy more or not, and if yes, then how much?"

"You should of course buy more. But I can understand your situation as well. It is just like the oxidation effect, which we studied earlier. Do you remember that?"

"Yes, that was in one of your sessions. And I remember you were talking about dividends, right?"

"Correct. So, you lose big time if you don't reduce your average cost, and the more you adopt cost averaging, the less effective it gets. So, you got to use it very judiciously."

"OK... So how do I decide whether I need to buy more and apply rupee cost averaging?"

"To understand that, we must first understand two key factors."

"OK, please explain me."

"First is the AC-MP Factor, which you have already seen (Formula 13). It denotes the percentage by which the current market price (CMP) of the stock is down with respect to its average cost (AC). Also called as Price vs. Cost Factor.

"Second is the IV-MP factor©. This denotes the percentage by which the current market price (CMP) of the stock is down with respect to its intrinsic value (IV) considering Average Cost (AC) as its base. Just look at this."

$$\text{IV-MP factor}^© = \frac{\text{Intrinsic Value (IV) – Current Market Price(CMP)}}{\text{Average Cost}}$$

Formula 14: *Value vs. Price factor© or IV-MP factor©*

"OK... I get these two factors. Now tell me, how do I decide whether I should go for rupee cost averaging or not..."

"Yes, there are two simple rules to take a decision on triggering this rule."

"Tell me please..."

"Rule# 1, The AC-MP factor should be 10 percent+ and Rule# 2, the rupee cost averaging should not be triggered more than once a month.

"Ah, interesting! But these values keep changing rapidly especially the CMP – so how often should I be monitoring these factors?"

"Keep looking for more buying opportunities after your first purchase. Look at your stock at least once a week to monitor its performance."

"OK... and why should I trigger rupee cost averaging only once a month?"

"This is the cooling off period to detect any sudden price movements and look if there is a market crash on the way."

"OK, I get what you say... so, I know that I must buy more if the Market price goes down. But I should be judicious enough to decide not to keep buying at every dip. So, I buy if the AC-MP factor is 10 percent+, and that too only once a month... Have I got it right?"

"Absolutely, You are my ideal student, Gobind."

"I still have a question..."

"Shoot"

"Based on the AC-MP factor, I know when to buy. But the next obvious challenge is to find out how much to buy?"

"Right, and that is precisely where WRCA© will help you..."

"WRCA?"

"Yes, WRCA© is a set of special weighted buying rules which help you decide the optimum number of shares to be purchased to make the most effective use of Rupee Cost Averaging."

"Wow, go on please... I am all ears."

"If the AC-MP factor is x-percent, then buy:

    a. Additional shares worth IV-MP factor percentage (if IV-MP-percent is greater than 20 percent), OR

    b. Additional shares worth AC-MP factor percentage (if IV-MP percent is less than 20 percent)

"OK, so today is December 17, 2014 and I see that the stock is hovering around INR 670 and INR 680, which is more than 10 percent down from my average cost (currently INR 765). Also, there has been no rupee cost averaging triggered in the last 30 days. So, you are saying that I should trigger rupee cost averaging?"

"Why not, Gobind? And you know how much to buy, right?"

"Yes, let me work out and show it to you."

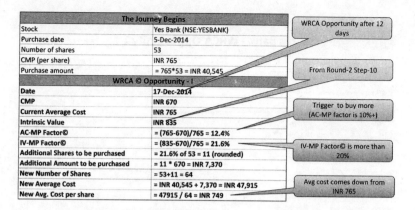

The Journey Begins	
Stock	Yes Bank (NSE:YESBANK)
Purchase date	5-Dec-2014
Number of shares	53
CMP (per share)	INR 765
Purchase amount	= 765*53 = INR 40,545
WRCA © Opportunity - I	
Date	17-Dec-2014
CMP	INR 670
Current Average Cost	INR 765
Intrinsic Value	INR 835
AC-MP Factor©	= (765-670)/765 = 12.4%
IV-MP Factor©	= (835-670)/765 = 21.6%
Additional Shares to be purchased	= 21.6% of 53 = 11 (rounded)
Additional Amount to be purchased	= 11 * 670 = INR 7,370
New Number of Shares	= 53+11 = 64
New Average Cost	= INR 40,545 + 7,370 = INR 47,915
New Avg. Cost per share	= 47915 / 64 = INR 749

Annotations: WRCA Opportunity after 12 days; From Round-2 Step-10; Trigger to buy more (AC-MP factor is 10%+); IV-MP Factor© is more than 20%; Avg cost comes down from INR 765

Table 49: *WRCA© Opportunity-I executed on Yes Bank (December 17, 2014)*

Month	Average Cost (AC)	Market Price (MP)	Intrinsic Value (IV)	AC-MP Factor ©	IV-MP Factor ©
Initial	765	765	835	0.00%	9.15%
17-Dec-2014 (Before)	765	670	835	12.42%	21.57%
17-Dec-2014 (After)	749	670	835	10.55%	22.03%

Table 50: *AC-MP-IV Tracking©at WRCA©Opportunity-I for Yes Bank (December 17, 2014)*

"I bought 21.6 percent additional shares because IV-MP factor© was more than 20 percent, or else I should have bought only 12.4 percent more shares. Is that understanding right?"

"Absolutely right, Gobind. So, now your average cost has come down from INR 765 to INR 749; that's your new baseline whenever you are looking for the next buying opportunity. Now, you will cool off for this month and from January 2015 onwards, you will keep a watch if the stock price falls below more than 10 percent of INR 749, got it?"

"Ah got it! I think I now know how to apply rupee cost averaging. Have a look at Chart 3 before I ask you the next question…"

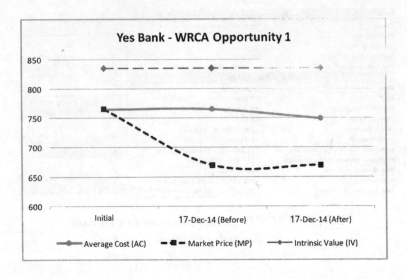

Chart 3: *AC-MP-IV Tracking©at WRCA©Opportunity-I for Yes Bank (December 17, 2014)*

"Looks great, Gobind. So, what you see is that we have reduced the average cost and widened the gap between average cost and intrinsic value."

"Yes, super. But tell me, every time if the market price of the stock is crossing 10 percent threshold below the average cost, if I apply WRCA© technique, then will there ever be a case of market price going 20 percent below average cost or 30 percent or 40 percent ?"

"There still could be many scenarios when you will see that the market price goes much beyond 10 percent dip…"

"Like?"

"First, there may be a scenario when after applying rupee cost averaging once in a month, the stock continues to spiral downward and even hits the 20 percent or 30 percent or even more before the next month. One of the WRCA© rule does not permit you to buy more than once in a month. In that case, you will have to deal with probably 30 percent price cut in the coming month."

LESSON 72

Use WRCA© technique to use rupee cost averaging effectively and efficiently.

Rupee cost averaging can be effectively and efficiently used by using the WRCA© technique.

It uses IV-MP factor© and AC-MP factor© to influence when and how to apply the averaging strategy.

"Right, I remember that rule."

"You may also be short of funds or short of liquidity in a specific month to invest that kind of amount. It all depends on the liquidity of your portfolio. It is highly advisable for an aggressive stock investor to keep enough liquidity in the portfolio to take advantage of these temporary dips. Besides, investing more money in stocks, especially in large amounts, might tweak your portfolio out of balance. You could also be envisaging certain impact on the stock market based on economic situation around you, and may want to wait for the stock to go down further."

"I understand, but if we wait because of any of the above scenarios, we might miss bringing the average cost down, as the stock may turn up in the other direction before we buy on dips."

"Yes, it's possible, and it is perfectly OK. Remember that the initial buying decision itself was done after taking comprehensive care of all data points. We are now just trying to do some aggressive investing by using techniques like WRCA© to bring down the average cost further. It is OK even if you miss a few such opportunities. I will provide you with enough such opportunities. Keep abundance in mind."

LESSON 73

Every stock dip below 10 percent of average cost may not result in buying more, and that's perfectly fine.

You may not buy on every dip, because of:

c. Once a month buy rule, based on WRCA© strategy

d. Lack of liquidity in your portfolio

e. Portfolio unbalancing worries

f. Macroeconomic situation

"I get it. This was useful. Thanks, buddy. Will be back soon in the coming month to try and search for another buying opportunity."

Gobind logged off and was in the New Year's celebration mode for the remaining part of the month. He knew he was learning something that could change not only his destiny but the future of the entire coming generation on this planet. And that is what my aim was. I hoped he remembered his promise. The elevation of the world on this planet depended so much on his shoulders. And I was quite confident that I had picked the right person.

Over the next 2-3 months, Gobind did login sometimes in between just to connect with me, and to express the fact that he was getting bored, though my price had started to pick up. For him, the boring part of the journey was that my current market price was neither low enough to implement further rupee cost averaging, nor it was high enough to exceed the intrinsic value. Caught in between the average cost and intrinsic value, these three months were not very exciting for Gobind, until one day he lost his patience and came back to me with this proposal:

"Hello, Yes Bank. How have you been?"

"Hello, Gobind. You know my current situation much better than I do. You seem to have been monitoring me up close."

"Yes, that is true. I have been monitoring you. I should be. But you know, this is all so boring. I mean there is no action for me to take."

"Right."

"What do you mean by that?"

"Remember, Gobind that it is not necessary to do extraordinary things to get extraordinary results. In fact, most successful investors do nothing most of the time. You should not confuse movement with action. The agents make money on your action, while you make money on inaction. Waiting and demonstrating monumental patience is one of the key attributes that makes an investor successful. You do not trade with me, just because everyone around you is."

"I thought I have been quite patient already. What else are you expecting?"

"You see that is the problem. You feel you have touched your extreme levels of patience, but I can prove that your patience has only been diminishing ."

"How can you say that?"

"Here is the data that should be enough to convince you, Gobind. The data that I have from India clearly shows that 27 percent of my investments are withdrawn within one year, and another 47 percent in two years. And trust me, the problem is not India-specific. Human beings are running out of patience. The average holding period for stocks in 1960 was 100 months. Currently, it is 8 months. Now you know why most investors do not really make wealth from me? And you are talking 'patience' after 2-3 months of investment... huh..."

"I understand your point, but how long should we actually be waiting and sitting on a stock?"

"There is no defined rule here, Gobind. Just as children take their time to grow into adults, businesses do take time to grow in value. You are waiting for the right investment situation or a selling situation. It could be a general bear market, an industry recession, a one-time recoverable company event, a panic sell off – all these situations will create opportunities. The only challenge is to be patient and wait for such opportunities to occur, and they do occur, not everyday, not every month, and may be not every year – but with enough regularity to make you wealthy."

Most successful investors do nothing most of the time.

Waiting and watching with monumental patience is one of the key attributes of a successful investor.

Movement should not be confused with action.

Gobind perhaps understood that he needed to stretch his levels of patience. He logged off that day and then came back after another couple of weeks.

"Hello YB. Today, I am planning to sell you."

"Ah, it has only been three months, isn't it?"

"Yes, but look at your market price. It has gone up to INR 900 in these 2-3 months. To be precise, your value has appreciated 20.2 percent in 3-month time (from the average cost of INR 749 to the current price of INR 900 today, i.e. on March 4, 2015). Now, 20.2 percent returns in three months is almost equivalent to 80 percent annualized returns. What else should I wait for? And look at this chart. Homecoming has already happened. The current price of the stock is already above the intrinsic value."

Month	Average Cost (AC)	Market Price (MP)	Intrinsic Value (IV)	AC-MP Factor ©	IV-MP Factor ©	
Initial	765	765	835	0.00%	9.15%	Stock Homecoming has occurred but it is too soon to sell
17-Dec-2014 (Before)	765	670	835	12.42%	21.57%	
17-Dec-2014 (After)	749	670	835	10.55%		
31-Dec-2014	749	773	835	-3.20%	8.28%	
31-Jan-2015	749	863	835	-15.22%	-3.74%	
28-Feb-2015	749	863	835	-15.22%	-3.74%	
4-Mar-2015	749	900	835	-20.16%	-8.68%	

Table 51: *AC-MP-IV Tracking© at Sell Opportunity-I on Yes Bank (March 4, 2015)*

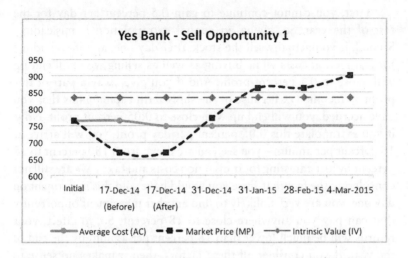

Chart 4: *AC-MP-IV Tracking© at Sell Opportunity-Ion Yes Bank*
(March 4,2015)

"Ah! You have a beautiful perspective of looking at things, Gobind. Of course, you are free to sell me anytime. But I would want you to just keep a few things in mind before you make up your mind to sell."

"I knew, you will be difficult to convince Mr. Yes Bank. You were difficult to convince when we were buying, and you are difficult still, when we are trying to sell. Tell me on reason why should I not sell you right now? I can see a clear homecoming."

"You do not have to convince anyone. It is your money, your decision. I can only recommend and suggest based on my knowledge and experience, and that too if you permit me to do so."

"Go ahead YB, I was just kidding. I have learnt so much from you. I will not take a decision without consulting you."

"OK, here is the first thing. Never try to extrapolate a short-term profit to look at things from a long-term perspective."

"OK, but why? What is the issue there?"

"You see, Gobind. Extrapolating 20 percent profit in three months to 80 percent per annum is not right. It is like if your stock gains 0.5percent in a day, you say that you have earned 180 percent per annum growth – this is not practical because of many reasons."

"Like?"

"First, you cannot continue to gain 0.5 percent per day for the rest of the year. So, giving an annual extrapolation is misleading. Second, if you actually sell the stock after day one, and if you adjust for transaction costs while buying as well as selling, you will end up with close to 0.1 percent profit. And if you give away a part of this profit as income tax because of the short-term capital gains that you have accrued, you will end up with close to 0.05 percent profit. Now, if you extrapolate this 0.05 percent per day profit, you will arrive at 18 percent per annum – you see you are down from 180 percent to 18 percent by just adjusting for transaction costs and taxes. We are still not considering the fact that since you would have sold this investment on day one, you are very unlikely to find another investment opportunity that can pay you anywhere close to 18 percent. So, in effect, your returns will be much lower than 18 percent per annum by the end of the year. If you consider all these factors, then it makes no sense to extrapolate a short-term gain and consider it as an annual return."

"Ah! I suddenly find myself talking so foolish."

"Good!"

"Good? What is so good about being foolish?"

"Being foolish may not be good, but acceptance of your ignorance is a wonderful display of great attitude. Remember Gobind, only those who agree that they have been ignorant, have an opportunity to improve. The experts often get stuck at the same intellectual level where they already are. So, it is good that you realize your mistake."

"Thanks, YB. In a fraction of a minute, you make me sound so wise too. You talked about taxes getting deducted. How much tax will I have to pay if I sell it in the short-term?"

"Any capital gains realized in short-term attract income tax. In the case of stocks in India, short term is 12 months, and the prevailing tax is 15 percent flat. So, if you were to sell your stock within 12 months, remember that you would have to part with 15 percent of the profits made, and pay it to the government."

Do not base your sell decisions by extrapolating short-term profits.

A 0.5 percent profit in a day does not translate to 180 percent per annum returns.

Short-term selling often attracts capital gains taxes, higher transaction charges and exit charges.

"Right, I get that."

"Also, do you know what you will do with the money that you'll get from selling me? Do you really need the money? If yes, then it's fine, else it will only rot in a fixed deposit generating only a fraction of the returns that you could have received from me."

"Yeah, I do not know where I will invest, but it is primarily because of the fear of losing this handsome potential profit that I wish to sell. I am not sure if this homecoming will happen again."

"I can understand that emotion very well, Gobind. Fear is one of the emotions you got to conquer. You must have confidence and belief in your calculations. You must understand that Stock Homecoming is bound to happen regularly. It is not a onetime phenomenon. It is a regular feature of any stock. Sooner or later, everyone has to come back to their home – the way I did."

Stock homecoming is not a onetime phenomenon.

Stock homecoming is not a onetime phenomenon. It will happen regularly in the life of a stock.

Once you have entered the stock at the right price, do not be too concerned with missing a homecoming.

"Hmm…"

"And last, but not the least, have you analyzed the impact of selling one asset type (stocks) and moving the funds to another asset type (say a fixed deposit) on your portfolio? Will it change your portfolio balance? If it does, is it for good? Or will it make your portfolio more imbalanced than it is right now?"

"Portfolio balance?"

"Balancing your portfolio is one of the key factors that determine your money's wealth creation ability in the long run. *An imbalanced portfolio can only yield muted returns.* An optimally balanced portfolio will continue to fetch great returns in spite of the market scenario. As homework for you, I recommend that you must study more about balancing your portfolio."

LESSON 77

A regularly balanced portfolio is vital for optimal wealth generation.
An imbalanced portfolio will yield muted returns.
An optimally balanced portfolio will continue to fetch great returns in spite of the market scenario.

"Sure, I will. Today, I am not even sure what selling you will do to my portfolio balance. So, what do you propose should be the minimum waiting period before we sell?"

"Unless there is an emergency life situation, you should not think about selling before 12 months. Re-assess my average cost, market price as well as the revised intrinsic value after 12 months and then see what you need to do."

"OK, then it makes sense for me to come back to you only after 12 months, unless there is anything drastic happening in between, right?"

"That sounds logical. However, do keep a watch for buying opportunities, as well as for some serious spike because of unexpected events, during that period."

"Sure, thanks, Yes Bank."

"No worries. Will catch you soon, Gobind."

Gobind logged off. He was now part of an emotional roller coaster, for which there was no defined end date.

He was nowhere to be heard for the next many months, until he showed up exactly after a year of his first purchase.

"Hey buddy, how have you been? It has been a real long time," I asked Gobind.

"I've been good. It has been a year of only wait and watch for me..."

"OK, can you show me your latest table and graph, please?"

"Yeah, I was about to do that anyway. Here you go..."

Month	Average Cost (AC)	Market Price (MP)	Intrinsic Value (IV)	AC-MP Factor ©	IV-MP Factor ©
Initial	765	765	835	0.00%	9.15%
17-Dec-2014 (Before)	765	670	835	12.42%	21.57%
17-Dec-2014 (After)	749	670	835	10.55%	22.03%
31-Dec-2014	749	773	835	-3.20%	8.28%
31-Jan-2015	749	863	835	-15.22%	-3.74%
28-Feb-2015	749	863	835	-15.22%	-3.74%
4-Mar-2015	749	900	835	-20.16%	-8.68%
31-Mar-2015	749	817	835	-9.08%	2.40%
30-Apr-2015	749	840	835	-12.15%	-0.67%
31-May-2015	749	882	835	-17.76%	-6.28%
30-Jun-2015	749	843	835	-12.55%	-1.07%
31-Jul-2015	749	829	835	-10.68%	0.80%
31-Aug-2015	749	690	835	7.88%	19.36%
30-Sep-2015	749	730	835	2.54%	14.02%
31-Oct-2015	749	759	835	-1.34%	10.15%
30-Nov-2015	749	767	835	-2.40%	9.08%

Table 52: *AC-MP-IV Tracking© 12-month status for Yes Bank*
(November 30, 2015)

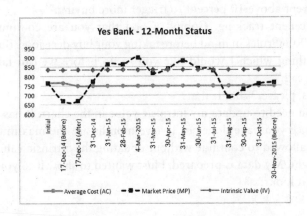

Chart 5: *AC-MP-IV Tracking©12-month status for Yes Bank*
(November 30, 2015)

"Interesting plot... do you have any observations on this 12-month status chart, Gobind?"

"Yes, I do have a few. You see, YB, you never touched the peak of March 4, 2015 when I came to you with my first sell request."

"Right, and do you repent that?"

"I think I do to an extent, but it is just my faith in you that is keeping me here, hanging around with no end in sight."

"Ah! Faith is a big thing. Keep it up! Keep hanging in there till the storm has gone and sanity has prevailed. That is what is going to make you wealthy, Gobind. Keep the faith alive. Hang on there, a bit more..."

"Yeah," said Gobind. He did not seem as excited as he was on March 4, 2015. His emotions were driven by the stock price movement. He was sitting on the front seat of a roller coaster whose engine is driven by my market price. He would need to overcome this dependency of emotions based on stock market price movements. He will need all the faith to be able to overcome that.

Gobind continued, "and that's why I did not sell you. There were no new buying opportunities either, since you never dipped below the low of December 17, 2014. You have just been hovering around your intrinsic value. There were chances somewhere in August, 2015 when your price came down to INR 690 or so, but then AC-MP factor© never went above 10 percent to trigger more buying."

"Excellent tracking, Gobind. Good that you are continuing to keep WRCA©rules in mind before taking your buy decisions. But there is one thing which I would like you to do before we can take any further call."

"Yes, please. What is that?"

"You need to update my intrinsic value in the chart. It has been a year since you have done so. Twelve months are the maximum you can be allowed to continue without updating the intrinsic value."

"Right. My data is prepared. I just wanted to show it to you. Here is how it looks..."

The Journey Begins	
Stock	Yes Bank (NSE:YESBANK)
Purchase date	5-Dec-2014
Number of shares	53
CMP (per share)	INR 765
Purchase amount	= 765*53 = INR 40,545
WRCA © Opportunity – I	
Date	17-Dec-2014
CMP	INR 670
New Number of Shares	= 53+11 = 64
New Average Cost	= INR 40,545 + 7,370 = INR 47,915
New Avg. Cost per share	= 47915 / 64 = INR 749
Recalculating Intrinsic Value after Year 1	
EPS (2014-15)	49.34
EPS-GR(up to 2014-15)	= (49.34/2.20) ^ (1/9) = 22.43^0.111 = 1.413 = 41.30% growth
Current P/E (as on Nov 2015)	= 767/41.3 = 18.57
Avg. P/E (2005-06 to 2014-15)	18.06 (Intrinsic P/E)
Intrinsic Value	= 18.06*49.34 = INR 891.08

Actual EPS

In continuation from Round-2 Step-4

INR 767 is the CMP

After incl. 13.40 (avg. P/E for 2014-15) to the prev. average

Table 53: *Recalculating intrinsic value after 12 months for Yes Bank (November 30, 2015)*

Financial Year	Apr	May	Jun	Jul	Aug	Sep	Oct	Nov	Dec	Jan	Feb	Mar	Avg. Price	EPS	P/E
2014/15	440	569	542	541	572	559	684	710	773	863	863	817	**661.09**	**49.34**	**13.40**

Table 54: *Calculating P/E for 2014-15 for Yes Bank (November 30, 2015)*

"Great Gobind. You are now a master in your calculations, which tells me how well you have understood the concepts. So your revised intrinsic value to be tracked now is INR 891.08. Can I also see your updated chart please?"

"Yes, here you go…"

Month	Average Cost (AC)	Market Price (MP)	Intrinsic Value (IV)	AC-MP Factor ©	IV-MP Factor ©
Initial	765	765	835	0.00%	9.15%
17-Dec-14 (Before)	765	670	835	12.42%	21.57%
17-Dec-14 (After)	749	670	835	10.55%	22.03%
31-Dec-14	749	773	835	-3.20%	8.28%
31-Jan-15	749	863	835	-15.22%	-3.74%
28-Feb-15	749	863	835	-15.22%	-3.74%
04-Mar-15	749	900	835	-20.16%	-8.68%
31-Mar-15	749	817	835	-9.08%	2.40%
30-Apr-15	749	840	835	-12.15%	-0.67%
31-May-15	749	882	835	-17.76%	-6.28%
30-Jun-15	749	843	835	-12.55%	-1.07%
31-Jul-15	749	829	835	-10.68%	0.80%
31-Aug-15	749	690	835	7.88%	19.36%
30-Sep-15	749	730	835	2.54%	
31-Oct-15	749	759	835	-1.34%	10.15%
30-Nov-2015 (Before)	749	767	835	-2.40%	9.08%
30-Nov-2015 (After)	749	767	891	-2.40%	16.56%

Updated Intrinsic Value

Table 55: *AC-MP-IV Tracking© with updated Intrinsic Value for Yes Bank Stock (November 30, 2015)*

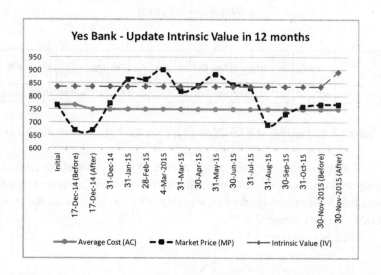

Chart 6: *AC-MP-IV Tracking© with updated intrinsic value for Yes Bank (November 30, 2015)*

"Super, now note what is happening. Although there has been a homecoming once or twice in the very first year, which we had to let go for multiple reasons, the key point here is that your intrinsic value is going up, and average cost is coming down. The gap between the two represents your potential profit or gains. This means that whenever you get the next homecoming, you are in for a much fatter profits, much higher than what you planned for, when you first purchased me."

"Wow, this tracking really gives me the complete picture. So, what should be my next target: wait for the next homecoming and keep looking at opportunities to reduce my average cost?"

"Yes, but you have to be careful of one thing. Over time, the fundamentals of the stock may change."

"I hear this quite often. But tell me, what do we really mean by the fundamentals of a stock changing over time?"

"See Gobind, We purchase the stock initially after having been convinced ourselves of various factors over and above the current market price and intrinsic value. Some of these were the quality of management, the macroeconomic scenario in which the company operates, the business potential, the long-term competitive advantage etc. One or many of these may change over time – because of technology disruption, a new competitor, management reshuffling, new laws passed by the Government, global political situations and a host of other uncontrollable reasons."

"Right. I agree that it is possible. So, what is likely to be the first visible sign for these fundamentals to change over time?"

"You see, with experience, you become the best judge of these fundamental changes. It is important that you keep a track of the news from the companies you are invested in."

"And how do I do that?"

"Read their annual financial reports, go through quarterly results to see if the company is on track or not, subscribe to news about your stock via some financial portals like *moneycontrol.com*, watch some financial channels on TV. This is what you can surely do, and do so pretty easily."

"Ah OK! Tracking at this level for all the companies that I have invested in: won't that be a tough task?"

"Yes, it can become quite cumbersome if you are invested in too many companies. And that is why I advise not to spread too much. Select a limited number of companies and then go deep. Invest more on dips rather than buying new companies."

"Yes, makes perfect sense, and how much would be too many companies for me?"

"Well Gobind, I would never recommend holding more than 20

carefully selected companies at any given point in time. With anything more than that, you will end up with a zoo in which none of the animals would get the attention they deserve. It is like being a juggler with too many balls in the air. You do not end dropping just one or two – you drop them all. But this is also easier said than done. You will always have that temptation to buy a new set of problems than to fix the old set. You ought to have immense self-control to be able to implement this tightly."

"OK. I get that point. But I heard that we also need to diversify. Don't we? Aren't you limiting our diversification by restricting the number of companies?"

"Yes, you must diversify, but not more in the number of stocks you hold. Diversifying more than these is like a protection you are seeking for your ignorance. Diversification makes very little sense for those who know what they are doing. Great successes of life are made by concentration and not by scattering too much. Rather, think about diversification in the industries to which your 20 stocks belong. Not all industries are likely to grow at the same pace in every age."

LESSON 78

Diversify, not much with the number of stocks, but with the set of industries you hold.

20 stocks is a big enough portfolio for regular monitoring. Do not diversify beyond that.

But ensure that these 20 stocks do not overexpose you to one or two industries only.

"Interesting point. I will keep that in mind. By the way, is there anything specific information you want me to read in the financial reports?"

"Yes, start reading them backwards."

"Backwards? Why?"

"Because anything that the company does not want you to find is buried in the back."

"Wow. What else?"

"Read the footnotes carefully, watch out for disclaimers and disclosures and go through the risk factors. Do not read with the intent that you doubt the company and do not wish to buy the stock, but with the intent to make sure that you continue the long-term association with this company."

"OK, will take care of these points. But tell me, what happens if I still miss seeing the initial signs of fundamentals getting deviated from what I originally thought?"

"If you miss the initial signs, it is quite likely that in such cases, you will see the after effects of those on your intrinsic value. You might find your intrinsic value coming down, and that is an alarming sign indeed – if a stock starts to lose its intrinsic value."

LESSON 79

A stock losing its intrinsic value is an alarming sign.

A stock starting to lose intrinsic value demands prompt action.

An in-depth study of the reasons is a must, and if the reasons point towards instability or weakened stock fundamentals, exiting the stock must be considered as one of the action items, irrespective of the current market price or average cost.

"So, re-calculation of intrinsic value is a must, not only from the perspective of viewing the right information in the chart or booking profits, but also for preventing losses, right?"

"Absolutely, if you find the intrinsic value coming down, you will have to get deeper into the problem and take immediate action. And if your study reveals an alarming story, or if the intrinsic value starts to inch close to your average cost, then you might even consider exiting your stock – ignoring the capital gains that you had planned for, when you had initially invested in it."

"OK, so are you saying that I must take prompt action, even if that means selling the stock at lower than planned margins or even at negative margins?"

"Yes, of course. No matter, how careful you have been with your calculations, one risk that no investor can eliminate is the risk of going wrong. The probability of making at least one mistake at some point of your investing life is virtually 100 percent and the factors controlling this may be completely out of your control. But on your first knowledge of this fact, quick action is the key. You see, the moment your intrinsic value dips below the current market price of the stock, it is anyway a virtual homecoming situation, though not very good news for you. Since, it is the intrinsic value that has dipped to touch the current market price, rather than the current market price elevating to touch the intrinsic value. In either case, it is a homecoming – and therefore a trigger to sell."

LESSON 80

Get ready to sell if the intrinsic value starts to dip below market price or average cost.

A dipping intrinsic value is an ominous sign.

If the intrinsic value dips below either of market price or average cost, get mentally prepared to sell post in-depth investigation.

"Ah, OK."

"This will not happen usually, but just in case this happens, you know that you have to be mentally prepared to sell the stock if the stock price is hovering above the intrinsic value. Selling at this point would mean selling the stock probably at 0 percent profit or even at a loss after one year of investment. But that is the risk that you always carry with stock investments. Now, you are a business owner, and every business carries these kinds of risks."

"Hmm... One word of advice for me?"

"At all stages, you have got to stay focused on your AC-MP-IV tracking© chart and cut off your intervention of media, news, friends and financial experts."

LESSON 81

Stock investing isn't about winning every battle. It is also about losing a few battles to win the war.

Get mentally prepared. There will be stocks which you will have to exit quickly – even if it means booking losses.

The idea is to stay invested only as long as the fundamentals hold good.

"Right."

"Remember that there are good chances that as your intrinsic value dips, the market price will also take a beating and it may very well happen that both the intrinsic value and the market price start dipping in unison – and you never see a situation where market price is higher than intrinsic value."

"Yes, what do I do in that case?"

"See, in general, intrinsic value coming down in itself is an ominous sign. So, in most situations where you see intrinsic value coming down, get mentally prepared to sell. But if the intrinsic value has come down close to your average cost, then you should be ready to sell the stock at its current level, irrespective of its current market price."

"Hmm, I get it. Anyway, I will keep these things in my mind. I have noted a few vital points as well. But for now, you are doing very good in terms of intrinsic value, and there seems to be no reason to worry for me. I will take your leave for now, YB."

"Sure, Gobind. Keep in touch. Keep monitoring."

Gobind left with a very cautious state of mind. He seemed apprehensive about selling stocks at a loss, especially after the hard work he had already put in. But it was important for him to understand that stock market is not only about winning every small battle. It is also about losing a few battles in an attempt to win the war.

Hardly a month had passed when Gobind came back. It was January 20, 2016 and he seemed excited and worried at the same time – a typical symptom of someone on a stock market roller coaster. Was it the end of my journey? Only time would have told.

"What excites you, Gobind?" I was the first one to shoot a message, trying to start the conversation on a positive note.

"Frankly YB, for the first time in my life, I am excited as well as worried about falling stocks."

"Why are you worried, Gobind? If you trust your calculations, then neither spikes nor dips should worry you. Both are awesome opportunities for you. Isn't it?"

"Why worried? It is easier said than done, Mr. Yes Bank. It is not the first time that you are falling. You have already fallen more than 15 percent below the average cost. I am really worried whether it is really worth putting more money in you. I do not know how long will you keep falling. Or should I rather invest more money in any assured investment option like a fixed deposit? I am confused. I know you will tell me to have belief in our calculation. But it is so difficult to continue to have that belief when all I see is that you are either stagnant or falling."

"I can understand your emotion of fear and lack of belief. There is no shortcut to develop that belief, except for having faith and going ahead."

"Yeah, maybe you are right. I will trust you, yet again, and invest. Once I put a belief in our calculation, I do become excited about this entire fall in your current market price. I see this as another wonderful buying opportunity. I just saw a dip which is close to 15 percent below our average cost. Here is the data and chart that might interest you:"

Month	Average Cost (AC)	Market Price (MP)	Intrinsic Value (IV)	AC-MP Factor ©	IV-MP Factor ©
Initial	765	765	835	0.00%	9.15%
17-Dec-14 (Before)	765	670	835	12.42%	21.57%
17-Dec-14 (After)	749	670	835	10.55%	22.03%
31-Dec-14	749	773	835	-3.20%	8.28%
31-Jan-15	749	863	835	-15.22%	-3.74%
28-Feb-15	749	863	835	-15.22%	-3.74%
04-Mar-15	749	900	835	-20.16%	-8.68%
31-Mar-15	749	817	835	-9.08%	2.40%
30-Apr-15	749	840	835	-12.15%	-0.67%
31-May-15	749	882	835	-17.76%	-6.28%
30-Jun-15	749	843	835	-12.55%	-1.07%
31-Jul-15	749	829	835	-10.68%	0.80%
31-Aug-15	749	690	835	7.88%	19.36%
30-Sep-15	749	730	835	2.54%	14.02%
31-Oct-15	749	759	835	-1.34%	10.%
30-Nov-2015 (Before)	749	767	835	-2.40%	.08%
30-Nov-2015 (After)	749	767	891	-2.40%	16.56%
31-Dec-2015	749	726	891	3.07%	22.03%
20-Jan-2016	749	640	891	14.55%	33.51%

AC-MP Factor of 10%+ is WRCA trigger

IV-MP Factor of 20%+ guides us to buy 33.5% more shares

Table 56: *AC-MP-IV Tracking© WRCA© Opportunity-II for Yes Bank*
(January 20, 2016)

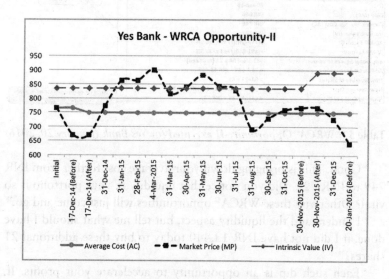

Chart 7: *AC-MP-IV Tracking© WRCA© Opportunity-II for Yes Bank*
(January 20, 2016)

"Great, this definitely looks another WRCA© opportunity. The AC-MP factor© in the table is running at 14.55 percent which is more than 10 percent, and thus is a trigger to implement WRCA©. This is also our first buy of the month – so I do not see any bottlenecks. The

IV-MP factor© tells us to buy 33.5 percent more."

"Yes, I calculated the same numbers. Here is how the situation will look post our new purchase:

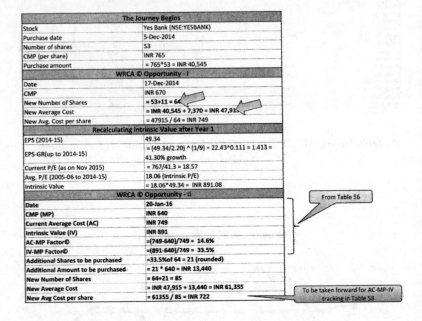

The Journey Begins	
Stock	Yes Bank (NSE:YESBANK)
Purchase date	5-Dec-2014
Number of shares	53
CMP (per share)	INR 765
Purchase amount	= 765*53 = INR 40,545
WRCA © Opportunity - I	
Date	17-Dec-2014
CMP	INR 670
New Number of Shares	= 53+11 = 64
New Average Cost	= INR 40,545 + 7,370 = INR 47,915
New Avg. Cost per share	= 47915 / 64 = INR 749
Recalculating Intrinsic Value after Year 1	
EPS (2014-15)	49.34
EPS-GR(up to 2014-15)	= (49.34/2.20) ^ (1/9) = 22.43^0.111 = 1.413 = 41.30% growth
Current P/E (as on Nov 2015)	= 767/41.3 = 18.57
Avg. P/E (2005-06 to 2014-15)	18.06 (Intrinsic P/E)
Intrinsic Value	= 18.06*49.34 = INR 891.08
WRCA © Opportunity - II	
Date	20-Jan-16
CMP (MP)	INR 640
Current Average Cost (AC)	INR 749
Intrinsic Value (IV)	INR 891
AC-MP Factor©	=(749-640)/749 = 14.6%
IV-MP Factor©	=(891-640)/749 = 33.5%
Additional Shares to be purchased	=33.5%of 64 = 21 (rounded)
Additional Amount to be purchased	= 21 * 640 = INR 13,440
New Number of Shares	= 64+21 = 85
New Average Cost	= INR 47,915 + 13,440 = INR 61,355
New Avg Cost per share	= 61355 / 85 = INR 722

From Table 56

To be taken forward for AC-MP-IV tracking in Table 58

Table 57: WRCA© Opportunity-II executed for Yes Bank (January 20, 2016)

"Good. This is bringing down your average cost further from INR 749 to INR 722. Did you notice that liquidity in your portfolio is so vital? Otherwise these WRCA© opportunities will just come and go."

"I understand the liquidity aspect, but tell me what should I have done, if I did not have INR 13,440 today to buy these additional 21 shares?"

"Each such dip is an opportunity to accelerate your profits. If, for any reason, you cannot spare INR 13,440 today, you can invest whatever you can. If you can manage INR 10,000 – that is also fine. It is just that you might miss the most optimal returns, but that is still better than missing the entire opportunity to bring down your average cost."

"Ah OK. For now, I can manage this liquidity and I will go ahead with this additional investment of INR 13,440."

Gobind went ahead to purchase another 21 shares and to bring down his average cost, though with some heavy feeling. His faith was increasing but wasn't yet there. But he was doing what he was supposed to do – *buying low*, and waiting patiently for *selling high*. Here is what he showed me as the table and chart post this purchase:

Month	Average Cost (AC)	Market Price (MP)	Intrinsic Value (IV)	AC-MP Factor ©	IV-MP Factor ©
Initial	765	765	835	0.00%	9.15%
17-Dec-14 (Before)	765	670	835	12.42%	21.57%
17-Dec-14 (After)	749	670	835	10.55%	22.03%
31-Dec-14	749	773	835	-3.20%	8.28%
31-Jan-15	749	863	835	-15.22%	-3.74%
28-Feb-15	749	863	835	-15.22%	-3.74%
04-Mar-15	749	900	835	-20.16%	-8.68%
31-Mar-15	749	817	835	-9.08%	2.40%
30-Apr-15	749	840	835	-12.15%	-0.67%
31-May-15	749	882	835	-17.76%	-6.28%
30-Jun-15	749	843	835	-12.55%	-1.07%
31-Jul-15	749	829	835	-10.68%	0.80%
31-Aug-15	749	690	835	7.88%	19.36%
30-Sep-15	749	730	835	2.54%	14.02%
31-Oct-15	749	759	835	-1.34%	10.15%
30-Nov-2015 (Before)	749	767	835	-2.40%	9.08%
30-Nov-2015 (After)	749	767	891	-2.40%	16.56%
31-Dec-2015	749	726	891	3.07%	22.03%
20-Jan-2016 (Before)	749	640	891	14.55%	33.51%
20-Jan-2016 (After)	722	640	891	11.36%	34.76%

Average Cost of Purchase comes down

Table 58: *AC-MP-IV Tracking© WRCA© Opportunity-II executed for Yes Bank Stock (January 20, 2016)*

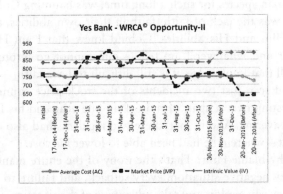

Chart 8: *AC-MP-IV Tracking© WRCA© Opportunity-II executed for Yes Bank Stock (January 20, 2016)*

"Cool, feels good to see the increasing gap between the intrinsic value (IV) and average cost (AC). Keep monitoring this chart. Wish

you good luck with your next homecoming or further WRCA©
implementation very soon."

"Thanks. But frankly, I am not sure if I will have the guts to invest
even more on further dips... I just hope some sanity prevails."

"I can understand. This strategy requires you to have 100 percent
belief in homecoming. Without that, it is easy to lose track and miss
on such opportunities."

"I do have faith, YB. But I really do not know what is getting me
anxious whenever the price dips nowadays?"

"That is a human psychology that you all have developed over the
last few centuries."

"What is that?"

"The pain of a financial loss to you is twice as intense as the
pleasure of an equivalent gain. I mean, an INR 20,000 loss wields an
emotional wallop twice as powerful as the feeling of INR 20,000 gain.
This could be perhaps because the gain is an intrinsic expectation
when you invest. Therefore, most investors either sell out in such dips
or refuse to buy more. But have 100 percent faith in what I am telling
you, and you will never be disappointed in the long run."

"Hmm. Keeping my fingers crossed!"

Gobind logged off. The same disease that has been haunting the
entire human species for such a long time, was haunting Gobind too.
And that was the lack of faith; faith in their own abilities, and even
faith in Him and His abilities. Gobind knew that I am His direct
messenger and whatever I am telling him cannot go wrong, but in
spite of all that knowledge, it is still difficult to have faith.

He had seen just two incidents of the stock price coming down
after investing over a span of more than one year and his faith was
already wavering. And in fact, these two incidents had also come for
his benefit – wherein he had been able to lower his cost.

But why blame Him? That's the irony of the entire mankind. *He*
gives every negative situation, every setback, and failure to humans,
so that they can exploit and take advantage of the situation and come
out wiser, stronger, better. *We* give it to them for their benefit, but they
feel otherwise.

A parent ensures that the child is immunized against all known
deadly diseases, though the child might feel the pain of the syringe and
feel that the parents are his worst enemies at that moment. Sooner or

later, the child realizes that the pain was worth it. Not only worth it, it was necessary for his own survival.

Similarly in life, in moments of pain, if someone remembers Him and invests his complete faith in Him, that is the person who stands to benefit the maximum with His blessings. Faith is that vital for success in life, as also in stock investing.

Gobind somehow held on to my spiraling down prices in spite of all negative media news being spread about my downfall, various charts predicting that the lower threshold had been broken, and his all-weather friends, who had been holding me for a long time, already selling me at some fair profit.

Even with diminished faith, if one can just hold on long enough, one is sure to be rewarded. And rewards came much sooner and grander than what Gobind would have ever thought of...

He came back after three months, at the end of April 2016, and seemed too excited to contain his feelings.

"Hello, Yes Bank. You there?" He fired in our chat window.

"Of course, I am here for you Gobind," I responded. Even before my message would have reached him, I saw the below table and chart on my screen, and could understand the reason for his excitement straightaway.

"I am all set to sell you now. Have a look at this table and graph. The homecoming has occurred once again and I cannot wait any more. Should I sell all, or only a part of it? That is all I want to know from you. Please tell me, quickly!" exclaimed Gobind, running desperately short of patience now.

Month	Average Cost (AC)	Market Price (MP)	Intrinsic Value (IV)	AC-MP Factor ©	IV-MP Factor ©
Initial	765	765	835	0.00%	9.15%
17-Dec-14 (Before)	765	670	835	12.42%	21.57%
17-Dec-14 (After)	749	670	835	10.55%	22.03%
31-Dec-14	749	773	835	-3.20%	8.28%
31-Jan-15	749	863	835	-15.22%	-3.74%
28-Feb-15	749	863	835	-15.22%	-3.74%
04-Mar-15	749	900	835	-20.16%	-8.68%
31-Mar-15	749	817	835	-9.08%	2.40%
30-Apr-15	749	840	835	-12.15%	-0.67%
31-May-15	749	882	835	-17.76%	-6.28%
30-Jun-15	749	843	835	-12.55%	-1.07%
31-Jul-15	749	829	835	-10.68%	0.80%
31-Aug-15	749	690	835	7.88%	19.36%
30-Sep-15	749	730	835	2.54%	14.02%
31-Oct-15	749	759	835	-1.34%	10.15%
30-Nov-2015 (Before)	749	767	835	-2.40%	9.08%
30-Nov-2015 (After)	749	767	891	-2.40%	16.56%
31-Dec-2015	749	726	891	3.07%	22.03%
20-Jan-2016 (Before)	749	640	891	14.55%	33.51%
20-Jan-2016 (After)	722	640	891	11.36%	34.76%
31-Jan-2016	722	747	891	-3.46%	19.94%
28-Feb-2016	722	688	891	4.71%	28.12%
31-Mar-2016	722	865	891	-19.81%	3.60%
28-Apr-2016	722	944	891	-30.75%	-7.34%

Homecoming has occured yet again with CMP touching and exceeding Intrinsic Value

Table 59: *AC-MP-IV Tracking© at Sell Opportunity-II on Yes Bank*
(April 28, 2016)

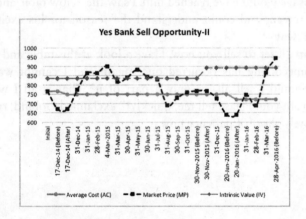

Chart 9: *AC-MP-IV Tracking© at Sell Opportunity-II on Yes Bank*
(April 28, 2016)

"Gobind, happy to see that you have been able to persist with me until now – overcoming the seesaw ride so far. This definitely seems a strong case to sell. But remember that whenever you are on the verge of taking a key decision of buying or selling, make sure that you always have the latest intrinsic value with you. We are already entering May. Last year's financial results must have been announced. I would suggest that you please get the updated intrinsic value and plot it to the chart before you actually go and sell."

"Now, this is not done. The moment I update the intrinsic value, I might not be able to sell it, because the intrinsic value may also have gone up too."

"The choice is always with you, Gobind."

"You have an attitude, boss."

"No. In fact, I would welcome your decision no matter what."

"You know that I am not going to go against you. OK, let me collate the data to recalibrate the intrinsic value for now."

The Journey Begins	
Stock	Yes Bank (NSE:YESBANK)
Purchase date	5-Dec-2014
Number of shares	53
CMP (per share)	INR 765
Purchase amount	= 765*53 = INR 40,545
WRCA © Opportunity - I	
Date	17-Dec-2014
CMP	INR 670
New Number of Shares	= 53+11 = 64
New Average Cost	= INR 40,545 + 7,370 = INR 47,915
New Avg. Cost per share	= 47915 / 64 = INR 749
Recalculating Intrinsic Value after Year 1	
EPS (2014-15)	49.34
EPS-GR(up to 2014-15)	= (49.34/2.20) ^ (1/9) = 22.43^0.111 = 1.413 = 41.30% growth
Current P/E (as on Nov 2015)	= 767/41.3 = 18.57
Avg. P/E (2005-06 to 2014-15)	18.06 (Intrinsic P/E)
Intrinsic Value	= 18.06*49.34 = INR 891.08
WRCA © Opportunity - II	
Date	20-Jan-16
CMP (MP)	INR 640
New Number of Shares	= 64+21 = 85
New Average Cost	= INR 47,915 + 13,440 = INR 61,355
New Avg Cost per share	= 61355 / 85 = INR 722
Recalculating Intrinsic Value at Sell Opportunity-II	
EPS (2015-16)	60.62
EPS-GR (up to 2015-16)	= (60.62/2.20) ^ (1/10) = 27.55^0.100 = 1.393 = 39.30% growth
Current P/E (as on April 2016)	=944/60.62 = 15.57
Avg. P/E (2005-06 to 2015-16)	17.83 (Intrinsic P/E)
Intrinsic Value	= 17.83*60.62 = INR 1081.07

Actual EPS

In continuation from Round-2 Step-4

INR 944 is the CMP

After incl. 15.57 (avg. P/E for 2015-16) to the prev. average

INR 1081 is the new Intrinsic Value

Table 60: *Re-calculating Intrinsic value at Sell Opportunity-II for Yes Bank (April 28, 2016)*

"Oh man, this is what I feared the most. The intrinsic value has gone up, yet again, and it is way beyond your current market price. This means that I cannot sell, it seems. Look at the below table and chart:

Month	Average Cost (AC)	Market Price (MP)	Intrinsic Value (IV)	AC-MP Factor ©	IV-MP Factor ©
Initial	765	765	835	0.00%	9.15%
17-Dec-14 (Before)	765	670	835	12.42%	21.57%
17-Dec-14 (After)	749	670	835	10.55%	22.03%
31-Dec-14	749	773	835	-3.20%	8.28%
31-Jan-15	749	863	835	-15.22%	-3.74%
28-Feb-15	749	863	835	-15.22%	-3.74%
04-Mar-15	749	900	835	-20.16%	-8.68%
31-Mar-15	749	817	835	-9.08%	2.40%
30-Apr-15	749	840	835	-12.15%	-0.67%
31-May-15	749	882	835	-17.76%	-6.28%
30-Jun-15	749	843	835	-12.55%	-1.07%
31-Jul-15	749	829	835	-10.68%	0.80%
31-Aug-15	749	690	835	7.88%	19.36%
30-Sep-15	749	730	835	2.54%	14.02%
31-Oct-15	749	759	835	-1.34%	10.15%
30-Nov-2015 (Before)	749	767	835	-2.40%	9.08%
30-Nov-2015 (After)	749	767	891	-2.40%	16.56%
31-Dec-2015	749	726	891	3.07%	22.03%
20-Jan-2016 (Before)	749	640	891	14.55%	33.51%
20-Jan-2016 (After)	722	640	891	11.36%	34.76%
31-Jan-2016	722	747	891	-3.46%	19.94%
28-Feb-2016	722	688	891	4.71%	22%
31-Mar-2016	722	865	891	-19.81%	3.60%
28-Apr-2016 (Before)	722	944	891	-30.75%	-7.34%
28-Apr-2016 (After)	722	944	1081	-30.75%	18.98%

CMP is below the new Intrinsic Value.
Decision is 'No Sell'

Table 61: *AC-MP-IV Tracking© with updated Intrinsic Value for Yes Bank Stock (April 28, 2016)*

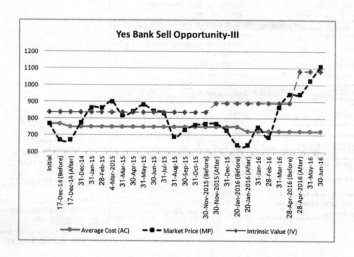

Chart 10: *AC-MP-IV Tracking© with updated Intrinsic Value for Yes Bank (April 28, 2016)*

"It is all for your good, Gobind. However, there is no need for either of us to get emotional. If you need the money, you are good to sell because, as of now, you are already making 30 percent profit in approximately 1.3 years of investment."

"Oh really?"

"Yes. My average cost is INR 722 while my current market price is INR 944, a neat 30 percent profit, and now no taxes on investment you did 12 months ago, though you might still have to pay some tax on the short-term gains arising of the investments that you did during the last 12 months – the ones that you did to reduce your average costs."

"Frankly, even if I have to pay a little bit of capital gains tax, I am tempted to sell at this lovely margin. I have never earned this much from any kind of investments; forget stocks, but from any other investment in my entire life. What if this stock plummets tomorrow? I won't even get this. And this stock has risen so sharply in the last couple of months. I do not think it can go much further."

"That risk is always there, Gobind. And that is precisely why most people don't make enough money in stocks. They enter and exit based on their feeling, the noise around them, their experiences, their urgency, their emotions and not their calculations."

"Are you saying that I should let this opportunity go?"

"That is what I would have done, unless of course there is a genuine reason to sell. Of the various reasons we discussed earlier: either an emergency or a need to rebalance your portfolio, or to invest in a more lucrative opportunity. Does your situation fall in any of those categories?"

"No."

"Then, I would recommend you keep moving on."

"Shit!" and Gobind closed the chat window.

Gobind was extremely frustrated, and that is natural to humans. They come with a bias and pre-conceived notion in their minds. They are not open-minded enough and are not prepared to listen to contrarian views – views that can only make them wiser in the long-run. But He has his own way of teaching them.

Gobind came back running after exactly two months.

"Boss, this visit is just for your information. I do not want any decision from you. I just want to give you a hug. Where are you? Is it possible for you to appear before me just one more time?"

"Hey, Gobind. What happened?"

"As if you don't know, YB."

I simply smiled.

"Look at this chart. We are past our revised intrinsic value also. Homecoming has happened yet again."

Month	Average Cost (AC)	Market Price (MP)	Intrinsic Value (IV)	AC-MP Factor ©	IV-MP Factor ©
Initial	765	765	835	0.00%	9.15%
17-Dec-14 (Before)	765	670	835	12.42%	21.57%
17-Dec-14 (After)	749	670	835	10.55%	22.03%
31-Dec-14	749	773	835	-3.20%	8.28%
31-Jan-15	749	863	835	-15.22%	-3.74%
28-Feb-15	749	863	835	-15.22%	-3.74%
04-Mar-15	749	900	835	-20.16%	-8.68%
31-Mar-15	749	817	835	-9.08%	2.40%
30-Apr-15	749	840	835	12.15%	-0.67%
31-May-15	749	882	835	-17.76%	-6.28%
30-Jun-15	749	843	835	-12.55%	-1.07%
31-Jul-15	749	829	835	-10.68%	0.80%
31-Aug-15	749	690	835	7.88%	19.36%
30-Sep-15	749	730	835	2.54%	14.02%
31-Oct-15	749	759	835	-1.34%	10.15%
30-Nov-2015 (Before)	749	767	835	-2.40%	9.08%
30-Nov-2015 (After)	749	767	891	-2.40%	16.56%
31-Dec-2015	749	726	891	3.07%	22.03%
20-Jan-2016 (Before)	749	640	891	14.55%	33.51%
20-Jan-2016 (After)	722	640	891	11.36%	34.76%
31-Jan-2016	722	747	891	-3.46%	19.94%
28-Feb-2016	722	688	891	4.71%	28.12%
31-Mar-2016	722	865	891	-19.81%	3.60%
28-Apr-2016 (Before)	722	944	891	-30.75%	
28-Apr-2016 (After)	722	944	1081	-30.75%	18.98%
31-May-2016	722	1026	1081	-42.11%	7.62%
30-Jun-2016	722	1111	1081	-53.88%	-4.16%

> Homecoming has occured yet again

Table 62: *AC-MP-IV Tracking©at Sell Opportunity-III on Yes Bank Stock (June 30, 2016)*

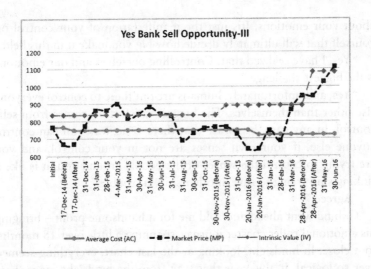

Chart 11: *AC-MP-IV Tracking©at Sell Opportunity-III on Yes Bank (June 30, 2016)*

"Wow! Good things always come to those who wait, provided of course that they have picked the right stock. And you did pick the right stock, Gobind."

"You are very right. I will always remember this lesson."

"Great! You are all set to sell, Gobind. And I assume that you have a reason to sell this time."

"Yes, my portfolio."

"What happened to your portfolio?"

"It has swollen more than what equity portion should be."

"Will selling me balance it?"

"Not fully, but to some extent. I have to sell a few more."

"Great. So you have been making good profits elsewhere as well and I am really happy about that."

"I have been using all the learning from you and applying them in all my stocks that I have been holding."

"Awesome. Go ahead then, Gobind. This might be our last ever chat."

"That is my only fear now, when I sell. I will never have your company. Who will answer my questions? Who will support me?"

"You. You have all the knowledge. You just need to be careful about your emotions. Itis just the manifestation of your control on yourself that will ultimately decide how big you make it in this field."

"Yes, I have realized that. Controlling ourselves and our emotions is the biggest challenge."

"Yes, and unfortunately, humans are out there to control everyone else other than themselves. The biggest satisfaction comes from self-control. In any case, be aware that there is no way you can control anyone else. If your own senses are not in your control, and you are trying to control the senses of the people around you, it is like a sinking ship trying to save another ship in trouble."

"Agreed."

Gobind went ahead and sold me for a handsome profit – bringing his emotional roller coaster journey, spanning a little over 18 months, to a close. In hindsight, looking at the last chart, everything seemed ever so logical. It always is that way from the hindsight, since there are no emotions involved when looking back. And that is the reason it is so easy for the TV channels to analyze and report what has already happened. It is an absolutely different ball game when you go out and play with your foresight.

It was time to say good bye to Gobind. But just before that, I felt it was prudent to push through some of the most important aspects that he must keep in mind – skills that will differentiate him from the crowd.

The parting lesson

"**O**K Gobind. A couple of last minute suggestions before I sign off..."

"Please. That'd be my honour."

"First, you are fortunate enough to be yielding more than 50 percent profits and selling off the stock in less than 1.5 years' time frame. This fairy tale may not repeat in many other stocks. In some cases, you may get more than the required yield but the patience required may be much longer than 1.5 years. In some other cases, you will sell at less than the planned yield. In a few cases, you will be forced to sell them in loss as well. You, therefore, need to practice a lot of self-control and continue to have belief in your calculations."

"I agree. I can see that some of the other stocks that I had purchased are still far off from being in a position to be sold."

"Yes, and if there is one trait that is most difficult to inculcate, it is the monumental patience that you need to exhibit. Stocks may move up to the intrinsic value today, next week, next month, next year, and sometimes even in the next decade. It may trade sideways for seven years and then quadruple in a few months. There is simply no way to find out when will this happen. There will be frustrating times when our strategy will yield lesser returns than other short-term strategies. There will also be times when your friends will be talking big profits and you wouldn't be able find a single stock worth buying. You will be tested quite frequently for your patience and faith in your own calculations."

"I completely understand your point. I am not sure whether I should I ask this, but could you also share with me some technique to practice self-control? I realize that as my weak area and I was getting reluctant to buy more at dips and was too eager to sell quickly in your case. I want to conquer myself. Tell me the way. I am ready to put in the hard work."

"If you are serious, then you must start practicing it with those little things in life."

"Like?"

"Which is your favourite snack, which hardly adds any nutritional value to your daily diet?"

"Biscuits. I eat too many of them in a day. And I know they do more harm than good."

"Leave them!"

"Means?"

"Means stop eating them from today itself. Can you try and practice this?"

"OK for how long? Will that increase my patience and improve my self-control?"

"You leave them today, for the rest of your life."

"What?"

"Yes. Why is this decision so tough for you to take, Gobind? I mean, you already know that it is not good for you, and it is your sense of taste that pulls you towards it. Start controlling your senses. You are the master. Do not behave like a slave to your senses. C'mon! Take charge of your own senses, at least."

LESSON 82

Rigorously practice self-control to succeed in stocks.

You are the master and your senses must obey you. It is not the other way round.

Practice self-control rigorously to succeed big time in stocks.

"Seems tough."

"It is the easiest experiment to start with. Controlling greed and insulating from outside noise is much tougher. Start with this, and slowly, keep adding one thing to your list every month – something that you like to eat but does not really add any nutritional value. Keep leaving them for the rest of your life, and see your self-control shooting up."

"Very interesting, as well as challenging. I will take this up."

"Great! Wish you luck!"

"Thanks, buddy!"

"The other advice I have for you is that once you have sold me, never try and look back at how I have been performing, unless you buy me again and I am a part of your portfolio. It is possible that I may go up or down after you sell me. That should not waiver your confidence in your calculations and should never influence your future buy and sell decisions on other stocks. You bought me and are now selling, after achieving your target, and that's it. Only those who are not confident of what they are doing, go and look back at a sold stock."

LESSON 83

Do not look back at the price of a sold stock with the intent of validating your decision.

Your buying or selling decisions are based on certain fundamentals which were valid only until you possessed the stock.

A post-mortem should not influence your future calculations.

"Point taken. I will remember that."

"Good. And stay humble, at all times. It is very easy to make a few quick gains and feel smug. Stay focused and continue to seek opinion and information that do not go with your confirmation bias. Do not overrule them. Consider them, carefully evaluate them with an open mind and then take a decision. In fact, go and update your bias and beliefs if the evidence suggests so."

"Point taken."

"One more point. You are a value investor now, which means that you do not jump on to the bandwagon. You insulate yourself from the noise, do your calculations and take a decision. When you do that, mostly you will find yourself as a contrarian. Get comfortable in that zone."

"This is engrained in me now!"

"Wonderful! And remember that you are not here to beat anyone else in terms of the returns you are able to accumulate. You don't have to beat your friend, neighbour or even the market index. The whole point of investing is not in beating anyone, but in creating enough wealth for yourself and your needs."

"Awesome. I loved this one."

"Good. And last, but not the least, with wealth, you will get the power to make choices others cannot, to make decisions that others find difficult. If you do not channelize that power to make a difference to the lives of people outside your immediate circle, of what use is the rebellious streak you displayed as youth, of what use has been my 200 years of effort, and of what use will be your money if it cannot help the living beings around you? All of this is His creation – each one created with immense love and care by none other than Him. So, my last request to you is not to forget your promise to me."

"That's a gentleman's word, till my last breath, I will keep spreading your message and learnings to the entire world, so that they can all make money and make this world a better place to live. Money in the right hands can do great service to this planet."

"I trust you, Gobind. You have been a great student. Good bye then!"

The window flashed and closed.

It was the end, end of a two-year long relationship that taught Gobind the most effective way to make money from stocks. Or was it a beginning of a new era, a new world? Only time would tell that."

On my side of the universe, I had this meeting with Him, which I had been longing for more than 200 years now.

"Almighty…"

"Yes, Stock. Come on in."

"Majesty, our proof of concept is over."

"Oh, that is great news."

"Gobind has sold off his holding at a handsome 53.88 percent profit in 1.5 years. He has promised to spread the learnings across to the world. And I trust him as my student."

"That's very nice to hear, Stock. Do keep me posted of the progress," responded the Almighty.

"Yes, Boss," I said as I took leave of Him.

Both of us knew that the mission was far from over.

This was just the beginning of a new era, where people on the planet Earth would become wiser and richer. They would start living their lives, not in the pursuit of money, but in the pursuit of finding their true self – something that needs them to invest a lot of time with themselves. They would be able to spare that time once they have accumulated enough wealth. This wealth, along with the passive income it generates, would take care of their day-to-day needs. This would spare them the time to elevate themselves by elevating lives of others around them.

A lot will depend on what Gobind was going to do with this mission.

Over the next few months, Gobind streamlined the entire process, experimented with a few more stocks and started to look for opportunities that can help him spread the message. When it is God's work, avenues open up of their own.

Coincidentally, Gobind connected with a dreamer, author and social worker – Manoj, who helped him create a website where all the stock selection and monitoring calculations could be automated for use by the general public. Gobind actually fell in love with the process. His love for the process and people far exceeded his love for the proceeds. And when humans do that, miracles happen and proceeds follow them of their own. He became financially free, quit his job and dedicated himself for the upliftment of the world around him.

However small his attempts may be, he kept his promise. And the Almighty has special love and blessings for all humans who are ready to keep their promise made to themselves. If someone like Gobind takes one step, He is ready to take ten steps forward and help.

How He helps may not be explicit: it could be a message on your WhatsApp that hits you, a thought in your mind or someone coming and talking about the topic on whichyou always wanted a solution.

A thought was kindled in Gobind's mind about writing a book on this topic. That was one sure way to reach out to millions and billions out there – so that His message could spread. That is where Manoj agreed to write my life's journey as one of his bestselling books. I, lovingly referred to as Mr. Stock, must sign off now, for my role on this planet got over sometime back. I will continue to monitor the status frequently, but the primary responsibility is now with Gobind and many others like him who will get inspired, learn the basics of investing, make wealth and teach others around them – with the intent of elevating everyone's life. At some stage, people also need to realize that lives cannot be elevated in isolation. It is the society as a whole, which gets elevated. Individual wealth creation is a short term phenomenon since nature knows how to bring the state of the society back to equilibrium.

I am sure Gobind and Manoj's efforts would not go in vain. I and God look forward to meeting again someday in this beautiful world when they would be able to make a significant difference. There are many like Gobind and Manoj – they are just looking for an opportunity to beat the day-to-day chaos and compulsion to earn money and then help the people around them.

The world is made beautiful when people live with the intent of giving and not of taking. Those who give, also get more – because they are directly blessed by the biggest giver of all – and that is Him.

At no stage do we wish to claim that the methodology, techniques and practices mentioned in the book is the most optimum way to wealth generation in stocks. There never is any best way.

Readers of the book are recommended to weigh the reasoning given in the book against the contrary reasoning they will hear from most competent and experienced people in the market. In the end, each one of us must make our own decision and accept responsibility thereof.

We suggest that if the investor is in doubt as to which course to pursue, one should choose the path of caution.

Data Sources

moneycontrol.com
equitymaster.com
valueresearchonline.com
nseindia.com
profit.ndtv.com
money.rediff.com
ycharts.comfinancials.morningstar.com
4-traders.com

Pointers

Lessons

Lesson No.	Lesson Summary
1	Do not let your child lose the 'Time Leverage' edge.
2	Never ever invest on tips.
3	Never have a short-term horizon.
4	Stock market volatility is what helps it to give stellar returns.
5	Do not invest with borrowed money or a faint heart; both are fatal.
6	Your portfolio must beat inflation after paying taxes – year on year.
7	Real estate is no match to stock investing.
8	Mutual fund is next best to stock investing.
9	Mutual funds do not allow for your intellectual growth, stocks do.
10	Stock returns far outweigh returns from mutual funds, with almost similar risk.
11	Wealth creation is not complex. Follow the simple steps, over and over again – with faith and commitment.
12	You do not just buy a stock; you buy a part of the company.
13	A lower share price of an IPO gives you no clue of its worthiness to buy or sell.
14	A stock's current market price (CMP) alone gives you no clue of its worthiness to buy or sell.
15	A blue chip or a brand gives you no clue of its worthiness to buy or sell.
16	One of the key ingredients to amass massive wealth in stocks is to be a good human being with a great attitude.

Lesson No.	Lesson Summary
17	Buy or sell Decemberision should be based on comparison of a stock's current market price (CMP) with its intrinsic value.
18	Great investors wait patiently for a bargain price – much below intrinsic value.
19	Herd mentality drives irrational behaviour.
20	Most technical analysis strategies are as fallacious as they are popular.
21	The 'collective' 'perceived' worth by investors determines its market price dynamically.
22	Between periods of fluctuating collective perception, the price of a stock will always hit close to its true intrinsic value .
23	Keeping faith during testing times does not come easy to human race.
24	An investor's job is not to predict tomorrow's market price of a stock
25	'Buy' when CMP is significantly below intrinsic value. 'Sell' when CMP meets or exceeds intrinsic value.
26	Book losses without hesitation, if your CMP-intrinsic value calculation guides you to do so.
27	In stock investing, as in the real world, there are no guarantees; but only probabilities.
28	Dividend payout ratio signifies a company's intent towards distributing profit. Dividend yield tells you the returns on invested money.
29	Dividend paying stocks outsmart the non-dividend ones in the long run.
30	Dividend oxidation effect© leads to capping the possible capital gains.
31	Stock movement can be quite different from market movement.
32	Timing the market is a myth.
33	Stock investments need to be predicted and protected for at least next 10 years. Strong company fundamentals help here.
34	A stable industry, even if old-fashioned, mitigates your investment risk over a 10-year period.
35	Look for companies with a competitive advantage.
36	Between a great business and great management, former holds much more weight.
37	Four golden rules to stock selection: Industry, company, management, intrinsic price (ICMI).

Lesson No.	Lesson Summary
38	Insulate yourself from outside noise and focus on fundamentals and intrinsic value calculation. Then, trust what you had calculated.
39	Relax! One hurriedly made investment can kill your 10 good investments.
40	Investing is not about beating the market or anyone else.
41	The very first thing you check on a stock is its stability.
42	Earnings represent profit. Revenue represent sales.
43	Price represents market's perception. Cost represents actual value.
44	Eliminate luck and add predictability to your selection.
45	Trailing Twelve Months EPS (TTM EPS) is preferred over a full year EPS.
46	Company growth rate and your investment growth can be significantly different. A lot depends on the entry price.
47	P/E ratio indicates the premium investors are paying per rupee of current earning.
48	P/E ratio comparison makes sense only within similar industries.
49	P/E ratio alone does not give you any idea about a stock's worthiness.
50	A high P/E ratio could indicate high confidence in the company or a highly overpriced stock.
51	An intrinsic P/E ratio of the company tends to maintain its value in spite of changing P or E.
52	A 'No Buy' Decemberision is as good as a 'Buy' Decemberision, if not more.
53	PEG ratio connects the past performance with future growth potential, and is more informative for value analysis.
54	PEG ratio more than one suggests an overvalued stock.
55	There is only one guarantee in stock market – stock homecoming.
56	Recalibrate a stock's intrinsic value at least once a year.
57	Stock investing is simple, predictable and carries no additional risks.
58	True human emotions come to the fore for the period when you are holding the stock.
59	Book value is the price paid to buy an asset. Market value is the current price of the asset .
60	P/B ratio should ideally be less than one. A value up to three is still tolerable.

Lesson No.	Lesson Summary
61	Low P/B and High ROE is a beautiful combination of a fundamentally strong and undervalued stock.
62	High Debt / Equity Ratio is definitely more risky, if not bad.
63	D/E Ratio is highly industry specific. Anything between 0.5 and 2 is acceptable. Less than 0.5 is awesome.
64	Earnings can be volatile and subject to accounting gimmick. Sales are much more stable measuring criteria.
65	Free cash flow (FCF) is the free cash available with the company.
66	FCF ratio above 50 percent is considered very good.
67	Visualize your futuristic capital gains estimate before investing.
68	Rupee cost averaging allows you to bring down your average cost.
69	Weight of *Top-Up shares*© signifies the efficiency of rupee cost averaging for your stock.
70	Price vs. *Cost factor*© indicates the proportion of shares you should be buying.
71	Rupee cost averaging is a double edged sword – the more you use, the less effective it becomes.
72	Use *WRCA*© technique to use Rupee Cost Averaging effectively and efficiently.
73	Every stock dip below 10 percent of average cost may not result in buying more, and that's perfectly fine.
74	Most successful investors do nothing most of the time.
75	Do not base your sell Decemberisions by extrapolating short term profits.
76	Stock homecoming is not a onetime phenomenon.
77	A regularly balanced portfolio is vital for optimal wealth generation.
78	Diversify, not much with the number of stocks, but with the set of industries you hold.
79	A stock losing its intrinsic value is an alarming sign.
80	Get ready to sell if the intrinsic value starts to dip below market price or average cost.
81	Stock investing isn't about winning every battle. It is also about losing a few battles to win the war.
82	Rigorously practice self-control to succeed in stocks.
83	Do not look back at the price of a sold stock with the intent of validating your decision.

Formulas

Formula No.	Formula Title
1	Dividend Payout Ratio
2	Dividend Yield
3	Earnings per share (EPS)
4	P/E Ratio
5	PEG Ratio
6	P/B Ratio
7	ROE
8	D/E Ratio
9	P/S Ratio
10	Free Cash Flow
11	FCF Ratio
12	Weight of Top-Up shares©
13	Price vs. Cost factor© or AC-MP factor©
14	Price vs. Value factor© or IV-MP factor©

Tables

Table No.	Table Title
1	Round-0 Results of Stock Selection
2	Snapshot from Voltas Annual Report
3	Round-1 Result of Stock Selection (Voltas)
4	Snapshot from SBI Annual Report
5	Round-1 Final Results
6	Finding Industry (Round-2 of Stock Selection)
7	Finding CMP (Round-2 of Stock Selection)
8	Finding Historical EPS data (Round-2 of Stock Selection)
9	Calculating EPS-GR data (Round-2 of Stock Selection)
10	Calculating P/E Ratio (Round-2 of Stock Selection)
11	Finding Industry P/E (Round-2 of Stock Selection)
12	Calculating Average P/E for 2013-14 for Asian Paints
13	Average P/E for 9 years for Asian Paints
14	Average P/E for 8 years for Asian Paints (excl outlier year)
15	P/E Growth Rate for Asian Paints
16	Calculating Intrinsic P/E & Best Case P/E for Asian Paints
17	Calculating Intrinsic Value & Most Optimistic Value for Asian Paints
18	Calculating PEG Ratio for Asian Paints
19	Round 2 Results for Asian Paints
20	Finding Industry (Round-2 Step-1 of Stock Selection for Yes Bank)
21	Finding CMP (Round-2 Step-2 of Stock Selection for Yes Bank)
22	Finding EPS Data (Round-2 Step-3 of Stock Selection for Yes Bank)
23	Calculating overall EPS-GR (Round-2 Step-4 of Stock Selection for Yes Bank)

Table No.	Table Title
24	Calculating year wise EPS-GR (Round-2 Step-5 of Stock Selection for Yes Bank)
25	Calculating the current P/E (Round-2 Step-6 of Stock Selection for Yes Bank)
26	Finding the industry P/E (Round-2 Step-7 of Stock Selection for Yes Bank)
27	Calculating the Intrinsic P/E (Round-2 Step-8 of Stock Selection for Yes Bank)
28	Calculating Intrinsic & Best Case P/E (Round-2 Step-9 of Stock Selection for Yes Bank)
29	Calculating Intrinsic Value (Round-2 Step-10 of Stock Selection for Yes Bank)
30	Calculating PEG Ratio (Round-2 Step-11 of Stock Selection for Yes Bank)
31	Calculating P/B Ratio (Round-3 Step-1 of Stock Selection for Yes Bank)
32	Calculating ROE (Round-3 Step-2 of Stock Selection for Yes Bank)
33	Finding D/E Ratio (Round-3 Step-3 of Stock Selection for Yes Bank)
34	Finding P/S Ratio (Round-3 Step-4 of Stock Selection for Yes Bank)
35	Finding Free Cash flow (Round-3 Step-5 of Stock Selection for Yes Bank)
36	Calculating FCF Ratio (Round-3 Step-6 of Stock Selection for Yes Bank)
37	Calculating Current Capital Gains Potential (Round-4 Step-1 of Stock Selection for Yes Bank)
38	Establishing Projected Growth Rate (Round-4 Step-2 of Stock Selection for Yes Bank)
39	Establishing Consensus Growth Rate (Round-4 Step-3 of Stock Selection for Yes Bank)
40	Calculating Projected EPS (Round-4 Step-4 of Stock Selection for Yes Bank)
41	Calculating Projected Price (Round-4 Step-5 of Stock Selection for Yes Bank)
42	Calculating Projected Capital Gains Potential (Round-4 Step-6 of Stock Selection for Yes Bank)
43	Calculating Dividend / share (Round-4 Step-7 of Stock Selection for Yes Bank)
44	Calculating Average Dividend Payout Ratio (Round-4 Step-8 of Stock Selection for Yes Bank)
45	Calculating Projected Year Wise Dividends (Round-4 Step-9 of Stock Selection for Yes Bank)

Table No.	Table Title
46	Calculating overall projected CAGR (Round-4 Step-10 of Stock Selection for Yes Bank)
47	Initial Purchase of Yes Bank Stock (5-December-2014)
48	AC-MP-IV Tracking©for Yes Bank Stock (5-December-2014)
49	WRCA©Opportunity I executed on Yes Bank Stock (17-December-2014)
50	AC-MP-IV Tracking©at WRCA©Opportunity-I for Yes Bank Stock (5-December-2014)
51	AC-MP-IV Tracking©at Sell Opportunity-I on Yes Bank Stock (4-Mar-2015)
52	AC-MP-IV Tracking©12 months Status with Yes Bank Stock (30-November-2015)
53	Re-calculating Intrinsic Value after 12 months for Yes Bank Stock (30-November-2015)
54	Calculating P/E for 2014-15 for Yes Bank Stock (30-November-2015)
55	AC-MP-IV Tracking©with updated Intrinsic Value for Yes Bank Stock (30-November-2015)
56	AC-MP-IV Tracking©WRCA©Opportunity-II for Yes Bank Stock (20-January-2016)
57	WRCA© Opportunity-II executed for Yes Bank Stock (20-January-2016)
58	AC-MP-IV Tracking©WRCA©Opportunity-II executed for Yes Bank Stock (20-January-2016)
59	AC-MP-IV Tracking©at Sell Opportunity-II on Yes Bank Stock (28-April-2016)
60	Re-calculating Intrinsic Value at Sell Opportunity-II for Yes Bank Stock (28-April-2016)
61	AC-MP-IV Tracking©with updated Intrinsic Value for Yes Bank Stock (28-April-2016)
62	AC-MP-IV Tracking©at Sell Opportunity-III on Yes Bank Stock (30-Jun-2016)

Charts

Chart No.	Chart Title
1	Stock Homecoming
2	Initial Purchase of Yes Bank Stock (December 05,2014)
3	AC-MP-IV Tracking© at WRCA© Opportunity-1 for Yes Bank Stock (December 17, 2014)
4	AC-MP-IV Tracking© at Sell Opportunity-I on Yes Bank Stock (March 04, 2015)
5	AC-MP-IV Tracking© 12 months Status for Yes Bank Stock (November 30, 2015)
6	AC-MP-IV Tracking© with updated Intrinsic Value for Yes Bank Stock (Novembe 30, 2015)
7	AC-MP-IV Tracking© WRCA© Opportunity-II for Yes Bank Stock (20-January-2016)
8	AC-MP-IV Tracking© WRCA© Opportunity-II executed for Yes Bank Stock (20-January-2016)
9	AC-MP-IV Tracking© at Sell Opportunity-II on Yes Bank Stock (28-April-2016)
10	AC-MP-IV Tracking© with updated Intrinsic Value for Yes Bank Stock (28-April-2016)
11	AC-MP-IV Tracking© at Sell Opportunity-III on Yes Bank Stock (30-June-2016)

Copyrighted Innovations in this Book

Term	Explanation
Dividend Oxidation Effect	This effect improves returns, liquidity, limits downside risk. At the same time, it also limits the upside potential of a stock, thus limiting the potential capital gains
Client Inertia	The effect because of which the clients tend to stay with the existing product or service provider
Intrinsic P/E	The average P/E calculated over a 5 to 10 year history of the stock. This P/E tends to remain constant through the life of the stock
AC-MP-IV tracking	Tracking the trio of Actual Cost-Market Price-Intrinsic Value of a Stock for most optimized control on the Stock movements enabling right Decemberision making
Weight of Top-Up Shares	It is the number of top-up shares you wish to buy with respect to the current number of shares you are already holding for a particular stock
Price Vs Cost Factor OR AC-MP Factor	It depicts the gap between the running average cost and the price at which you want to buy additional top up stocks
IV-MP Factor	It is the percent difference between the Intrinsic Value and CMP (calculated with Average Cost as the base)
Weighted Rupee Cost Averaging	A special set of weighted buying rules which ensures that rupee cost averaging is applied effectively and efficiently

My Commitment to You

I am passionate about YOU. I am committed to YOU.

It is my life's mission to elevate my society, in whatever ways I can. As with all my other books (From the Rat Race to Financial Freedom, Happiness Unlimited & Dream On), this book comes with a 100% commitment to help you, guide you; mentor you on your journey.

We will walk this journey together. No charges, no fees, no constraints...

You have an absolute right to connect with me, and I will be more than delighted to help you elevate your life.

Feel free to connect with us at our:

Official Website	:	http://www.manoj-arora.com
Blog	:	http://elevate-your-life.blogspot.in/
Email	:	help@manoj-arora.com
Whats App	:	+91-9871133619

Manoj Arora
Dreams • Financial Freedom • Happiness